Groove
Interrupted

Groove Interrupted

*Loss, Renewal, and
the Music of New Orleans*

Keith Spera

St. Martin's Press   New York

GROOVE INTERRUPTED. Copyright © 2011 by Keith Spera. Foreword
copyright © 2011 by Harry Shearer. All rights reserved. Printed in the
United States of America. For information, address St. Martin's Press,
175 Fifth Avenue, New York, N.Y. 10010.

www.stmartins.com

Library of Congress Cataloging-in-Publication Data

Spera, Keith.
  Groove interrupted : loss, renewal, and the music of New Orleans /
Keith Spera.—1st ed.
    p. cm.
  ISBN 978-0-312-55225-1
  1. Musicians—Louisiana—New Orleans—Biography. 2. Disaster
victims—Louisiana—New Orleans—Biography. 3. Hurricane Katrina,
2005—Personal narratives. I. Title.
  ML385.S635 2011
  780.92'276335—dc22
  [B]   2011010122

First Edition: August 2011

For Mary, Sophie, and Sam,
my favorite melodies

Contents

Foreword

Keith Spera knows the New Orleans music world well. He knows that, unlike other cities with a music-business heritage, that world isn't a "scene"; it's a culture. It's a culture born of loss and recovery, the cycle repeated like a chorus of a Mardi Gras Indian chant over and over again, with new details interspersed. Sure, most major cities have some moments of loss in their story. But New Orleans, through the gifts of geography, history, and human malfeasance, has had more than its share. This, after all, was the site of the last yellow-fever epidemic in North America which took place in the twentieth century.

In this book, Keith is focusing not so much on the stories of loss in the catastrophic 2005 flood that followed the landfall of Hurricane Katrina, but more on the individual paths to recovery of a group of New Orleans musicians. Those paths, as befit a city where parallel streets intersect, are sometimes tentative, sometimes treacherous, sometimes funny, sometimes bordered with tragedy.

Keith tells the stories from a position halfway between reporter and confidante. Aaron Neville opens up to him about just how difficult it was to travel the road home. Fats Domino, always wondering "who's that guy?", takes him along on a promotional trip to New York and a triumphant return to New Orleans. At times, the wounds of the existential crisis of a major American city are on the surface for all to see. Other times, they appear just as accompaniment to, amplification of, the ravages of time.

What emerges from Keith's clear-eyed but empathetic view of these people, the people he's covered for years in the pages of the local daily, is the conclusion that these folks are neither heroes nor victims. They are extraordinarily gifted members of a unique music culture, their world flooded away in an historical instant—family splintered, neighborhood rubbished, support system shattered—and, in these knowing, loving portraits, they are, each at their own speed, in their own way, doing what New Orleanians have always done: getting the groove back.

—Harry Shearer

Groove
Interrupted

Introduction

In the spring of 2007, Robert Plant traveled to New Orleans to lend his Led pipes to a Fats Domino tribute CD. As a mere lad in England, he was smitten by the sounds of the faraway city. He devoured the latest rhythm-and-blues singles from New Orleans, pouring over the record jackets for clues to the music's mysterious origins. Forty years later, he accurately recalled an orange, black, and white Par-Lo Productions label on Aaron Neville's original 1966 recording of "Tell It Like It Is."

"I was intoxicated by the sound of New Orleans," Plant enthused during a break in the Domino session. "When I came here in Led Zeppelin, I realized that the culture was just so radically different than anything else in the whole of the United States. I could feel something that was still alive, that hadn't been too Americanized and too messed with. I found it exotic, frightening, a little bit intimidating."

As he prowled the city's streets and clubs in 2007, Plant realized the song remained largely the same. In New Orleans, "the past is right up level with the present. It's local music for people who understand it. It's how it ought to be."

The music, in all its manifestations, is very much a reflection of the city itself—its history, neighborhoods, street culture, schools, Mardi Gras, and a pursuit of happiness that doesn't entirely erase the sadness and frustration that result from New Orleans' unwillingness or inability to rid itself of incompetence, corruption and crime. As much as anyplace, if not more, New Orleans musicians are a product of their environment. The concept of *terroir*—that a region's air, soil, water, etc., instill a distinct set of characteristics—doesn't only apply to grapes.

Often described as the northernmost point of the Caribbean, New Orleans is unique among North American cities. A commingling of French, Spanish and various African cultures—coupled with a port town's naturally decadent inclinations—cultivated a healthy appetite for food and music. The vibrant, idiosyncratic music community is essential to its hometown's identity, and to the larger world of popular music.

Casual fans may be vaguely aware that "New Orleans music" is its own entity. The more intimately attuned understand that the Big Easy incubated jazz and rock and roll in their infancy. That a direct line connects the homeland rhythms enslaved Africans perpetuated in the city's Congo Square to the syncopated cadence of brass, funk and R&B bands and the rappers who sample those beats.

Like the proverbial blind men who announce different parts of an elephant as its defining characteristic, partisans of various music genres tend to assign a homogeneous identity to the city's musical legacy. To jazz fans, New Orleans is Louis Armstrong, Pete Fountain, Wynton Marsalis and Terence Blanchard. To fans of classic rhythm and blues and rock and roll, New Orleans is synonymous with Fats Domino, Ernie K-Doe and Irma Thomas. To hip-hop devotees, New Orleans is the "bounce" beat and Juvenile, Lil Wayne, Mystikal and Master P.

In reality, it is everything from Louis Armstrong to Lil Wayne, and much more. It has never been homogenous. As jazz took shape in and around downtown brothels in the earliest days of the twentieth century, it had already fractured into a kaleidoscope of styles, from the bold cornet improvisations of Buddy Bolden—who perished in a mental institution and whose remains were lost in a pauper's cemetery—to the intricate ensemble work of the Dukes of Dixieland. Decades later, modern jazz musicians moonlighted on R&B records.

The 2009 Grammy Awards' tribute to New Orleans featured Lil Wayne, trumpeter Terence Blanchard, classic rhythm and blues song-writer, producer and pianist Allen Toussaint, and the Dirty Dozen Brass Band. That felt about right.

New Orleans music is its own self-contained universe, one that remains largely unknown to outsiders even as it informs, directly or indirectly, the soundtrack of their lives. The Dave Matthews Band recorded its *Big Whiskey & the GrooGrux King* CD in New Orleans in 2009. Matthews, a frequent visitor, subsequently declared New Orleans "the most musical city that I've ever been to. Somehow it's in the roots and in the ground in New Orleans. It's in the blood. It's in the celebration, and the suffering."

The recent history of New Orleans, of course, contains plenty of both.

I first heard the indigenous music of New Orleans as an infant in the city's Ninth Ward; local records constantly spun on the home stereo, courtesy of my father. As a suburban teenager under the thrall of eighties hard rock, I tended to regard his vinyl as "old man's music"; only later did I realize how special my hometown's music was, and is. I've written about it for my entire professional career, first at the monthly *OffBeat* magazine and, since 1996, at *The Times-Picayune*.

On August 29, 2005, I rode out Hurricane Katrina inside the newspaper's stout brick headquarters. As a music critic, death and destruction are not normally my beat, but when rising floodwaters forced the paper's staff to evacuate eighty miles to Baton Rouge, I joined a small band of reporters and photographers who remained behind to chronicle the unfolding devastation. We were an unconventional disaster team: the music and art critics, the editorial page editor, the sports editor, the education reporter, and the religion reporter (all things considered, probably not a bad guy to have around). Our fleet consisted of a *Picayune* delivery truck, two cars, assorted bicycles, a kayak and a canoe. In sweltering heat, we dodged noxious waters, downed power lines and brazen looters as New Orleans descended into chaos. I witnessed firsthand the suffering caused by official ineptitude and negligence at the Ernest N. Morial Convention Center and elsewhere.

Roaming Uptown the day after the storm, I was heartened to discover Tipitina's, the city's flagship music club, largely undisturbed on a swath of high, dry ground along the Mississippi River. From the street, the nearby home of legendary keyboardist Art Neville—founder of seminal funk band the Meters, a Neville Brother, and one of New

Orleans' most beloved musicians—also appeared undamaged. Only later did I learn that wind and rain conspired to ruin much of its meticulously decorated interior. The storm did not discriminate. Fats Domino, Allen Toussaint, and Art's brother Aaron, three of the city's most successful music makers, lost their homes just as surely as any number of musicians who still worked day jobs on the side.

Given the life-and-death struggles of those first, desperate days after Katrina, pondering the fate of the music community felt trite. But it soon became apparent that if New Orleans was to recover, the city must rekindle its carefree spirit and once again seduce the tourists and conventioneers who drive its economy. Music would play a vital role in that seduction.

For locals, music served as a rallying cry. Ten days after the storm, on Thursday, September 8, 2005, good-time jazz trumpeter Kermit Ruffins was in his element: onstage, black fedora over a blue bandana, cold beers at the ready, easing into "When It's Sleepy Time Down South." But he was not at Vaughan's Lounge, the tumbledown watering hole in New Orleans' Bywater neighborhood, where he spent most Thursdays for more than a decade. He was 350 miles west at Sammy's, a downtown Houston nightclub. Dozens of newly displaced New Orleanians—who normally consider wearing Mardi Gras beads out of season the mark of a tourist—flaunted beads as a badge of honor. After midnight, Lil' Rascals Brass Band trombonist Corey Henry led a cheer: "New Orleans, we're gonna rebuild, y'all!" The response was long and loud, fists and voices raised in defiance of the creeping realization of what might be lost. Later, a recording of the Rebirth Brass Band's "Do Whatcha Wanna" filled the dance floor once again. No one wanted the night, or New Orleans, to end.

On September 20, New Orleans Jazz and Heritage Festival producer/director Quint Davis co-produced *From the Big Apple to the Big Easy*, an all-star benefit concert at Madison Square Garden. Scattered, shell-shocked musicians came together for the first time since the storm, bolstered by an outpouring of support from the larger world of popular music and the people of New York. Emotions ran high both backstage and onstage.

For weeks, New Orleans itself was unplugged in a way that had nothing to do with acoustic guitars. The earliest post-storm gigs, such as blues/funk/soul guitarist Walter "Wolfman" Washington's at the

Maple Leaf, were powered by generators and cut short by curfews. No touring band found its way back to the city until James Low, a singer-songwriter from Portland, Oregon, performed at a Frenchmen Street bar called d.b.a. on October 21—nearly two months after the storm. Before Katrina, he was initially scheduled for a Wednesday night, because the club's owner feared rowdy weekend crowds would drown out the music. But after the storm, Low's gig got promoted to a Friday—with the local colleges all shuttered, there were no rowdy weekend crowds, at least temporarily.

Remarkably, two months after Katrina, New Orleans hosted a music festival. On Halloween weekend, Voodoo Experience founder Stephen Rehage managed to stage a downsized yet scrappy version of his annual music festival on an improvised site behind Audubon Zoo alongside the Mississippi River. Industrial rockers Nine Inch Nails, fronted by Trent Reznor, a former resident of New Orleans' Garden District, topped a roster of visiting and local acts determined to provide a brief respite from the hard business of recovery. That same weekend, Tipitina's reopened with a raucous set by, appropriately, the Rebirth Brass Band.

On November 17, some 1,200 souls filled Christ Church Cathedral, a 119-year-old Episcopal church on New Orleans' grand St. Charles Avenue, for the New Orleans Jazz Orchestra (NOJO) premiere of "All the Saints," a commissioned piece of grief and resolve. At the time, NOJO's young artistic director, trumpeter Irvin Mayfield, had yet to learn the fate of his father, who disappeared in the storm's chaotic aftermath—and whose body was found days after the concert. Mayfield, a protégé of Wynton Marsalis, breathed a somber blues for the eulogistic opening of "All the Saints." The full orchestra eased in behind him with one voice, built around a funereal progression of four notes. When it ended, the sanctuary was silent. Applause did not seem appropriate.

But soon enough, Clarence Johnson III's alto saxophone lit up the cathedral, followed closely by Steve Walker's gutbucket trombone and Ed "Sweetbread" Petersen's tenor saxophone, laced with humor, determination and resolve. Applause broke in waves. In Mayfield's finest moment, his trumpet caressed the opening bars of "Just a Closer Walk With Thee." Accompanied only by his old friend Ronald Markham on piano, his touch and tone were subdued, reverent and gorgeous; more than one listener cried. He brought the hymn down for a soft landing, inspiring the night's first standing ovation. "Ninth Ward Blues" earned another ovation, as did the final second-line. "If we don't believe in our city," Mayfield sang, "nobody else will."

As New Orleans repopulated itself over the coming weeks and months, a cheeky sense of humor helped. Before the storm, singer-songwriter Susan Cowsill established a monthly series at Carrollton Station, a cozy corner bar/music club near a streetcar barn, called Covered in Vinyl. Each month, she and her band covered a classic album in its entirety. During two months of post-Katrina exile, Cowsill, her drummer/husband Russ Broussard, and their family crisscrossed the country in search of lodging. In November, they relaunched Covered in Vinyl with Paul McCartney & Wings' "Band on the Run."

For some musicians, the deck would remain reshuffled indefinitely. Katrina blew Soul Rebels Brass Band snare drummer Lumar LeBlanc and trumpeter Marcus Hubbard to Houston. They found housing, enrolled their kids in school and decided to stay. But five-plus years after Katrina, they still drive 350 miles each way between Houston and New Orleans for the Rebels' weekly Thursday night gig at Le Bon Temps Roule, a roadhouse-like bar on Magazine Street. Maintaining that connection is essential, whatever the toll on their vehicles' odometers. "We still consider New Orleans our home," LeBlanc said. "I'm New Orleans till the day I die."

Today, patrons of Jazz Fest or the Frenchmen Street entertainment district would be hard-pressed to find any lingering effect of the storm. A symbolic circle was completed in early 2010 when the Saints' Super Bowl XLIV victory parade triggered a hurricane evacuation in reverse: All *inbound* arteries were clogged, as tens of thousands of fans from throughout the region flooded New Orleans to join in the celebration. Later that night, my wife's car was stolen—another indication, however unfortunate, that life in the city was back to normal.

Each of the following chapters presents a New Orleans musician confronting a challenge or staring down adversity that threatens his ability to make music. Some names are familiar, others less so. Each story is contemporary, set in roughly the same post-Katrina timeframe as David Simon's acclaimed *Treme* series on HBO. Not every tale is a Katrina story per se, but the storm is a common thread woven into the biography of every New Orleanian, musician or otherwise. Scratch a New Orleanian and you'll find a Katrina story that may involve horror and hardship, extreme good fortunate and miraculous reprieve, an epic evacuation, the kindness of strangers, and/or infuriation courtesy of insurance companies, bureaucrats and contractors.

The stories in *Groove, Interrupted* involve hope, humor and heartache, perseverance and pathos, framed by trumpets, guitars, drums and voices and set against the neon glow of New Orleans nightlife. By telling these stories, many of which originated with articles I wrote for *The Times-Picayune*, my intention was not only to provide insights into the recent lives—and in some cases, deaths—of the individuals, but to give an overall sense of what constitutes New Orleans music, in all its variety.

Featured musicians struggle with mortality, advancing age, decisions that will redirect the course of their lives and careers. They square off against their own insecurities, or pain, or prison. For more than one, Katrina yielded not only turmoil and hardship, but opportunity. They try to make sense of the storm through music, comforting themselves and uplifting those around them.

The Big Easy good-time ethos is coupled with the resiliency and resolve required to resuscitate an entire region after the most destructive natural/man-made disaster in American history. Each story stands on its own; together, they convey a sense of what New Orleans music was and is, in spite of Katrina's disruption.

To date, my father's collection of 1950s-era 45-rpm records has survived two catastrophes. In 1965, Hurricane Betsy swamped his home in the upper Ninth Ward. Forty years later, Katrina inundated his brick ranch house in suburban New Orleans East with six feet of foul floodwater. The contents festered for weeks.

After resettling high above sea level in central Texas, he spent countless hours scrubbing muck and mold from his vintage vinyl. When he finished, the labels on the records had disintegrated.

But the music sounded fine.

The fate of my father's 45s mirrors that of the entire New Orleans music community. That community, and the individual musicians who comprise it, survived Katrina and other traumas, though not un-scathed. Their groove was interrupted, but not for long.

K.S.
New Orleans, LA
January 2011

Chapter One

Gatemouth Brown's Last Ride

―――――――――――――――――――――――――――――――――――――――

In the fall of 1997, photographer Jennifer Zdon and I visited the notoriously cantankerous Clarence "Gatemouth" Brown at his ramshackle bayou-side bachelor's pad outside Slidell, Louisiana. He immediately antagonized Zdon. He'd rather marry a gorilla and keep it in his lemon tree, the thrice-divorced Brown informed her, than marry another woman. Not amused, she struggled to maintain her professional composure even as Brown refused pleas to pose with his trademark cowboy hat.

Eight years later, as Brown wasted away from cancer, heart disease and emphysema, Zdon asked to document his struggle for The Times-Picayune. *He agreed, with one provision: That he be allowed to preview the photographs before publication. In the end, the dying musician objected to only one image of himself, shirtless and skeletal, being helped into bed. It was too intimate, too revealing, too raw.*

As evidenced by his frequently impolitic assertions and boasts, Gatemouth Brown didn't worry all that much about other folks' opinions of him. But to expose his own weakness so nakedly was more than he could stomach. Even Gatemouth, at some point, was vulnerable.

Zdon honored his request. The photo never ran.

The black-and-red backpack never strayed from Clarence "Gatemouth" Brown's side. Inside were the tools of the guitarist's trade as a living legend of Gulf Coast music: copies of his latest CD; promotional photos; a Sharpie for signing autographs.

The backpack also contained personal items: a reserve sheriff's deputy badge from St. Tammany Parish, Louisiana; assorted pipes and tobacco; an ashtray for use in establishments that didn't ordinarily accommodate smokers.

Most critically, it concealed the realities of his precarious day-to-day existence in the spring of 2005: two portable oxygen tanks; an inhaler; an electronic blood pressure gauge; a supply of pills.

The previous September, Brown, then eighty, announced that he had lung cancer. After consulting with doctors at the MD Anderson Cancer Center in Houston, he opted to forgo treatment. He would ride it out, one day at a time, puffing calmly on the pipe that was his constant companion and a likely culprit.

Cancer was not his only ailment. He also suffered from emphysema and partial blockage in his arteries. Doctors wouldn't risk an operation because of his diminished lung capacity.

Clearly, Brown was nearing the end of his remarkable run. During a fifty-year career, commercial success on par with that of fellow blues traveler B. B. King had eluded him. But to fans and admirers, including Eric Clapton, the broad scope of his musicianship was unparalleled. Fluent on guitar, fiddle, mandola, harmonica, drums, viola and piano, he released his seminal single, the horn-heavy instrumental "Okie Dokie Stomp," in 1954. Like many of his roots-music peers, he faded into obscurity until European blues enthusiasts "rediscovered" him.

Brown stormed back, a font of jump blues, big band swing, country, jazz and Cajun music. Long, elegant fingers teased out precise licks; he demanded similar perfection from his musicians. "He's a very opinionated, hardheaded person sometimes," said Kenny Wayne Shepherd, the young blues-rock guitarist from north Louisiana who recruited Brown for his Grammy-nominated *10 Days Out: Blues from the Backroads* project. "I mean that in an endearing way. If he wasn't like that, he wouldn't be Gatemouth."

A string of acclaimed albums in the 1990s—*American Music, Texas Style, Long Way Home, Gate Swings*—found him at the peak of his powers. Clapton enlisted Brown and his band, Gate's Express, as the opening act on arena tours of Europe and North America. Brown was riding high once again. Not surprisingly, as illness encroached on his world, he refused to relinquish it quietly.

A weekday afternoon in October 1997 found Gatemouth Brown at his home near Slidell, a sleepy bedroom community east of New Orleans on the edge of Lake Pontchartrain. His abode alongside Highway 11 teetered above a canal on wood pilings; the back porch overlooked an expanse of marshland stretching to the Big Branch Marsh National Wildlife Refuge. Parked among the banana, plum, pecan and lemon trees out front was his barge-like black 1976 Cadillac DeVille. A side window bore a caricature of him as a lean cowboy guitar-slinger.

The arrival of visitors roused him from a siesta necessitated by a late night in Baton Rouge. "Gimme a few minutes to wake up," he mumbled, embarking on a quest for coffee and his trusty pipe. The restless Brown was rarely that idle. That July, at age seventy-three, he performed in both China and South Africa. Tours of the West Coast, France, Slovenia, Austria and Belgium followed.

Slowly coming alive at his kitchen table, he reflected on his epic life. He was born in 1924 in the southwest Louisiana town of Vinton, months before his family moved across the Sabine River to Orange, Texas. Accounts of the origin of his nickname varied. Some say the source was an exasperated schoolteacher who said young Brown's mouth swung open and shut like a gate; others claim it was Don Robey, Brown's first manager, who concocted "Gatemouth" as a stage name. Brown generally declined to elaborate—he planned to save the story for his autobiography.

Music abounded at home. His father, a railroad engineer, was also a bluegrass and Cajun fiddler; Brown's brothers played guitar and drums. In his late teens, he cut his teeth with various Texas bands, then served a stretch in the Army. Back in Texas, he worked as a journeyman guitarist. One evening at Houston's Bronze Peacock nightclub, he picked up an ailing T-Bone Walker's guitar and improvised a song. Impressed, Robey, the club's owner, resolved to get Brown a record deal.

Starting in 1947, Brown cut singles first for Los Angeles–based Aladdin Records, then Robey's own Peacock label. Those early sides contributed to the development of Texas blues; the Lone Star State would continue to claim him even after he settled in Slidell in 1983.

After the blues market dried up in the mid-1960s, Brown rambled around Colorado and New Mexico. In 1966 in Nashville, he fronted the house band for an R&B-based TV variety show called *The!!!!*

Beat; he and The Beat Boys performed alongside African-American go-go dancers in white boots and fringed miniskirts. After the show's one-year run, he dropped out of sight.

But roots music rewards longevity. Like many blues-based artists, Brown endured a long, fallow period as a has-been only to reemerge, like a butterfly from a cocoon, as an elder statesman. By the mid-1970s, he was appearing on *Hee Haw*. His 1982 release *Alright Again!* won a Grammy as Best Traditional Blues Album.

The 1990s proved to be the most lucrative period of his career. He could afford to record and occasionally perform with big bands, indulging his fondness for the arrangements of Duke Ellington and Count Basie. "Guys get on their knees bowing to me," he said, not altogether unpleased. "I get very embarrassed sometimes, but that's what they do."

Eric Clapton became an unabashed Brown booster on November 22, 1994, the second of Clapton's three consecutive nights at the New Orleans House of Blues. During his encore, Clapton invited Brown to sit in. After warming up, Brown stepped to the microphone and announced, "For my next song . . ." He essentially hijacked the show as a grinning Clapton shrugged and slipped into his newly assigned role as sideman.

"How many people would get up onstage with Clapton and do that, and not even hesitate?" said Shepherd. "Only guys from that generation can do something like that and get away with it."

Weeks later, Clapton invited Brown to join him at London's Royal Albert Hall. He then asked Brown to open dozens of concerts across Europe and North America, exposing the old master to thousands of fresh ears. "I was doing damn good before Clapton," Brown noted. "That just helped a little."

When not on the road, he made the rounds in New Orleans or holed up at his Slidell hideaway. Following his third divorce, he lived alone amid a confirmed bachelor's clutter. Dozens of elaborate model ships gave the den/living room/kitchen of his glorified fishing camp a nautical cast. He was especially proud of one vessel with a hull consisting of lacquered bones.

In one corner stood a copy of his plaster bas-relief portrait that is set in the ceiling of the New Orleans House of Blues; the club permanently reserved a booth in his honor. A photo of his Grammy award substituted for the actual trophy that resides in a Baton Rouge museum. Five W. C. Handy statuettes—the Grammy of the blues world—sat atop a dormant organ. A Rhythm & Blues Foundation plaque naming him 1997's "Pioneer Artist" was a particular favorite—it came with a substantial check.

Brown relished the role of curmudgeon, but a sly smile often followed his most outrageous pronouncements. He hated posing for pictures and loved to let photographers know. He loathed rap and "head-banging" hard rock. His definition of love? "A misunderstanding between two damn fools."

Initially, he declined an offer to contribute to a Rolling Stones tribute album. "I didn't want to do it, because I didn't like Mick Jagger's writing. It don't make no sense." He finally relented and recorded "Ventilator Blues."

Years later, when asked his opinion of *Me and Mr. Johnson*, Clapton's 2004 homage to blues pioneer Robert Johnson, Brown said, "I didn't like those songs the first time, so why in the hell you think I'm gonna like 'em now?"

He complimented Clapton only grudgingly. "He's all right," Brown allowed, before correcting himself. "No, no—he's a good guitar player. But what I notice is most guitar players in the white society figure the Delta blues is it. They don't know that there's a helluva lot more music than Delta blues. That's the kind of music I avoid, because it's depressing. It's negative, and I won't play it.

"Don't get me wrong," he continued. "I play the blues, but it's positive. It's not about 'my woman done left me'—a woman done left everyone who ever walked upright. That's what's wrong—every son of a bitch out there is trying to tell the world his woman deserted him, but that's nothing to teach our kids.

"Blues players can't give no information—they don't know what to say. A certain individual, I won't give his name, was on TV and they asked, 'What is the blues to you?' You know what his answer was? 'A feeling.' I cracked up, boy."

Given such perceived absurdities, he intended his then-current album, *Gate Swings*, as a musical primer. "I could see son-of-a-guns out there trying to play big-band music and couldn't even voice their instruments, didn't know what they were doing. I showed them how it's supposed to be voiced, what kind of dynamics it's supposed to have. I play big-band lines—it's not just twang, twang, twang. You've got to be making a statement."

On *Gate Swings*, the big band interacts with, but does not overwhelm, his guitar. As he listened to the CD at his kitchen table, arched eyebrows, slight grimaces, quick smiles and a fist that clenched and pumped for emphasis all reflected his nuanced guitar work. "See how smooth that is?" he said, reveling in the moment. "That's how music is supposed to be."

He knew the arrangements intimately. Unlike some other blues legends who may only trot out token licks, he was clearly the conductor of Gate's Express. After fifty years, he still strove for excellence.

"One time I was telling Clapton and my band, 'You see that staircase? I started years ago at this bottom step.' Then I didn't point to the top step—I said, 'I'm right here [in the middle], still climbing.' And I don't look back. What was is gone. What will be, who knows? But what is, counts."

He refused to speculate about the future, about what his next album might be or whether he would continue to tour incessantly. "Who knows? I have no idea from one day to another. People ask, 'What are you going to do next?' I don't know."

After the sun had sunk into Lake Pontchartrain, a fully engaged Brown saddled up for the evening's adventures. He pulled on black boots, positioned a matching cowboy hat atop his head, slipped his reserve sheriff's deputy badge into a back pocket and tucked a holstered .38 into his waistband.

His immediate itinerary was uncertain. He might drive into New Orleans for a late supper at the House of Blues. Maybe he'd cruise around Slidell "hollerin' at people I know." Outside, he fired up an old pickup with a new set of brakes, and Gate's express pulled out of the station.

Not surprisingly, a defiant Gatemouth Brown rejected farewell scenarios when diagnosed with cancer seven years later.

On a cloudy afternoon in October 2004, he ambled into the bunker-like Studio in the Country, a favorite haunt north of Lake Pontchartrain in the pine woods of Bogalusa. Looking every bit the cowboy depicted in his silhouette logo, he was the honored guest during a recording session by Japanese punk band Highway 61.

Gene Foster, the studio's engineer, greeted him with an all-too-familiar query: "How you feeling, Gate?"

As usual, he was in no mood to discuss his illness. He'd rather talk about his latest CD, *Timeless*. The disc swung through a variety of styles, as was Brown's habit onstage. He paired his country fiddle with a pedal steel guitar on Bobby Charles's "Tennessee Blues" and his own "Six Levels Below Plant Life." He injected "Unchained Melody" with crisp, bell-tone lead guitar lines. In the spoken-word intro to "The Drifter," he expounded on a favorite topic: woman trouble. *Timeless*, he said, was intended to demonstrate "the purity of music. The positive in music. The dynamic of music. The discipline in music."

The record's second track is "For Now, So Long," a song he wrote in the 1950s and first recorded for Peacock. "Good-bye, I hate to leave you now, good-bye," he sings. "So long for now." Given his grim medical prognosis, such lyrics could be especially poignant.

But he had no use for sentimentality. While in Texas in September 2004 for the Austin City Limits Music Festival, he agreed to contribute to an album by Lone Star State all-star band Los Super Seven. The morning of the session, he learned what song he'd been assigned: Blind Lemon Jefferson's "See That My Grave is Kept Clean," which Bob Dylan popularized.

The graveyard imagery did not unnerve him as much as the arrangement—straight-ahead blues, of the sort he normally disdained. "I didn't want to do it, but they paid enough money," he recalled. "I changed the music so I could tolerate it."

In Bogalusa a month later, he still felt like himself, save a slight cough and the general wear and tear accumulated during five decades on the road. He clearly enjoyed the commotion triggered by his visit to a diner near Studio in the Country. He asked a waitress for twenty dollars, a mischievous stunt he often pulled with both strangers and acquaintances. "I try to mess with 'em, get 'em grinnin'. I can tell if you're a good candidate. If you're not, I don't want to mess with you."

After lunch, Brown piloted his Cadillac DeVille back to the studio where the members of Highway 61 were hard at work. A long-ago incident at the same studio with another Japanese rock band, the Privates, is the stuff of legend. Like many Japanese musicians, the Privates idolized traditional American bluesmen. They were thrilled to meet Gatemouth Brown. Showing off, he whipped out a .38 and fired a round into a pine tree as the Japanese scattered. Later, they dug out the slug as a souvenir.

This time, perhaps not quite as confident about the steadiness of his hand, he waved his gun around outside, but did not fire. Instead of a spent slug, the Highway 61 crew collected video footage of his Cadillac. Given their limited English and inherent respect, they did not inquire about his health.

Had they asked, "I'd tell them I feel fine," Brown said, chuckling. "And I do. You ought to see my Web site. Messages from all over the world, wishing me well. It makes me feel real good to know people think that much of you."

He was less amused by rumors that circulated online before he announced his diagnosis. "People spook easy. But I'm not going to let nobody gut me like a pig and kill me because they want big money. Them doctors—it's all about money. Everybody's got some kind of medical problem. I know some eighteen-year-old kids that have cancer."

He bristled at the suggestion that he might "try" to make another album.

"Try? What do you mean 'try'? You goddamn right I'm going to make another record! Several records. I'm going to do a bluegrass album next. All fiddle, maybe some vocals and guitar."

And he intended to maintain his concert schedule. His longtime friend and manager, Jim Bateman, had approached Carlos Santana, Gregg Allman, Bonnie Raitt and Kenny Wayne Shepherd about performing with Brown to boost his profile and payday. "I'll work as much as I want," Brown said. "When I don't want, I won't."

As his visit to Studio in the Country wound down, he listened politely to the howls and distorted guitars of a Highway 61 track called, appropriately enough, "Power to Live." As the final chord faded away, the Japanese asked to take a picture with their honored guest. The camera's flash failed on the first two attempts. Moment finally captured, they bowed in thanks. "That'll be twenty dollars each," Brown said. "And that's American money, too. I don't want no yen."

The Japanese laughed nervously, not entirely sure if he's joking.

Brown offered some final words of encouragement: "Keep it up, fellas. Keep it up."

He planned to do the same, as long as possible.

Mortality came calling on Brown weeks later. One night that December, he climbed the stairs to Rock 'n' Bowl, a famed New Orleans nightspot that, at the time, occupied a second-floor, 1940s-era bowling alley. The ascent left him winded, but he still played two sets with a combo fronted by Joe Krown, the longtime keyboardist in Gate's Express. Nine days later, Brown collapsed onstage at actor Steven Seagal's New Year's Eve party in Memphis, Tennessee, and landed in a hospital. "He was pissed off about that," Krown said. "He's not a big doctor guy."

Over the objections of the hospital staff, Brown checked out and boarded a train for a gig in Atlanta. Barbara Peterson, a longtime friend from Austin who would later move into Brown's house to help care for him, ranked that show on January 8, 2005, among his best. Gregg Allman and guitarist Susan Tedeschi were on hand to fill in if Brown couldn't finish. "They only got to play *with* him," Peterson said. "They didn't play *for* him."

Back in New Orleans two weeks later for *OffBeat* magazine's "Best of the Beat" Awards, Brown was honored for a lifetime of achievement. In front of hundreds of fellow musicians and music industry insiders, he sat on a stool and coaxed a few notes from his guitar. But new antianxiety medication had left him groggy. After two songs, he signaled to Krown that he'd had enough.

The weekend after Mardi Gras, Brown and Gate's Express traveled to the Northeast for three grueling shows, starting at B. B. King's Blues Club in Manhattan. "His hands wouldn't work," Krown said. "He couldn't even play 'Unchained Melody,' which is his favorite moment in the night. He couldn't find the notes. It was heart-wrenching."

Offstage, Brown rode in a wheelchair and piled on hats, coats and blankets in a futile effort to keep warm. Medical technicians met the band at each airport and set up oxygen generators at hotels. In Columbus, Ohio, the hotel's power failed, shutting down the oxygen machine. "He had a panic attack," Krown said. "He couldn't get enough air. He got headaches, his arms and chest hurt, like a little heart attack. It was painful to watch."

Back in Louisiana, Brown grudgingly forfeited more of his fiercely guarded independence. For months, he'd been unable to drive; his beloved Cadillac DeVille languished outside his house, collecting dust. He depended on friends to provide round-the-clock assistance and shuttle him around in a decidedly less iconic 2003 Toyota Sienna minivan.

With traditional medicine offering little hope, Brown turned to alternative therapies, including a "white light" treatment. The month of March was especially rough; he struggled to even get out of bed. But he painstakingly completed one important task: autographing several hundred copies of the 2005 New Orleans Jazz & Heritage Festival's commemorative Congo Square poster bearing his likeness.

Meanwhile, manager Jim Bateman canceled Brown's spring performances, resigned to the possibility that the guitarist might never play again.

What happened next, those around him say, was a miracle.

On March 27, 2005, Joe Krown looked up from the tiny stage of the Maple Leaf Bar, a dim, low-slung music club with pressed-tin walls in New Orleans' Carrollton neighborhood. He watched in amazement as Gatemouth Brown sauntered in, decked out in full cowboy regalia.

"I'd seen him two weeks before, and he looked horrible," Krown said. "He had that glazed-over look in his eyes. He hadn't been out of bed in two weeks." Now here he was wearing cowboy boots again, "which was a big thing. For two months, his feet had been too swollen to wear them."

Four nights later, Krown met Gatemouth at Lucky's, a twenty-four-hour bar on St. Charles Avenue. "Every other time I'd seen him, he was so lethargic that he couldn't hold his head up," Krown said. "But I don't think his chin touched his chest once. He was cutting up on people. He said he felt really good and that he had energy. It was like, 'What's going on?'"

Brown's hands shook as he tried to light his pipe, but otherwise he seemed fine. When Krown left at two A.M., Brown was still holding court. "Everybody said he was like the old Gate," Bateman said. "It's like he got a second wind. I guess he made up his mind that he was going to get out of bed and keep going."

Suddenly it seemed possible that he might fulfill the only two engagements remaining on his 2005 calendar: a free show April 13 in a downtown New Orleans park, and the all-important April 28 appearance at Jazz Fest. To prepare, Krown suggested Brown—who hadn't touched a guitar in weeks—join him for a handful of informal gigs. "I told him that it would be a real shame if he walked out onstage at Jazz Fest in front of five thousand people and his hands were too shaky to play."

So on April 1, Brown showed up for Krown's weekly happy hour gig at Le Bon Temps Roule, a scruffy, roadhouse-like Uptown bar on Magazine Street. Fifty people filled the bar's back covered patio. Most ignored the elderly black man in the gray Levi slacks, black boots, beaver-skin cowboy hat and black leather Hard Rock Cafe jacket. He settled alongside the weathered upright piano armed with his signature guitar, a 1966 Gibson Firebird with GATEMOUTH stamped on the brown leather pick guard.

He wiggled his fingers and adjusted the guitar's knobs. He braced a pinky against the instrument's body, tapped the strings with three fingers and strummed with his thumb. Clean, tidy solos, the sort he'd spun for five decades, cut through the din.

The song? "Don't Get Around Much Anymore."

After twenty minutes, he retired to a nearby table and tucked into a dozen fried oysters, sipping beer through a straw. "Does that look like a dead man to you?" Barbara Peterson said, somewhat hopefully. "I've never seen anybody on their death bed eat oysters like that."

Later that night, Brown played two sets with Krown's band several miles away at the Banks Street Bar & Grill, an equally informal joint in Mid-City. The benefit of such activity "goes beyond the gig," Krown said. "It's psychological therapy. He's so much happier that he's out. I was waiting for the call that said it was over. And then here he is, calling me and telling me to book some dates. I don't know how long it's going to last, but he's back."

In the hopes of making a few extra dollars, Brown advertised his next guest appearance on April 10 at the Maple Leaf. As long as he toured, he had earned enough to help out his grown children. But as Bateman once noted, "Savings accounts don't exist in his world."

Brown's inability to tour put him in a precarious financial position. Medicare and a supplement covered most of his hospital and doctor bills, but not the stipend paid to his caretakers or the $600 monthly tab for medicine.

Carlos Santana sent a $10,000 check, but money remained tight. Bateman contacted organizations that provide a safety net for musicians: the Rhythm & Blues Foundation, the MusiCares arm of the Recording Academy, the New Orleans Jazz & Heritage Foundation and the New Orleans Musicians Clinic, among others. But assistance from such organizations was limited. Even a low-key gig at the Maple Leaf helped.

Two months earlier, Brown could not draw enough breath to sing or raise his arms to play fiddle. He did both, briefly, at the Maple Leaf. Three nights later, he faced 3,000 people at Lafayette Square, a magnolia-lined park in the heart of downtown New Orleans, as that week's headliner for the free Wednesday at the Square spring concert series. Seated on a padded stool center stage, with a tube from a small oxygen tank running to his nose, he played only intermittently early in the set. Mostly he deferred to country-blues singer and harmonica player Delbert McClinton, whom Bateman had added to the show as backup. Later, Brown played a bit more.

Afterward, he settled into a van parked behind the stage. He faced the open cargo door and received well-wishers for thirty minutes, posing for pictures and signing autographs until fatigue set in. His fingers, he reported, were less stiff than at previous shows. "Delbert helped me out, and my band did great," he said. "I had a great time."

McClinton, too, was impressed. "He's an amazing character. He's gonna go down swingin'."

Emboldened by the guitarist's newfound stamina, Terry Phillips, a friend and caretaker, drove Brown to Dallas for an April 17 benefit in his honor. "He's played at so many benefits over the years," Phillips said. "Why not have one for him?"

To make the Dallas journey as comfortable as possible, Brown's mattress was laid across the floor of Phillips's minivan. Following the show, they left Dallas at midnight and drove all night. Exhausted, Brown rested at home for most of April 18, a Monday, then celebrated his eighty-first birthday that night at Palmetto's, a Slidell restaurant.

In hindsight, the Dallas adventure might have been too strenuous.

Soon afterward, Phillips—who had befriended Brown two years earlier while working at Smokin' Blues, a Slidell barbecue joint the guitarist frequented—moved in as a full-time caregiver.

Brown, though feeble, still resisted the idea of hospice care. "When you go with hospice, you're pretty much resigned that there's no hope," Bateman said. "And Gate's reluctant to make that resignation."

Days before the first weekend of Jazz Fest, his weight had dropped to 100 pounds—nineteen pounds fewer than a weigh-in weeks earlier, an ominous sign. But Joe Krown, for one, wouldn't bet against his boss's resolve. "In January, doctors gave him another month or two. Maybe the powers above have given him a break so that he can play Jazz Fest. He's beaten the odds so many times. He's a warrior."

On the eve of the festival, Brown attended an afternoon reception at the swank Ogden Museum of Southern Art in honor of his commemorative Jazz Fest poster. As was his habit, he lit up a pipe. A museum official asked him to extinguish it, as smoking is strictly prohibited inside. Instead, Brown—still as stubborn as ever—left.

The next night, he accompanied Krown to the fabled New Orleans nightclub Tipitina's to see Austin rhythm-and-blues pianist Marcia Ball, an old friend. Ball embraced Brown for a long good-bye hug. "Gate's going out the way he wants—in the clubs," Krown said. "It's not even about playing. He just wants to be out there, around music he likes, as much as he possibly can. And he's doing exactly that."

The Monday between Jazz Fest weekends, Brown was to be inducted into the Tipitina's Walk of Fame with a commemorative plaque set into the sidewalk on the Napoleon Avenue side of the club. That night, the skies over New Orleans opened up with a deluge. The induction ceremony's organizers erected white canopies over the sidewalk. Dozens of fans and photographers huddled together, waiting for Brown and the other inductees: 1960s girl group the Dixie Cups, and acclaimed rhythm-and-blues arranger Wardell Quezergue.

Brown arrived early with his entourage and holed up inside the Tchoup House, a refurbished home/private clubhouse next door to Tipitina's. He stretched out on a bed wearing black jeans and, on his right hip, the new .38 Taurus pistol he purchased that afternoon.

At the appointed time, Quezergue, who is nearly blind, and the three Dixie Cups took their places outside Tip's under a canopy on a low riser the size of a table top. Before Brown could exit the Tchoup House, he required oxygen and a blood pressure check. Terry Phillips handed him a pill.

"What pill is this?" Brown asked.

"Anxiety," Phillips said.

Finally, Gate pulled on his leather Hard Rock Cafe jacket and headed out the back door. The forty-five-second walk from the Tchoup House through Tipitina's to the sidewalk left him breathless.

As the Walk of Fame ceremony commenced, Brown needed to sit down. Someone set a metal folding chair next to the riser where the Dixie Cups and Quezergue stood. A knot of fans quietly sang "Chapel of Love," the Dixie Cups' biggest hit, as the three women hugged, smiled, laughed and posed with Quezergue.

Off to the side, Brown sat motionless in the shadows, leaning forward, elbows at rest on rail-thin thighs, fingers clasped over his knees. A tube in his nose tethered him to a portable oxygen tank.

From below the brim of his beige cowboy hat, he stared up at his fellow honorees, eyes wide, willing himself to join them, not having the strength to do it.

The rain fell harder.

Former Tipitina's Foundation director Bill Taylor saluted the Dixie Cups and Quezergue. The honorees spoke briefly.

Finally it was Gatemouth's turn. As Taylor listed his accomplishments, Brown bolted upright and made his way to the microphone, eyeing leaks at the canopy's seams. Cameras flashed and people cheered.

"All I can say is thank you," he said, his voice steady, his eyes moist from the rain or maybe something else. "Thank you very much."

And then he hustled back to the folding chair.

He never did see the steel Walk of Fame plaque that was carved with his name and set in the sidewalk. As Quezergue and the Dixie Cups clustered under umbrellas for the unveiling, he was already in Phillips's minivan, his sanctuary. Where it was quiet, warm and dry. Where he could rest undisturbed, breathe pure oxygen, and stave off shortness of breath.

He had arranged to inspect a motor home the next day, with an eye toward buying it with money he did not have. Because after Jazz Fest, Gatemouth Brown fully intended to hit the road again.

Only he knew the destination.

That destination turned out to be Orange, his boyhood home in southeast Texas. First, though, he rose to the occasion at Jazz Fest.

At the Gentilly Stage, one of two main stages flanking the Fair Grounds' twenty-six-acre infield, Brown cut a sharp figure in a blue-gray embroidered Western shirt, suspenders, a crisp straw cowboy hat and mirrored shades. His oxygen tank sat unused at his side as he finger-picked lean, lyrical guitar solos throughout "Grape Jelly." In the auto-biographical "Born in Louisiana," he sang with authority, sawed on a fiddle, and switched back to guitar for yet another solo. He dedicated a song to his youngest daughter, Renee, who would soon make him a grandfather once again. "It's hard to take," he said with good-humored resignation, "but I have to accept it."

During Joe Krown's Hammond B-3 organ solo in "Jumpin' the Blues," Brown pointed at the vast audience and swept his extended arm across the field as if bestowing a benediction. At the set's conclusion, he turned and walked off, tall and proud, under his own power.

Backstage, he greeted B. B. King, who would follow him on the same stage. He boarded a golf cart and crossed the infield to the festival's on-site record tent, where he signed autographs. A determined Gatemouth Brown was clearly still a force with which to be reckoned.

However, determination could only carry him so far. In the weeks after Jazz Fest, his condition deteriorated rapidly as his body wasted away. His dream of touring again proved impossible; sheer force of will no longer sufficed.

In late August, as Hurricane Katrina stalked southeast Louisiana, a weakened Brown finally consented to evacuate to Orange with his ex-wife Yvonne and their daughter, Renee. Heavy traffic stretched what is normally a five-hour drive into a twelve-hour ordeal.

On August 29, Katrina's winds and storm surge obliterated Brown's beloved Slidell abode, washing the entire house and its contents—the gun collection, the awards, the photos, the memorabilia, the model ship built out of bones—into the nearby canal and marsh. All that reminded were lonely pilings upon which the house once stood and scattered debris—a sodden guitar case, stained and smeared pictures, the ruined black Cadillac.

After several days in Orange, an effort was made to move Brown to Austin, where club owner Clifford Antone had agreed to look after him. Longtime Gate's Express saxophonist Eric Demmer and his wife, Dusty, traveled from Houston to Orange in a borrowed limousine on the night of September 5, 2005, planning to drive Brown three hundred miles to the Texas capital.

But they discovered that he was much frailer than when they'd last seen him in Slidell on August 21. "I was shocked at his condition," Dusty Demmer said. "I was afraid he might die if we took him to Austin."

Instead, they summoned an ambulance, which rushed Brown to the Medical Center of Southeast Texas in nearby Port Arthur. Doctors inserted a stent to relieve pressure on his blocked arteries. Four days later, on September 9, he checked out of the hospital, apparently against the advice of doctors.

He died less than twenty-four hours later at a grandniece's apartment in Orange.

On the afternoon of September 17, 2005, family, friends and fans gathered at Mount Calvary Baptist Church in a leafy, working-class neighborhood of Orange. The sanctuary was decidedly humble: low ceiling, cheap paneling, frosted glass windows, uneven, creaky floor. The Sunday before the funeral, Mount Calvary hosted fifty-four congregants.

Nearly four times as many souls settled into the cushioned pews for ninety minutes of music and memories in honor of Gatemouth Brown. A banner above the lectern spelled out the house rules: LET THE PREACHER DO THE TALKING! LET THE USHERS DO THE WALKING!

Brown, lying beneath the banner in a bronze-tinted steel casket, likely would have appreciated the no-nonsense directive: on the bandstand, as in life, he did not suffer fools or foolishness gladly. Had he been able, he likely would have halted the Mount Calvary band after the guitarist's first sloppy chord change. Later that afternoon, at a repast stocked with barbecue chicken, ribs, potato salad and spicy "dirty" rice, friends joked that God had forced Brown to endure the subpar music. "I'm surprised Gate didn't get up out of that coffin and take that guitar," said Terry Phillips, his former caretaker.

Had he arisen, Brown would have been dressed for the occasion. In repose he wore his trademark black cowboy hat, a black Western shirt embroidered with elaborate yellow and green flowers, and an oversize belt buckle borrowed from his brother; his own buckles lay buried in the marsh outside Slidell.

The funeral functioned as a reunion for Brown's far-flung family. Two of his four children by different women had never met. A great-nephew who spoke during the service confessed that he "wasn't real close" to Uncle Gatemouth. "I was just scared of him."

B. B. King and Delbert McClinton sent flowers. Famed Austin guitarist Jimmie Vaughan attended the service, as did members of Baton Rouge–based guitar-pop band the Benjy Davis Project. Bateman managed the young band; Brown's guest appearance on the Benjy Davis Project's 2006 CD *The Angie House* was his final recording.

Gold embroidering inside the coffin lid trumpeted his 1982 Grammy for *Alright Again!* The album's artwork dominated the cover of the glossy funeral bulletin. "He was the number-one guitar slinger from the Gulf Coast," said a somber Vaughan. "I learned a lot from his records. I never dreamed that I would grow up to meet him and play with him."

During the service, Brown's friend and collaborator Gene Gunulfsen reprised an a cappella "For Now, So Long," from the *Timeless* album. Backed by an electric keyboard, guitar and an eight-man choir, Pastor Joe Roberson sent up an exhilarating "I Got Nothing But the Holy Ghost." Urging mourners to "put your hands together," he gripped the lectern, hunched his shoulders in time with the rhythm, and rocked the house with a gritty high tenor.

Pastor George H. Brown—no relation to the deceased—delivered a thirty-minute sermon that only occasionally referenced the Grammy winner lying before him. His cadence was that of Bill Cosby posing as an elderly preacher. In a knee-length cream jacket and matching vest, he described how he was once "crazy in my mind and no sense in my soul," then found salvation.

Having concluded his speech, Pastor Brown abruptly announced "the undertakers are coming." The undertakers slowly wheeled the casket down the center aisle, preceding pastors, family and friends who quietly sang "I'll Fly Away." A black Cadillac hearse—Brown always loved black Caddies—transported the body two miles to Hollywood Cemetery. He was laid to rest between a water tower and a drainage canal, alongside his mother, sister and uncle in a grassy field studded by magnolia and cedar trees and cement slabs.

Under a punishing sun, a seven-man honor guard—Brown's honorable discharge from the Army qualified him for a military funeral—fired three volleys. A trumpeter sounded "Taps" before a chaplain oversaw the ceremonial folding of the flag draped over the casket. The mourners drifted away to eat and drink and share stories about Gatemouth Brown, of which there were many.

His long road had finally circled back to where it began.

Gatemouth Brown's adult children were civil to one another at his funeral, but two years later they tangled in court over his modest estate, which Jim Bateman—whom a judge would eventually name executor—valued at around $120,000. The most precious artifacts were the musician's fiddle and his 1966 Gibson Firebird guitar; according to Bateman, both Steven Seagal and a Japanese collector had offered Brown tens of thousands of dollars for the guitar. The instruments were in Renee Brown's possession after her father's death. Bateman wanted them held in trust by a museum, and insured. Renee then testified that the guitar and fiddle had been stolen from a storage shed, and burned.

In the early morning hours of September 13, 2008, Hurricane Ike slammed into the Texas Gulf Coast near Orange. Storm surge and rainwater flooded Hollywood Cemetery. The water forced open Brown's subterranean vault and flushed out his bronze-tinted casket, which came to rest against a nearby fence.

Not even death could halt Gatemouth Brown's rambles.

Chapter Two

Aaron Neville's Hardest Homecoming

For years, Aaron Neville collected scraps of poetry—scraps that would yield "Yellow Moon" and "Brother Jake," two of the most evocative songs in the Neville Brothers canon—in a paper bag. A friend finally gathered the scraps, typed them up and printed them on legal-size paper, color-coordinated by subject matter: yellow for the theme "In God's Hands," green for "Reality of the Streets," pink for "Love," blue for "My Family/Myself."

During a 2000 interview at his home, Neville presented me with one of these rainbow-hued poetry collections. Before his writings were collated, he said, "I lost a lot of stuff. I didn't think it was worth anything. I'd just write down my thoughts. That's how I would get over things: If something happened, I would just write. It was like somebody was telling me the words, to calm me down."

I identified with such compulsion: Writing about tribulation restores some measure of control. And for all his blessings, Aaron Neville, especially in his younger years, suffered more tribulation than most: heroin, criminal escapades, jail, crushing career disappointments, family strife.

He eventually realized the success his remarkable voice warranted, only to have his world crash down around him once again. In quick succession, he lost his city to Hurricane Katrina and his beloved wife of nearly fifty years to cancer.

If he still maintains his color-coded poetry book, he's likely added more pages.

It was not the homecoming he or anyone else wanted.

Aaron Neville was on tour with the Neville Brothers in August 2005 when Hurricane Katrina ransacked New Orleans. For sixteen months he stayed away in self-imposed exile, monitoring the news, absorbing the horror.

He didn't dare return. Following the 2004 New Orleans Jazz & Heritage Festival, an acute onset of asthma landed him in a hospital; an inhaler became his constant companion. Despite assurances that the air in the city after Katrina was no more hostile to asthmatics, he chose not to tempt fate.

And he would not endanger Joel.

Before the storm, the former Joel Roux, Neville's wife and the mother of his four children, battled lung cancer into remission. But her health was still precarious. Post-Katrina New Orleans, they decided, was no place for her.

The couple bought a hilltop house in leafy Brentwood, Tennessee, just down the road from Dolly Parton. The newly established Nevilles of Nashville circled the wagons and settled in with Joel's brother and elderly mother, who had lost their own home in New Orleans' Pontchartrain Park neighborhood.

Despite his self-imposed exile, Aaron celebrated his hometown across the country: on *The Tonight Show with Jay Leno*; onstage with Simon & Garfunkel at Madison Square Garden in New York; with Aretha Franklin at the 2006 Super Bowl in Detroit; on the road with the Neville Brothers.

Everywhere but New Orleans.

Throughout his exile, Aaron and his manager contemplated when, and how, the singer might return. The longer he waited, the more dramatic such a homecoming would be. They envisioned a public celebration to demonstrate how much Aaron and his brothers still loved the city that forged their identity.

In the end, it was Joel who brought Aaron home . . . to bury her.

Joel (pronounced Jo-EL) Roux grew up in Uptown New Orleans on Burdette Street, the daughter of a golf pro and a public housing administrator. Achievement runs in her family. Her oldest brother, Dr. Vincent J. Roux, is a surgeon and associate dean of the Howard University College of Medicine in Washington D.C. During her senior year at Xavier Prep, a Catholic high school for girls of African-American descent, Joel met a sixteen-year-old boy named Aaron Neville.

His left cheek sported a crude cross/dagger tattoo, applied by a buddy with India ink and two sewing needles tied to a matchstick. Neville's father made him "scrub it with a Brillo pad and soap. The skin came off, but the tattoo stayed." It could have been worse: His buddy, a fellow student at Samuel James Green Junior High, sported a cross between his eyebrows; another acquaintance rocked a skull and crossbones on his face. "I thought about that one," Neville said, "but I'm glad I didn't get it. I think my dad would have killed me." (Decades later, his cheek tat came in handy. When he released *The Tattooed Heart* in 1995, he had a professional tattoo artist in Los Angeles trace the outline; it became part of the CD's promotional campaign.)

His menacing exterior, a protective shell hardened by a childhood spent in the Calliope housing development, did not completely mask an inherent sweetness. He first spotted this "cute Creole girl" at a party in May 1957. A few days later, he and Leo Morris—who would become Idris Muhammad, a formidable jazz drummer—were "bippity-bopping" down Valence Street. They crossed paths with the girl from the party, en route to have her prom dress altered. Morris introduced her to Neville, who was smitten. He courted her. She sang with a group called the Debettes; he showed up to play piano with them at St. Joan of Arc Church and Lincoln Beach, an amusement park for the segregated city's black population.

The Roux family was not pleased. They expected Joel go to college, not fall for a Walter L. Cohen High School dropout and aspiring singer with a homemade face tattoo. "I don't think they liked that too much," Aaron recalled decades later, chuckling. "They thought she was crazy. But I knew I loved her, and I knew she loved me, so it didn't matter."

The couple married on January 10, 1959. Joel was eighteen. Aaron was two weeks shy of that mark; his mother signed the marriage license. The precise date of their wedding eventually slipped from their collective memory. So they celebrated on three consecutive days—January 10, 11 and 12—even after their marriage license resurfaced and confirmed the 10th as their anniversary.

Aaron's young bride enrolled at New Orleans' historically black

Xavier University, but quit after the couple's first child, Ivan, arrived in August 1959. Over the next four decades, their roller coaster of a marriage endured more peaks and valleys than most. Aaron possessed a remarkable talent, an angelic, delicate voice modeled on cowboy yodelers and soul singers. But his gift could not overcome the lure of the streets. Juvenile crime and car theft gave way to more serious offenses and heroin use; he spent time at Angola, Louisiana's notorious state prison.

In the early 1960s, Aaron moved to Los Angeles, hoping to jumpstart his career. Instead, he was busted during a break-in at a clothing store. He spent a year fighting fires with a jailhouse work gang, then returned to New Orleans. Through it all, Joel encouraged her husband's musical career and that of his youngest brother, Cyril, a firebrand soul singer with a massive chip on his shoulder. Cyril referred to Joel as "my second mother," a confidant for whom he would audition new songs.

Aaron finally notched a major national hit, "Tell It Like It Is," in early 1967, but made little money. To make ends meet, he worked on the Mississippi River docks, painted houses, dug ditches and drove trucks. Frustration mounted, trouble followed, and he took solace in drugs. One day in 1972, soon after the arrival of his youngest son, Jason, Aaron returned to an empty house in the 1000 block of Valence: Joel had packed up the kids and moved in with her parents in the leafy suburb of Pontchartrain Park.

That, he recalled in early 2007, "was about the lowest part of my life. Besides now."

With his life in New Orleans completely unraveled, Aaron joined Cyril and another brother, Charles, a saxophonist, in New York. Even from afar, Joel "kept me safe, really. Where I'd normally have done something wrong, maybe I thought about them and I wouldn't do it. So it gave me a purpose."

Months later, he returned to New Orleans. Joel's parents had forbidden her to see him. But he hung out in a park near the Roux house. Ivan would sneak outside and remind his pop of the family life he was missing.

Aaron secretly contacted Joel and promised to change. "I told her

I was going to be right, that I wasn't going to be doing the things I was doing, messing with drugs. We got back together, and she stuck with me through the rest. She helped me grow up."

In 1977, Aaron realized his parents' dream and formed a band with his three brothers, Art, Charles and Cyril. The Neville Brothers trafficked in a potent mix of second-line rhythms and chants passed down by their uncle George "Jolly" Landry, Big Chief of the Wild Tchoupitoulas Mardi Gras Indian tribe, and percolating funk carried over from Cyril and oldest brother Art's time in the groundbreaking Meters.

Meanwhile, Joel earned a steady paycheck in the business department of Charity Hospital. She provided stability until the Neville Brothers finally started making decent money in the early 1980s. At first glance, Joel and Aaron formed an incongruous couple. She was petite, short and gregarious, fond of stylish pantsuits and always up for an outing with friends. With his weight lifter's build, Aaron dwarfed his wife. When not on stage, he preferred to be home. Regardless of the setting, he favored sleeveless shirts and denim jackets.

Yet they had forged an unbreakable bond. The week of their twenty-fifth anniversary, Joel took a cruise with her siblings. Back home on Valence Street, a lonely Aaron gazed at the full moon as lyrics formed in his head. "That's how I got through a lot of things, writing about it. I'd write it, and it would help me out. I was missing her, and there was a big yellow moon out my window."

Because of Joel's inspiration, he credited her as a co-writer of "Yellow Moon." The bewitching song, laced with a snake-charmer saxophone solo by Charles, served as the title track of what is considered the Neville Brothers' best album, 1989's Grammy-winning *Yellow Moon*.

That same year, Linda Ronstadt invited Aaron to sing on her *Cry Like a Rainstorm, Howl Like the Wind*. The album yielded two smash duets, "Don't Know Much" and "All My Life." Building on that momentum, he relaunched his solo career in 1991 with *Warm Your Heart* and the single "Everybody Plays the Fool," his biggest hit since "Tell It Like It Is."

This time, he got paid. "It was smooth sailing after that. I was able to give Joel things I wasn't able to give her before. She liked to shop. Her and my sister Athelgra were shopping buddies."

Aaron was now ranked among his hometown's most famous residents. With his imposing physique, tattoos and prominent facial mole, he was instantly recognizable. Joel retired from Charity. She and Aaron moved away from their deteriorating Uptown neighborhood to a new, ranch-style brick house at the end of a quiet cul-de-sac in eastern New Orleans, an expanse of drained swampland overlaid with new suburbs. They soon gave that house to their daughter Ernestine and upgraded to a spacious two-story alongside a golf course in the gated Eastover subdivision, a popular destination for the city's black upper-middle class.

They made the house a home. A stylized N adorned the wrought-iron gate, behind which sat Aaron's beloved Corvette. His Grammy awards occupied a shelf in a small office just off the foyer. Joel cooked her famous red beans in a large kitchen, which opened onto the family room. A white leather sectional sofa faced the big-screen TV on which her husband watched *The Young and the Restless*, his favorite soap opera. They specifically didn't install a pool so friends and relations wouldn't overrun their sanctuary.

The house inspired Aaron. The big bay window in the upstairs master bedroom framed the gentle green curves of the Eastover golf course, a lagoon and a distant tree line. One stormy summer evening, the singer sat on the edge of the bed, transfixed, as long lightning fingers fractured the dark sky. As the storm receded, the setting sun burned through the clouds. "It was bloodred—it looked like it was dripping. I sat there saying, 'Lord, thank you for letting me see this.'"

He envisioned living in that house in eastern New Orleans until he died. "I always thought Joel would bury me. I used to make plans with her, telling her what I wanted. But it didn't work out like that."

In 2004, Joel was diagnosed with inoperable lung cancer. Her prognosis was poor. "The doctors gave her three months," her husband said. "We started praying and doing our novenas. We prayed together every day."

Raised a Roman Catholic like his mother, even though his father was Methodist, Neville has long credited his Christian faith and St. Jude for his deliverance from drugs and crime, and his ultimate success. As a boy, he and his mother made pilgrimages to St. Ann's Shrine, a grotto at the corner of Ursulines Avenue and North Johnson Street in the city's 6th Ward. They ascended the steps on their knees, reciting a prayer at each stop. Years later, Neville accompanied his uncle George Landry to the same shrine, as cancer ate away at Landry's lungs.

Through the end of 2004 and into the following spring and summer, Joel bore her cross with quiet dignity, strength and humor. She also proved to be a tenacious fighter, forcing the cancer into remission with radiation and chemotherapy.

Then Hurricane Katrina roared ashore on August 29. Storm surge and floodwaters unleashed by broken levees destroyed most of eastern New Orleans; Eastover was decimated. Joel had evacuated ahead of the storm; Aaron, on tour with the Neville Brothers in upstate New York, met his displaced family in Tennessee. With New Orleans uninhabitable, they decided to settle right there, in Brentwood, Tennessee.

Aaron would not return to New Orleans, but he pled the city's case on television and at benefit concerts around the country. He delivered a haunting "Bridge Over Troubled Water" with Simon & Garfunkel during the *From the Big Apple to the Big Easy* benefit at Madison Square Garden on September 20, 2005—barely four weeks after his home was destroyed.

In part because of Aaron's fear of aggravating his asthma, the Neville Brothers elected to sit out the 2006 Jazz Fest—a decision that infuriated many longtime fans. The first Jazz Fest after the storm would be a major milestone on the city's road to recovery, a rallying point for citizens engaged in the epic struggle to rebuild. Thus, many believed, it was the brothers' duty to stand with the city that succored them in its time of greatest need.

Aaron, though, was not willing to risk his health. "I love New Orleans and I want to come back, but I want to be safe," he said at the time. "I don't want to chance it on the Fair Grounds and get real sick and have to go in the hospital. I've got to take medicine to keep my lungs clear. It's a scary thing."

By the spring of 2006, Jazz Fest was the least of his concerns: Joel's cancer had roared back with a vengeance. The stress and sadness brought on by Katrina likely did her body no favors. This time, the cancer invaded her bones and brain. Aaron doted on her through the long, terrible descent, as the disease laid waste to the woman who had sustained him through his own darkest days.

The extended Neville family gathered at the Brentwood house for New Year's Eve 2006—and to say good-bye. As the end drew near, Aaron maintained a constant vigil at Joel's bedside. He cradled her frail wrists in his hands, his physical strength of no use. "I couldn't help her. She was hurting. She prayed for God to come for her."

Before daybreak on the morning of January 5, her prayers were answered.

Joel had made her intentions clear: She wanted to be laid to rest in New Orleans, in the family's vault at Mount Olivet Cemetery on Gentilly Boulevard in the 7th Ward. So on January 10, 2007, their forty-eighth wedding anniversary, Aaron returned to New Orleans for the first time since Hurricane Katrina.

Aboard Southwest's ten A.M. nonstop from Nashville, he focused on a book of Sudoku puzzles, a favorite pastime. He traveled with one of Joel's brothers, John, and her mother, Beatrice Roux Taylor. Athelgra Neville Gabriel, Aaron's sister and one of Joel's closest friends, picked them up at Louis Armstrong International Airport. Gabriel drove Aaron to the downtown Sheraton hotel, where he holed up in a forty-eighth-floor room with a sweeping view of the Mississippi River. Family and friends stopped by to offer comfort and support.

The next day, he ventured onto the streets of New Orleans after a sixteen-month absence. With his brother-in-law Dr. Vincent Roux, he walked a block on bustling Canal Street to the upscale Rubenstein Bros. haberdashery and bought two shirts. He turned west onto St. Charles Avenue and stopped at the venerable Meyer the Hatter, a New Orleans institution since 1894. Aaron's late father, "Big" Arthur Neville, and his Uncle Jolly favored hats from Meyer. Aaron stocked up on New Orleans Saints caps, a flat "apple" cap, and a black Dobbs 5th Avenue dutton with a "stingy" brim.

And then he retreated to the Sheraton. Strangers encountered on his walk either offered condolences or asked if he would be singing at that weekend's Saints-Eagles game in the Superdome. "I'm afraid not," Aaron replied without further explanation. "I'm not here for the game."

He was not inclined to tour the city's flood-ravaged neighborhoods. His own ruined house in Eastover had been gutted and sold without his ever laying eyes on it. "I don't know if I'll get out or not," he said from the sanctity of the Sheraton. "I don't think I want to see it. I've got memories."

Joel loved Our Lady Star of the Sea, a turn-of-the-twentieth century Catholic church in a hardscrabble swath of the 8th Ward. During Katrina, six feet of water swamped the surrounding neighborhood, but only two inches topped the church steps and breached the sanctuary. The terrazzo floors and wooden pews survived.

On the night of January 12, 2007, neighborhood boys engaged in a street basketball game on a corner near the church. Tidy rows of boxy white FEMA trailers filled nearby St. Roch Playground. Blue flashes from police cars pierced the amber glow of streetlights, pointing the way for hundreds of mourners.

Inside the cavernous domed sanctuary, eight larger-than-life angels ascend the thirty-foot wall behind the altar. Painter Vernon Dobard had rendered the angels as sensual, beautiful women of various races with long, flowing locks. Some sprinkle flower petals; one strokes a pelican, the Louisiana state bird. Above them towers an equally radiant Virgin Mary.

At the base of the wall of angels lay Joel Neville, dressed in a black ensemble trimmed in leopard print. Aaron sat alone in the front pew, steps from her body. In an embroidered burgundy suit and sunglasses, he clasped hands with passing friends, family and musicians. Initially, the gathering felt more like a reunion than a funeral; as a young man, Aaron had even painted houses alongside an uncle of Our Lady's priest, Tony Ricard.

At the lectern, Ricard finally made the sign of the cross, a signal for the congregation to quiet down. In the ensuing service, Ricard explained, there would be no introductions of performers: "We're not having a concert. We're having a prayer service."

Yet it would be a decidedly musical prayer service. Jazz vocalist Phillip Manuel sang "Come Ye Disconsolate." Jason Neville eulogized his mother with a solo piano tribute titled "An Angel." His uncle Charles unspooled a lovely saxophone solo.

Cyril Neville stepped to the lectern with a statement Aaron wrote as a raw expression of loss. To read it, Cyril said, "is one of the greatest honors I've had in my life." With that, he channeled his brother's words: "I remember the first kiss back in 1957, and I'll never forget our last kiss. I held her head in my hands and was as gentle as I could be. I kissed her eyes, her face and her hands. I knew I was losing my best friend."

Cyril choked up and continued through tears. "She was everything a person could be to another. I still feel her lips on mine. I'll never get over losing her. But I know she's in a better place. She's gone home, and I'll see her again some day."

Aaron sat, head bowed, listening. Earlier, he had removed his dark sunglasses. Now they hid his eyes once again.

That week, he had stressed that he would not speak or sing during the service; he wanted only to mourn. So family and friends were stunned when he stood up, signaled the musicians to be silent, and made his way to the lectern. He recalled meeting Joel on Valence Street. Quiet laughter rippled through the church as he explained their fluctuating wedding anniversary. Then, abruptly, he declared, "It's going to be the hardest thing in the world for me to accept that Joel is not there no more."

Words caught in his throat; he could not continue. He moved stiffly toward the casket, where Vincent Roux embraced him. He leaned over his wife's body, then hurried back to his seat in the first row. Ernestine wrapped a reassuring arm around her father's broad shoulders.

The next morning, Our Lady Star of the Sea hosted Joel's funeral Mass. Aaron arrived at nine A.M. He had provided prerecorded music to play before the Mass; as he made his way down the center aisle, his recording of "Take It to the Lord in Prayer" wafted from the church speakers, a comforting voice that happened to be his own.

Early in the service, Art Neville delivered a piano eulogy. Art's daughter, the TV personality Arthel Neville, read "To My Lil Joel from Your Big Aaron," a final open letter from Aaron to his wife: "Through it all I've never seen anyone as strong and faithful as you. If I can be half that strong, I'll be all right."

Rev. Ricard's upbeat remarks acknowledged Joel's legendary shopping prowess: "She's going to let us know where the best deals are when we get up there" to heaven, where he imagined Joel sashaying down a line of friends and family.

After two hours, the Rebirth Brass Band, trumpeter James Andrews, and his younger brother Troy "Trombone Shorty" Andrews led the recessional with a dirge, "Just a Closer Walk with Thee." Outside, Aaron's sister Athelgra—she and the six other surviving members of Joel's pokeno club wore pins consisting of playing cards—orchestrated a brief second-line. As the white handkerchiefs fluttered, Aaron disappeared into a waiting limousine.

Thirty minutes later, Joel's casket arrived on the second floor of the Mount Olivet mausoleum. Accompanying it were dozens of floral arrangements from the likes of Trisha Yearwood and Garth Brooks, Linda Ronstadt, contemporary gospel group Take 6, and actor John Goodman.

Athelgra was the last to leave after the brief interment ceremony. With the pointed metal tip of a flower's stem-holder, she etched the names of loved ones into the polished mahogany of Joel's casket—a Neville family tradition established by an aunt who feared her coffin might be reused.

The next afternoon, Aaron visited Art's house Uptown. The following morning, he flew back to Tennessee. When he would return to New Orleans was unknown. He hoped to sing in his hometown "at some point. Right now I'm not even thinking about it. I'm taking it one minute at a time, and going through what I've got to go through. Right now, I'm missing Joel."

He canceled two shows with the San Diego Symphony scheduled for the weekend after the funeral, and planned to avoid solo gigs indefinitely. "With the Nevilles, I have them to take up the slack. When I'm doing solo stuff, it's on me, and I don't want to cheat nobody if I get emotional and can't perform."

Days before Joel's death, he performed a Christmas show with the Nashville Symphony. He broke down during Jimmie Rodgers's country lament "Why Should I Be Lonely." "I got halfway through and couldn't sing no more. It was like recording [the 2006 CD] *Bring It On Home: The Soul Classics*. Songs like 'Ain't No Sunshine When She's Gone' and 'Stand by Me' took on new meanings. They turned into prayers."

That Nashville Symphony concert would be his final performance for many weeks. Back home in Brentwood after the funeral, he rested, recuperated, wrote, sorted through a lifetime of memories and adjusted to the huge void left by Joel's passing. "I have good moments and bad moments. But I'm learning to make all of them good moments. If I'm crying, it's a good cry."

Ultimately, he anticipated at least one final trip to New Orleans, to Mount Olivet Cemetery. "Because that's where I'm going to be buried," he said. "With her."

By January 2008, a year after Joel's death, Aaron had begun to reconcile her passing. "It's been a heavy month," he said. "Everybody kept saying, 'You've got a few firsts coming up: The first year, the first birthday.' I got past a year."

Indicative of his forward progress, he slipped into New Orleans for brief, low-key visits. Two months after Joel's funeral, he rejoined the Neville Brothers on the road, marking the band's thirtieth anniversary and the fortieth anniversary of "Tell It Like It Is" topping the charts.

Additionally, Aaron and Mac "Dr. John" Rebennack finally explored a long-discussed collaboration. When his schedule allowed, Rebennack traveled to Nashville and bunked at Neville's house. They'd toy with voice-and-piano arrangements of vintage doo-wop and rhythm-and-blues songs, then record them at a nearby studio.

With no agenda, they focused on chestnuts. From the New Orleans repertoire, they borrowed Johnny Adams's "I Won't Cry," the Spiders' "Bells In My Heart" and the traditional "St. James Infirmary." They also recorded Johnny Ace's "The Clock" and "Pledging My Love," Chuck Willis's "It's Too Late (She's Gone)," Jesse Belvin's "Goodnight My Love" and the Platters' "Smoke Gets In Your Eyes." Paging through a tablet of Neville's writings, Rebennack came across a poem about Joel and wrote music for what became "My Leading Lady."

As he mourned, Neville found a kindred spirit in Don Hubbard, a friend from his days at Cohen High School. Like Neville, Hubbard met his future wife when they were teenagers. The Nevilles and the Hubbards married the same year. Hubbard's wife passed away just after Joel. "We get together on the phone and laugh and cry and help each other," Neville said. "We're probably the only ones who can understand what we're going through. It's hard for somebody else to give you advice, because they don't know."

To distract himself, Neville exercised more intensely than ever. "I have a ritual. I used to go to the Starbucks but I stopped drinking coffee. So now I just go pick up a paper at Walgreens and get on back home. I work out in the daytime. That's it."

He spoke to his children often, and they visited him in Brentwood. "So that's good. I help my kids, they help me. But I need to get down there to New Orleans." In New Orleans, however, he was surrounded by memories. Of the city before the storm. Of Joel. Some day it might be easier to walk among the ghosts. "It is something," he said, "that I need to do."

The pull of home and family finally proved too powerful: In the spring of 2008, Neville sold his Tennessee house and bought property near rural Covington, Louisiana, an hour's drive from New Orleans on the far side of Lake Pontchartrain. A plot of high ground north of Interstate 12, he believed, offered better protection from hurricanes than reclaimed swampland in New Orleans. His new place "is a hundred-and-something feet above sea level. I don't want to run every time a hurricane comes. [But] I wanted to get closer to my kids." In addition to the threat of hurricanes, New Orleans still held too many memories. "Me and Joel spent our life there. It would be hard."

His new spread in St. Tammany Parish included a pool and three acres alongside a man-made lake. "I'm Aquarius. That water draws me. I can sit outside and watch the sun go down, then drive on in to New Orleans. It's nice."

Aaron's return doubled the number of Neville Brothers living in the New Orleans area. Art had already reoccupied his repaired house in the family's old Uptown neighborhood. Cyril, whose home in Gentilly was claimed by Katrina's waters, was still displaced to Austin, Texas. Charles, the family wayfarer, had moved to western Massachusetts in the 1990s, his New Orleans exit hastened by the stray bullet that crashed through a window of his old house in the Carrollton area.

More aware than ever of mortality, Aaron intended to stay busy: "There's so much I want to do. I just hope I've got time enough."

The question of if and when to return to post-Katrina New Orleans is a complex decision based on the perception of what is best for a family's mental, physical and financial well-being at any given time. When your last name is Neville, that decision is played out in the court of public opinion, where verdicts are often rendered on emotion.

News of Aaron Neville's impending return to Louisiana was met with generally fond wishes—but not so the announcement that the Neville Brothers would close out the 2008 New Orleans Jazz & Heritage Festival. Some hometown fans still resented the brothers' long absence. Throughout the spring of 2008, naysayers peppered online message boards. Their vitriolic tone suggested the brothers were personally responsible for such Katrina nightmares as FEMA trailers contaminated with formaldehyde or botched Road Home recovery grants. Clearly the brothers misjudged the message they would inadvertently send by skipping the first two Jazz Fests after the storm.

What most detractors did not know was that the brothers had agreed to perform in 2007, but as the booking deadline loomed in the fall of 2006, Joel's prognosis was grave. Aaron's availability was bound to her uncertain fate, and the Neville Brothers would not appear without him. So they quietly withdrew from Jazz Fest before their booking was even announced; the festival replaced them with another home-grown favorite, Harry Connick Jr.

Following Joel's death, the Nevilles cut a lucrative deal to return in 2008. They had long believed the festival underpaid them relative to other headliners; thus, a bit of checkbook diplomacy on the part of Jazz Fest facilitated their return. Those who still questioned the brothers' motives "don't know the story," Aaron said. "They don't know what other people went through. I had a few blows. Losing my house and my children's houses and Joel getting sick. . . . It's been a heavy few years. That's all I can say."

Against that backdrop, he made the most of his highly anticipated homecoming. Appropriately enough, his post-Katrina debut on a New

Orleans stage was in support of brother Art, a primary inspiration. Growing up in the Calliope projects, the brothers often harmonized on doo-wop. Art was the family's first star as the lead singer on the Hawketts' 1954 single "Mardi Gras Mambo," an essential New Orleans carnival season anthem to this day.

In recent years, Art limited his performances to the Neville Brothers or some incarnation of the Meters. But he agreed to front his own all-star band at Jazz Fest's main Acura Stage on May 2, the second Friday of the 2008 festival. Aaron sang backup on "Mardi Gras Mambo," "Tick Tock"—a song dating to their days in the Calliope projects—and Fats Domino's "Please Don't Leave Me."

Supporting Art was a way for Aaron to ease into the weekend. The next afternoon, all eyes would be on him at the festival's AIG Gospel Tent. His Jazz Fest Gospel Tent appearances are extremely popular. In years past, veteran vocal group the Zion Harmonizers backed him, or he sang to prerecorded tapes. This time, he would use a quintet featuring brother Charles on saxophone.

As showtime approached, the sweltering white tent overflowed its 2,000-person capacity; latecomers pooled outside, straining to catch a glimpse through tent flaps. Emotions and anticipation ran high. "I felt the emotion," Neville said later. "I saw a lot of people dabbing their eyes with handkerchiefs." Joel had come to him in a dream the previous night. He took comfort in her "telling me everything was cool."

Throughout his hour-long set, he stuck mostly to standard fare: "Bridge Over Troubled Water," an intimate "Jesus Loves Me," a swinging "Mary Don't You Weep." Charles opened "Just a Closer Walk With Thee" with a hushed saxophone solo; when the entire band swung in and picked up the tempo, Aaron danced and waved a white towel as if second-lining on the street. He "couldn't help it. It was that kind of beat, that New Orleans thing I learned as a little bitty kid. I used to run behind the funeral parades. I didn't know who was dead, but the music drew me. I'd be right in that crowd.

"I've got to be careful," he continued, laughing. "I can't be doing it too much because I don't want to pull nothing out of whack."

A fresh arrangement of "Stand By Me" included the line "just as long as Jesus stands by me." Charles lit up "A Change Is Gonna Come" with an eloquent alto sax passage. An enlivened "I Saw the Light" sailed along on a funky undercurrent and doo-wop harmonies. Hitting his stride, Aaron led the ensemble through a medley of "Down By the Riverside," "Amen" and "This Little Light of Mine," followed by "The Lord's Prayer" and "Amazing Grace," a hymn he essentially owns. "When you're emotional, you've got stuff happening inside you that the notes may not come out right. Some of those songs were tugging at me, and I had to suck it up and get through them. If I had let go and started getting emotional, I wouldn't have been able to finish."

His musicians kept a close watch, reassuring the singer with smiles if they sensed emotion threatened to overcome him. Thousands of listeners attuned to every syllable also sustained his focus: "It was like, 'Hey, I'm at the Gospel Tent with my band. It's time for me to sing. I've got to go for what I know.'"

The audience stood, spellbound, during the final, spine-tingling encore: Randy Newman's "Louisiana 1927." "Louisiana, they're trying to wash us away," were the final words sung by Aaron Neville at his first full Jazz Fest performance since his house, and much of his city, were in fact washed away. In the crowd, second-line handkerchiefs and napkins now dabbed tears.

As he descended the stage steps into a throng of well-wishers, his default stoicism shattered. He broke into a broad, unabashed grin, part joy, part relief. "The people made me feel so elated. People say the music do them, but it do me, also. And I got through it without crying. I was on the verge a bunch of times. But I got through it."

The Gospel Tent was only a prelude of what was to come.

As the New Orleans heat melted away on the afternoon of May 4, 2008, Jazz Fest's final Sunday, tens of thousands of fans settled on the field facing the Acura Stage, primed for the Neville Brothers. Backstage, the brothers and their band huddled in a dressing room trailer. "This was the show of shows," Aaron said. "All of us felt the same way about the love affair we were coming back to, to the city, to the people and to the Jazz Fest. We said, 'Let's go out there and do it. We're the Neville Brothers, we're home, let's go give 'em us, and take them.' In other words, give out our energy and love and soul, and receive the love and soul and energy from the audience. And they gave it to us."

The love affair was rekindled soon after the band arrived onstage.

"How many people are happy to be in New Orleans?" Cyril shouted. "How many people are happy to be listening to the Neville Brothers?" Thousands of voices answered in the affirmative. Rumored protests by disgruntled fans did not materialize; lingering misgivings quickly dissipated. Out on the field, lifelong New Orleanian Johnny Sanchez watched his two-year-old daughter, Anna, stomp across a mud puddle, a remnant of the weekend's rains. He proudly noted that Anna had not missed a day of Jazz Fest "from the womb until now."

Sanchez said he "initially had apprehension" about the Nevilles skipping the first two post-Katrina Jazz Fests. "But I realized we all come back on our own time. I have to respect that." With their set underway, he summed up his feelings by pointing out one of dozens of homemade flags fluttering above the vast crowd. It proclaimed Sunday the "Best Day Ever."

From the set's opening moments, the Nevilles underscored their deep roots in Mardi Gras Indian culture. Indians in full, feathered regalia joined them for "Meet De Boys on the Battlefront," an age-old Indian anthem, and "Fiyo on the Bayou," a song Cyril and Art first recorded with the Meters. Meters bassist George Porter Jr. was also an onstage guest.

After the bewitching "Voodoo," Aaron crooned "A Change is Gonna Come." His son Ivan, a renowned musician with his own story of struggle and survival, buttressed a soulful "Tipitina" with keyboard fills. Aaron dedicated "Tell It Like It Is" to Joel. "Life is too short to live in sorrow," he sang, as much for his own benefit as anyone else's. "You may be here today, and gone tomorrow."

Carlos Santana, who preceded the Neville Brothers on the Acura Stage, returned to spike the Nevilles' "My Blood" with smoldering guitar lines. Art's singsongy Hammond organ, Cyril's percussion, Aaron's voice, Charles's sax and drummer "Mean" Willie Green's thunder and funk interlocked on "Ain't No Use," "Brother Jake" and a haunting "Yellow Moon" in quick succession. They swung back to the streets of New Orleans with "Brother John is Gone" and "Iko Iko." Nick Daniels and Tony Hall squared off on a double-bass groove.

Aaron still had one more river to cross. His voice quivered, but never broke, during a stunning "Amazing Grace." At its conclusion, he said simply, "Joel, y'all." That, he later confirmed, "was the heaviest moment. That was the only time I really cracked. I almost lost it . . . Joel is usually in front of the stage. I felt her there. I felt her in my heart."

And then the Neville Brothers eased into Bob Marley's reggae call for peace and understanding, "One Love," resurrecting a beloved pre-Katrina Jazz Fest tradition. They harmonized on the chorus of "let's get together and feel all right," underscoring the day's theme. Such were the happy feelings in the air that Cyril even saluted Jazz Fest producer Quint Davis, with whom he has occasionally clashed: "You've been keeping [Jazz Fest] together. I love you, bruh." Davis returned the compliment: "We're all Nevilles in New Orleans."

For the final "Big Chief," they pulled out all the stops. Troy "Trombone Shorty" Andrews set off trumpet fireworks, Green picked up the tempo as if powering a gospel revival, and Cyril, lost in the spirit, danced with knee-jerking, arm-swinging abandon. The brothers plugged into the music's power even as they generated it, restored to their rightful place in the city where it all began.

Aaron cherishes his memories of that day. "I was looking out at the crowd and looking at the sky. Every year I see a few birds pass over the people. I watched the birds pass, and I was glad. I was happy that the Neville Brothers were playing at the Jazz Fest, and closing it out like it's supposed to be on a sunny day."

Early in the set, they sang, "My brother Jake is finally home." So, too, were the Neville Brothers. "It was a rough week, but a great week," Aaron said. "It was like returning to a loved one that you hadn't seen for a while. Somebody that had been in your life since you can remember, and helped nurture you through the good, the bad and whatever else, and accepted you with open arms and loved you just as much as you loved them. The whole week, just walking through the streets, people telling me 'welcome home'—it was a great feeling."

Two days after Jazz Fest, Neville flew to Hawaii for a symphonic concert and a much-needed rest. But first he attended to one more task in New Orleans.

After months of delay, the Neville family crypt at Mount Olivet Cemetery was finally repaired. Barely twelve hours after the Neville Brothers lofted the last notes of Jazz Fest, Aaron and his family oversaw the transfer of Joel's remains from their temporary resting place in a mausoleum to the family vault. Once again he was reminded of his own mortality. His music—the sad songs, as well as the joyous—will outlive him.

"Ain't nobody got immortality. Everybody's got a time. A lot of people like to live like they're not going nowhere. But I'll welcome [death], because it's a part of life. Joel showed me how to do it. She was a strong woman. She gave me pointers: Go out with dignity and faith and love. So I ain't scared of nothing."

Prior to the 2008 Jazz Fest, *People* magazine dispatched a photographer from New York to New Orleans to shoot a portrait of the Neville Brothers. Sarah A. Friedman had documented dozens of prominent entertainers, athletes and businessmen. But that day in New Orleans, something other than a camera clicked.

Aaron called Friedman after she returned to New York. Shortly thereafter, they started dating. By October 2008, they were engaged. Even as he finished renovating his new home in Covington, Louisiana, he began shopping for an apartment in New York.

Their quick engagement and twenty-eight-year age difference raised some eyebrows, but Neville was unapologetic. "Two people on the planet at the same time that love each other and make each other happy—that's all that matters . . . If it had been on the other foot, I would have wanted Joel to go on with her life. I wouldn't want her to be lonely and grieving. I grieved; I'm going to still do that. That's going to be part of my life, because she was my whole life, up until now. I can't explain what my heart's been through. It needs some healing and nurturing." His marriage to Joel carried him "from a boy to a man. I was a teenager when I got married. I'm glad we were able to live out our vows."

On November 13, 2010, he made another one. He married Friedman before a handful of friends and relatives at New York's Eleven Madison Park restaurant. Presiding over the ceremony was the Rev. Tony R. Ricard of Our Lady Star of the Sea, the same priest who buried Joel.

Neville closed out 2010 as a man reborn. "I'm happy. I feel life," he said. "I love waking up in the morning. I'm in a good place." He and

Friedman settled into an apartment in Manhattan's Flatiron District with their two cats, Turks and Caicos. He hired a new manager for his solo career. He published his first book of poetry, *I Am a Song*. And four days before his wedding, he released an intimate album of gospel-soul songs. The title? *I Know I've Been Changed*.

Chapter Three

Quint Davis and the 2006 Jazz Fest Revival

When you listen to music for a living, cynicism is an occupational hazard; the merely ordinary no longer impresses. So on those rare occasions when I am deeply affected by a performance, I'm confident superlatives are justified.

The New Orleans Jazz & Heritage Festival has yielded more than its share of such moments. In 2005, Irma Thomas, the soul queen of New Orleans, lost herself in the spirit of gospel maverick Sister Rosetta Tharpe's "Beams of Heaven." By the song's conclusion, Thomas was fully caught up in the spirit; tears ran down her cheeks as a chill ran up my spine.

The 2006 Jazz Fest, staged eight months after Katrina, would by definition be emotional; much was at stake for the fest, and the city. Quint Davis, the festival's colorful producer/director, and his staff pulled off a minor miracle in presenting what sounded, looked, tasted and felt like a "regular" Jazz Fest. And lo and behold, it was not a local musician but a "visiting" artist, Bruce Springsteen, who supplied the literal watershed moment.

On the festival's first Sunday, my wife and I stood in the field facing the main Acura Stage alongside a half-dozen writers and journalists. Like me, they had witnessed countless concerts, and were not easily moved. By the conclusion of Springsteen's tour de force with his Seeger Sessions Band, all of us—myself, my wife, the other writers—were weeping.

It felt wonderful.

In the first two, terrible weeks after Hurricane Katrina, good news was hard to come by. But eleven surreal days after the storm, shell-shocked, scattered New Orleanians were momentarily cheered by a brief, boldly optimistic declaration: The 2006 New Orleans Jazz & Heritage Festival presented by Shell would go on as scheduled the following spring.

On September 9, 2005, the day the announcement appeared on Nola.com, swaths of the city were still submerged. The entire population was displaced. Not all the dead bodies had been discovered.

Yet producers of the annual springtime celebration of indigenous music, food and culture jabbed a defiant finger in Katrina's eye with their intention, in eight short months, to produce a major music festival in—or near—a city that was, at the moment, officially closed.

"We don't know when, we don't know where, we don't know what format," declared Quint Davis, the festival's longtime producer/director. "There will be a Jazz Fest in 2006. It will be in Louisiana. It will be as close to New Orleans as we can get it."

From humble origins in 1970, Jazz Fest had grown to rival Mardi Gras' cultural and economic impact. Staged annually over two weekends in late April and early May at the Fair Grounds horseracing track, it ballooned from hundreds of attendees to hundreds of thousands, from a budget in the tens of thousands to a budget in the millions. Even with such latter-day headliners as Pearl Jam, Rod Stewart, Billy Joel, Bon Jovi, Simon & Garfunkel, Bob Dylan, and My Morning Jacket, Jazz Fest remains firmly rooted in the swampy soil of south Louisiana.

To Davis, the festival "started out to be the world's greatest backyard barbecue, an indigenous self-celebration by a culture. Then at some phase, it was to promote and celebrate the culture annually, and bring it forward. Now, two or three generations later, it is a cultural institution."

The first four decades of Jazz Fest spanned the Nixon administration to the Obama administration, the Vietnam War to the Iraq and Afghanistan wars, and the myriad social, societal, cultural and economic upheavals in between. Jazz Fest has survived disco, punk, grunge and rap, tornados and lightning storms, a mammoth fire that destroyed the Fair Grounds grandstand months before the 1993 festival, a steep drop in travel after September 11, 2001, and Machiavellian behind-the-scenes power struggles. Bonnaroo, Austin City Limits, Coachella, Lollapalooza, the Voodoo Experience and most every other major American music festival of recent vintage borrowed in part from Jazz Fest's blueprint.

In Jazz Fest's egalitarian infancy, attendees were allowed to bring their own shade canopies and fully stocked ice chests. But even with the advent of corporate sponsorship, VIP ticket packages and premium seating, the festival retains what Davis terms a "handmade" feel, professional but not slick. "It's folksy, but underneath is one of the most complex infrastructures you can imagine. And it runs on time. We have hundreds of New Orleans bands starting and ending on time. Think about the miracle of that."

Festivals are, by nature, ephemeral. Known and unknown risks and variables can extinguish even the most established events. The 2006 Jazz Fest faced especially long odds. Normally, planning starts around September for the following spring's festival. In September 2005, given the deplorable state of south Louisiana, an enormous leap of faith was required to even consider the possibility of a Jazz Fest. Producers would, in essence, be laying down a multimillion-dollar bet with no guarantee the casino would be built and staffed in time to collect on it.

But if they made good on their brash promise, Jazz Fest would serve as a powerful symbol of recovery, a beacon for the rest of the world, and a morale and economic boost for a region badly in need of them.

The central character in this drama wasn't a musician at all, but a decidedly unconventional son of privilege who has spent his life immersed in African-derived music and culture. In the Camp Street headquarters of Festival Productions Inc.-New Orleans (FPI-NO), Quint Davis's "desk chair" is an African throne of goat hide and riveted metal, a gift from a troupe of Ghanaian dancers. Walls and flat surfaces erupt in photos, posters, mementos, folk art and alligators— Davis is way into alligators.

His ego is robust, his fashion sense, or lack thereof, legendary. He's a short white man with blondish hair who dons traditional African garb for public appearances. He is a patron and frequent attendee of Voodoo festivals in the West African nation of Benin, a fascination he shares with his father. A lifelong bachelor with no children, he cranks Howlin' Wolf in his '67 Corvette Stingray 427, dates women decades younger, and relishes late nights and an adult beverage or two.

He spent years on the road with Professor Longhair, reviving the long-lost piano legend's career; managed tours by Fats Domino, Duke Ellington, B. B. King and Muddy Waters; and went to jail with Chuck Berry at gunpoint in Spain, then talked his way out. He counts Paul Simon and Jimmy Buffett as friends and dated Linda Ronstadt. He has escorted U2's Bono and The Edge to a traditional New Orleans second-line parade and high-fived Lil Wayne court-side in celebration of Hornets star Chris Paul's heroics.

Yet he is equally at home marching among Mardi Gras Indians and Social Aide and Pleasure Club Grand Marshals, or demonstrating for shirtless villagers in Benin how New Orleanians drop to the ground to writhe on their bellies in a late-night practice known as "popping the gator."

He neither founded nor owns Jazz Fest, but he is the festival's primary mover and public face, the guy who careens around the Fair Grounds on a golf cart and emcees the main Acura Stage. As such, he is a lightning rod for complaints ranging from warm beer to the weather. Legendary East Coast festival promoter George Wein, Jazz Fest's founder and Davis's mentor, supplied the only job description that has ever applied to Davis: "If anything screws up, it's your fault."

His temperament suits his occupation. He is discrete, yet infinitely quotable. He is capable of putting a positive spin on anything. He remains cool amidst volatile personalities and controlled chaos, and accepts the fact that the seven festival dates he toils all year to plan are at the mercy of meteorological forces beyond his control. In his view, Jazz Fest has "helped give traditional music a place at the table in American popular culture."

But his lifelong love of street culture and noncommercial music is tempered by an understanding that it must pay for itself; the second-line must respect the bottom line. And so the presentation of live music is both his business and his art. "People think that I'm a funny guy in funny clothes that rides a golf cart and runs around. But it's a life, and a professional career. My mom once said, 'When are you going to stop with this music stuff and get a real job?' And I said, 'Mom, as long as I work twenty-four hours a day, seven days a week, I'll never have to get a real job.'"

As it turned out, no one else was better suited to orchestrate Jazz

Fest's resurrection than the man who helped bring it to life in the first place.

Arthur Quentin Davis Jr. was born in November 1947, the first of three children. His family's multigeneration history in Louisiana dates to the state's first rice mill, in Point à la Hache. His mother served on the state museum board. His father literally redrew the New Orleans skyline. Arthur Q. Davis Sr. and/or his architectural partners designed the Superdome, the New Orleans Arena, the UNO Lakefront Arena, the Marriott, Hyatt, Royal Sonesta and Royal Orleans hotels, the now-demolished Rivergate convention center, and elements of Louisiana State Penitentiary at Angola.

The bowtie-wearing senior Davis's interests were not necessarily those of the typical pillar of society; in his 2009 memoir *It Happened by Design*, he recounts his anointment with pigeon blood at a Voodoo ceremony in Haiti.

Growing up, young Quint tuned in to gospel and rhythm-and-blues radio stations with his family's domestic help. He'd sleep with the radio under his pillow, subconsciously soaking it in. Attendants at a neighborhood gas station escorted him to Dorothy's Medallion Lounge, a fabled R&B nightspot, to hear saxophonist James Rivers. Photographer Jules Kahn, a friend of Davis's parents, introduced him to New Orleans street culture: second-lines, jazz funerals, Mardi Gras Indian practices. Theirs were often the only white faces. Davis "thought that was normal life."

After graduating from high school in 1965—he'd been voted "best twister"—he set out for Lake Forest College near Chicago. The school wasn't a good fit; he returned to New Orleans to pursue a different kind of education in gospel churches and blues bars. He also embraced his inner hippie. He rattled a tambourine and danced in a psychedelic band named Yesterday's Children. He lived in the French Quarter and co-owned and "managed" a head shop called the Love Shop.

Awakened to the possibility of a career in music, he enrolled at Tulane University as a drama and ethnomusicology major. He let his freak flag fly: long hair; tortoise-shell glasses with yellow lenses; a "soul patch" under his bottom lip; a toothpick stuck in his mouth. He founded a student organization called Get It Together to book shows at the Tulane student center. One co-bill featured funk keyboardist Wilson "Willie Tee" Turbinton's band and the Wild Magnolias Mardi Gras Indians. During the Magnolias' set, Willie Tee took a seat at his keyboard and started vamping—quite possibly the first time Mardi Gras Indian chants and percussion were accompanied by electronic instruments.

On weekends the Indians gathered at scruffy bars in predominantly black, working-class neighborhoods to practice. Davis, a regular attendee, noticed that jukeboxes were switched off until rehearsals were over. He came to believe the Indians' music deserved a place on the jukebox, too. In 1970, he launched a record label, Crescent City 25—he is fond of multiples of five—and released the Wild Magnolias' first vinyl single, "Handa Wanda." The yellow label lists the record's producer as "Cosmic Q," aka Quint Davis.

Cosmic Q was not the most dedicated student. He eventually dropped out of Tulane, but not before meeting the man who would change the course of his life.

By 1969, George Wein was a music industry legend. A blunt-talking jazz pianist from Boston, he had built a lucrative business promoting jazz and blues tours, and pioneered contemporary music festivals with the Newport Jazz Festival in 1954. In the 1960s, New Orleans civic leaders hoping to boost tourism approached Wein about launching a jazz festival in New Orleans. City ordinances prohibiting interracial bandstands rendered the concept untenable. They tried again a few years later, only to discover that Wein, who is Jewish, had married an African-American woman. The idea was tabled once more.

The International Jazz Festival, staged without Wein in New Orleans in 1968 and '69, lost money. Propositioned for a third time, Wein agreed to produce the first New Orleans Jazz & Heritage Festival in the spring of 1970. He insisted that nighttime concerts at the Municipal Auditorium be augmented by a daytime "Louisiana Heritage Fair" of local music, food and crafts in what is now Armstrong Park.

Wein needed a "kid" to round up local musicians for the Heritage Fair. He consulted Preservation Hall founder Allan Jaffe, who steered him to Dick Allen, proprietor of the Hogan Jazz Archives at Tulane. Allen recommended Davis, a student worker at the archive. Wein hired him over beignets at Café du Monde. "George said, 'I want to do this festival that has blues and gospel and Cajun and zydeco.' I said, 'I know some of those people. I'll go ask them to come.'"

One afternoon Wein and Davis heard the Carnival season staple "Go to the Mardi Gras" on a jukebox. "George says, 'Who's that?' And I said, 'It's not anybody. It's just a song that comes on every year at Mardi Gras.' And George said, 'Well, it's somebody. You find that guy.'"

That led Davis to Professor Longhair, aka Henry Roeland Byrd. Destitute, unknown, and in poor health, the pianist's best days seemed far behind him. Davis took it upon himself to revive Longhair's career. They toured in a green station wagon and slept on floors. Allison Miner, Davis's girlfriend at the time, later took over Longhair's management; she also played a critical role in Jazz Fest's early development. By the time of his death in 1980, Longhair was a beloved icon of New Orleans music.

Once Wein hired him, Davis's career path was set. "After 1970, every spring it was either Jazz Fest or a geology exam," Davis said. Jazz Fest won. "My father went to Newman [a well-regarded private high school in New Orleans], then Tulane, then Harvard. And I tell him I'm dropping out of school to live in a green station wagon with someone named Professor Longhair."

The senior Davis rolled with it. "If that's the direction he wanted to go, I supported it," Arthur Davis said. "It turned out pretty well."

Wein took a shine to Davis and hired him for other festivals and tours promoted by Festival Productions Inc. Davis worked the 1971 Newport Jazz Festival, which ended with a riot triggered by gate crashers. "The first big festival I did, they burned the stage down under my feet. Everything after that's been calmer."

A firm believer in "sink or swim," Wein dispatched Davis as the assistant tour manager for Duke Ellington's first tour behind the Iron Curtain, in 1971. Armed troops flanked stages. In Romania, officials refused to let Ellington encore. Davis packed up the musicians' gear, hidden behind an actual iron curtain, as the defiant audience cheered. "I'm onstage by myself and the whole audience is standing out there pouring their hearts out. Little hippie me learned real quick what freedom was and wasn't on that trip."

Two years later, Wein assigned Davis to manage B. B. King's first tour of Africa, which touched down in Senegal, Ghana and Nigeria. Davis later shepherded Muddy Waters on his initial visit to Africa, and globe-trotted with Chuck Berry, Fats Domino and John Mayall. "This is like if a kid who collects baseball cards in his garage gets a call that says, 'Can you come pitch in the World Series next week at Yankee Stadium?'"

Working for Wein, Davis learned the concert business "from real music professionals, instead of coming up as some hippie in the rock business. George understood how to construct a bottom line, how to maintain it, how to work to it." Wein introduced him to the "economics of creativity." Davis "never thought of those two things in the same place before. Something important only comes out of longevity. And the only way to achieve longevity is to master the economics of creativity. Otherwise, you'll do something that will be great once, and lose a lot of money."

The economics of creativity took hold slowly at the New Orleans Jazz & Heritage Festival. The inaugural, 1970 festival, budgeted at $80,000, reportedly lost $40,000. In 1972, Wein and Davis moved Jazz Fest to the Fair Grounds. Davis's father signed a $25,000 line of credit to keep it afloat. More notes would be needed; the festival would not turn a profit until 1978.

In a decision he would later call the "biggest financial mistake I ever made," Wein acquiesced to the wishes of community leaders and did not exercise an option to buy the festival from the nonprofit foundation that owned it. Early on, the New Orleans Jazz & Heritage Foundation's board members included Arthur Davis and others who generally let Wein and Quint operate as they saw fit. But as the board grew, members sought more oversight and control.

In the early '80s, a frustrated Davis took a year off. He drove his Corvette to Winter Park, Florida, where he and Wein partnered in a new festival. "It was the first time I ever took a risk," Davis said. "It was a terrible failure. George said, 'OK, you owe forty thousand dollars.' It took me years to recover."

He soon returned to New Orleans and Jazz Fest. Wein ceded more responsibility to Davis, yet they didn't sign a contract with one another until 1995, when they formed Festival Productions Inc.-New Orleans to produce the first Essence Music Festival, a three-night celebration of urban contemporary music in the Superdome.

At Jazz Fest, Davis became a fixture onstage. "I only got to announce acts because nobody knew how to get them off. Running a show on time is not about an introduction; it's about an out-troduction. When a band's time is up, I had to learn to go out there and take the microphone."

Through the 1990s, Jazz Fest grew exponentially. In 2001, the Dave Matthews Band and the New Orleans rapper Mystikal headlined the single largest day in the festival's history, with an announced attendance of 160,000.

Depending on whom you ask, Jazz Fest is either too slow or too quick to change. "We're always 'ruining' the festival," Davis said, echoing a charge he has heard for decades. A common complaint is that closing acts on the largest stages are generally "visiting" artists. Such high-dollar headliners with little connection to New Orleans jazz or heritage are necessary, Davis says, to drive attendance, which benefits hundreds of lesser-known Louisiana acts. "In order to have a traditional music/jazz/blues/Cajun music festival that draws 400,000 people over seven days—how else could it happen? How many tickets and records do those acts sell? Those of us who have spent our lives producing and promoting blues, gospel, jazz in particular—we know. This is the least commercial music there is. But more really straight white people have seen gospel at Jazz Fest than anywhere else. These people go home and go to a blues club, or buy a Cajun or zydeco record."

When Jazz Fest added a tenth stage to the Fair Grounds in 2005, it wasn't a jam band or indie rock or rap stage, but the Jazz & Heritage Stage, dedicated to brass bands and Mardi Gras Indians. "If we're going to be a festival of the heritage of jazz and New Orleans, that's the taproot," Davis said. "That's the heart and soul. That's who we are."

He anticipates tooling around festivals on golf carts indefinitely. "People in all businesses get blasé and jaded. I can't understand that. It's just as unbelievable and thrilling to me, every day, every minute, as it was when I got the call to take B. B. King to Africa."

For Davis, the road always leads back to New Orleans. "There's no better place to come home to. You don't eat the same, you don't dance the same, you don't make love the same, none of that. In New York and L.A., if you start to fall, you're going to hit the ground. In New Orleans, you will never hit the ground. New Orleans people will catch you and hold you and put you back up."

He required such support after the rain-soaked 2004 Jazz Fest lost nearly one million dollars, exacerbating long-simmering tensions with the New Orleans Jazz & Heritage Foundation. The executive committee of the foundation board put production of the festival out to bid; for the first time in its history, Jazz Fest might move on without Davis and Wein. The board eventually voted to retain them, but demanded certain financial guarantees. Davis went searching for a partner with deep pockets and found one in AEG Live, the high-powered concert promoter that initially bid against him.

AEG Live is part of an international entertainment conglomerate that includes sports teams, a movie production company, and such venues as the O2 arena in London and the Staples Center in Los Angeles. AEG and Festival Productions hammered out a deal whereby Davis and his team would continue to coordinate Jazz Fest's complex logistics and politics and book talent, but with the support of AEG's vast financial resources, marketing muscle, business acumen and music industry connections. In late 2004, Davis and AEG signed a five-year agreement, with two five-year options, to co-produce the festival for the Jazz & Heritage Foundation.

The 2005 festival, the first offspring of this shotgun marriage, was a rousing success. Featuring Brian Wilson, James Taylor, Wilco, Widespread Panic, Isaac Hayes, the Roots, and a reunion of seminal New Orleans funk band the Meters, the festival finished in the black, thanks in part to staffers' resourcefulness. Early on the morning of April 30, hours before the Dave Matthews Band and Elvis Costello were to headline the main stages, a storm system parked itself over the Fair Grounds. It knocked out power and silenced pumps that drain water from the site; small lakes marooned stages and food booths. Staffers patched a generator into the Fair Grounds power grid; pumps sprang to life. With the dirt track around the infield too soggy to drive on, they carried musical gear to stages by hand. Gates opened forty-five minutes late, but the show went on; the day wasn't a washout.

The alliance between Festival Productions and AEG Live had delivered on the promise of a financially secure, artistically satisfying Jazz Fest. The future looked very bright. But four months later, Hurricane Katrina nearly rendered all that goodwill moot.

———

In August 2005, AEG Live president and CEO Randy Phillips sat in a New York hotel room, horrified, as the Katrina disaster unfolded on television. "We just didn't think there was going to be a Jazz Fest," he would later recall. "I thought there was just too much devastation. We had made so many strides restoring the festival's luster—how much more can they throw at us?"

Mitch Landrieu, Louisiana's lieutenant governor at the time—he would be elected mayor of New Orleans in 2010—had made it his mission to promote the state's "cultural economy," of which Jazz Fest was a cornerstone. Soon after Katrina, he delivered an unambiguous directive to Davis: "Not having Jazz Fest this year is *not* an option."

Publicly, Davis echoed Landrieu's resolve. Privately, he wasn't so sure. As the extent of Katrina's devastation became clear, the numbers did not add up. Production costs for the 2005 festival approached $11 million; post-Katrina, those costs would be even higher. Musicians who once drove to the Fair Grounds from eastern New Orleans, Gentilly, Central City or the 9th Ward were now exiled; they must be flown in and housed. How much of New Orleans' population would be restored by early 2006? And would tourists be able to find flights and hotel rooms?

George Wein and AEG fronted money to pay fest employees through the fall of 2005, even as Phillips debated whether to stage a full festival. "For the longest time, we were trying to figure out the economics," Phillips said. "In the beginning, it really seemed like a long shot. We knew the artist community would support the festival, and people would want to be part of restoring a great American city. But we were concerned that it would be difficult to get the attendance we needed."

Given the slow pace of recovery through the fall of 2005, the outlook was grim. Producers of the Halloween weekend Voodoo Experience learned just how difficult staging a festival in a disaster zone could be. Two months after the storm, City Park, Voodoo's traditional site, lay in ruins; the city's infrastructure was wobbly at best. Producer Stephen Rehage was resigned to remaking Voodoo in Memphis, Tennessee, as a benefit concert until Trent Reznor, a former Garden District resident and leader of platinum-selling industrial rock act Nine Inch Nails, pressed him to keep it in New Orleans.

Voodoo wound up in both cities. In New Orleans on October 29, it occupied Riverview Park, a grassy sliver alongside the Mississippi River behind Audubon Zoo; admission was free. Nine Inch Nails headlined, donating its services; the roster also included Queens of the Stone Age, the New York Dolls, and hometown favorites Jon Cleary, the Rebirth and Soul Rebels brass bands, Big Sam's Funky Nation, Bonerama, Theresa Andersson and Kermit Ruffins. Local rockers Cowboy Mouth unveiled two new songs, "Home" and "The Avenue," that spoke directly to displaced New Orleanians. Several thousand souls—first responders, National Guardsmen, police, firefighters, Red Cross volunteers, returning residents—sang along. It was a start.

Prospects for other major events remained precarious. In early November, city officials announced that the 2006 Mardi Gras would be scaled back: fewer days, fewer parades, shorter parade routes. Also in November, executives at *Essence* magazine decided to relocate the 2006 Essence Music Festival to Houston. Davis had produced the Essence Fest in the Superdome each July 4th weekend since its 1995 inception, but repairs to the badly damaged Dome would not be completed by July 2006.

On November 10, the Jazz and Heritage Foundation board met with Davis and executives from AEG Live and Churchill Downs, the new owners of the Fair Grounds. The next day, David Oestreicher, president of the foundation's governing board, stated his intention to mount a "major" Jazz Fest in the spring that would "jump-start the tourist economy for this part of the world," even as he allowed that "there are some 'ifs.' We are vigorously addressing logistical problems."

Tellingly, the festival's producers—the folks charged with solving those logistical problems and taking the financial risk—were more guarded. "We realize more than ever before, what happens with the festival will be a comment on the state of New Orleans culture post-Katrina," said Louis Edwards, an associate producer at Festival Productions. "With that in mind, we're focused and working hard to make the festival a reality."

Davis found himself caught between "people *asking* me if it was happening, and people *telling* me it was happening." His usual response? "I hope so." He and his staff still had no idea what size Jazz Fest was feasible. "Is it one stage on one day? Four days? Six days? Those are differences of millions of dollars."

For years, corporate sponsorships had underwritten specific Jazz Fest stages and other production costs. In 2006, more sponsors would be needed as a hedge against uncertain attendance projections and as a means for AEG and FPI-NO to limit financial exposure. An effort to recruit a "presenting sponsor" for the entire festival commenced in earnest.

At least four prospective deals fell apart in late December. The festival's producers gave themselves a deadline of January 15, 2006 to either secure adequate sponsorship dollars—or cancel the festival.

Tenet Health Choices was the first to sign on. "They got us on a respirator," Davis said, finding an appropriate metaphor. "So we had a pulse." In early January, Shell Exploration & Production Company, which had over the decades extracted vast amounts of oil and natural gas from Louisiana, signed on as Jazz Fest's first presenting sponsor. In return, the festival would officially become the New Orleans Jazz & Heritage Festival Presented by Shell. The company's commitment "allowed us to put on a full-fledged festival knowing that our ticket sales would not be the same as in the past," said Don Marshall, executive director of the foundation board.

Additional sponsors chipped in. Starwood Hotels & Resorts Worldwide Inc., owner of two W hotels and the Sheraton in New Orleans, housed Davis and his staff until they could return to their homes. The Louisiana Department of Culture, Recreation and Tourism, under Landrieu, funded a national marketing campaign urging potential visitors to "Bear Witness to the Healing Power of Music." The state also underwrote the festival's popular Congo Square Stage, rechristened the Congo Square/Louisiana Rebirth Stage.

Overall, Jazz Fest tripled its sponsorship revenue from 2005 to 2006. Money in hand, producers still needed a functioning venue. The Fair Grounds, Jazz Fest's home since 1972, required major repairs. The roof of the Grandstand had been torn off. Five feet of floodwater had trashed the grounds. Salt from the brackish water killed grass covering the twenty-six-acre infield; the subterranean irrigation and electrical systems were ruined.

Going forward, vast reserves of determination, ingenuity and commitment from festival staffers, volunteers, food and craft vendors, musicians and fans would be required. But the festival was most definitely on.

On February 8, 2006, Neil Portnow, president of the Recording Academy, signed off the 48th Grammy Awards by urging the telecast's 17 million viewers to attend Jazz Fest. A week later in a Sheraton Hotel conference room, Quint Davis faced a roomful of reporters for an annual ritual that New Orleans music fans equate to Christmas morning— the unveiling of the Jazz Fest talent roster.

Flanked by an honor guard of musicians, Davis ticked off the headliners: Paul Simon, Bob Dylan, Jimmy Buffett, the Dave Matthews Band, Lionel Richie, Keith Urban, Yolanda Adams, Elvis Costello. They would join Fats Domino, the reunited Meters, Irma Thomas, the Radiators, Galactic, Allen Toussaint, Deacon John, Irvin Mayfield & the New Orleans Jazz Orchestra, Paul S. Morton & the Greater St. Stephen Choir, Snooks Eaglin, Buckwheat Zydeco, Pete Fountain, Dr. John, and hundreds more Louisiana artists. "Jazz Fest this year is not about money or career," said Cowboy Mouth drummer Fred LeBlanc. "It's all about heart and soul. It's about singing to survive."

Davis rarely displays emotion in public, but that morning at the Sheraton, his voice caught as he invited displaced New Orleanians to come home for the celebration: "This is your homecoming dance, and this is your homecoming band." Later, he marveled at how Irma Thomas "started patting me like a church woman. Everybody had those 'Katrina moments,' where you're talking and all of a sudden you lose it. The musicians were coming back so that the festival could live, and New Orleans music could live. And it just hit me out of the blue."

Jazz Fest made concessions to Katrina reality. Thursday was dropped from the second weekend, reducing the total number of festival days from seven to six. The Blues Tent was scrapped and the Music Heritage and Lagniappe stages were combined. Overall, around one hundred performance slots were lost.

One glaring omission from the roster: the Neville Brothers, administrators of Jazz Fest's funky benediction for more than fifteen years. To the consternation of fans, the Nevilles decided to skip the '06 Jazz Fest, in part because of Aaron Neville's concerns about his wife's grievous health, and about airborne mold and dust aggravating his asthma.

Headliners Simon, Buffett, Matthews and Costello performed at the *From the Big Apple to the Big Easy* Katrina benefit concert in New York on September 20, 2005. Davis started recruiting Jazz Fest headliners that night. Simon was not scheduled to tour in the spring of 2006, but agreed to assemble a band specifically for Jazz Fest. Matthews, an avowed New Orleans fan and veteran of the 2005 festival, was eager to return.

Buffett, however, was a tough sell. A Gulf Coast native, he launched his career in the French Quarter. In 1967, while still a student at the University of Southern Mississippi in Hattiesburg, he landed a gig at the Bayou Room in the 500 block of Bourbon Street. Players from the new Saints expansion team occasionally showed up ("I think it was because we had a hot chick in our band," Buffett once told me). Someone gave him tickets to the first regular-season game, against the Los Angeles Rams. The Saints' John Gilliam returned the opening kickoff ninety-four yards for a touchdown. "Once I went to that first game," Buffett said, "they were my team for life." (Forty-three years and many losing seasons later, he would pilot his own Falcon 900 jet from a DVD shoot on the South Pacific island of Bora Bora to New Orleans to witness the Saints beat the Minnesota Vikings in the NFC Championship Game and advance to the Super Bowl for the first time.)

The margarita fantasies he sells for a living aside, Buffett is a shrewd businessman and consummate professional. Caught up in the moment at the *From the Big Apple* concert, he bought into Davis's show-must-go-on bravado. "Then we all went away and, after the emotions and the alcohol were gone, the serious business of whether we actually could do it came about," Buffett later recalled. "By that point, I'd gone down to Pascagoula, Mississippi, first and then New Orleans. When you see it, you're so overwhelmed: 'How could we possibly do this? Is it too early to try?' Those kinds of conversations happened for several months."

He "wasn't one of the big believers in 'hell or high water, here we come.' The emotional level was, 'Of course I'll do it.' [The hesitation] was more on a practical level of someone who does shows for a living."

Buffett required convincing. "Quint said, 'Whether it works or not, we need to step up here. Everybody is looking for something that's the first step back.' When he told me that, I understood what he was talking about, and that's when I said, 'I'm coming.'"

Given his longstanding ties to Davis and New Orleans, Buffett typically charged Jazz Fest a reduced rate. He'd intended to ask his full price, in the mid- to upper-six figures, in 2006. But after Katrina, he agreed to play for "about half" of his usual guarantee; Lionel Richie and others also took drastic pay cuts.

As with the first post-storm Mardi Gras and mayoral race, the media would descend en masse. In a normal year, one or two of the twenty-five largest daily newspapers might cover the festival. Most planned to send reporters in 2006. "I've pretty much been going to one festival a year, and it was a no-brainer to pick Jazz Fest this year," said Evelyn McDonnell, the *Miami Herald*'s pop culture writer at the time. "What happens with Jazz Fest will be symbolic of what is happening to New Orleans in the wake of the biggest news story of 2005. Jazz Fest is a prism through which to report post-Katrina recovery. Is this a revival, or a memorial?"

At the conclusion of the February 15 press conference announcing the roster, Irma Thomas led eighteen assembled musicians— representing rhythm and blues, jazz, rock, gospel, Cajun and Latin music—in "When the Saints Go Marching In." She sang alongside gospel patriarch Sherman Washington and R&B veteran Clarence "Frogman" Henry as saxophonists Donald Harrison Jr. and James Rivers, clarinetist Michael White, and trumpeter Gregg Stafford traded licks. "I think you get the message now," Davis said. "Jazz Fest is on."

But it wasn't complete. The festival still lacked a closer for the main Acura Stage on the first Sunday. Davis had one in mind: Bruce Springsteen. The courtship had begun in earnest after a post-Katrina breakfast meeting between George Wein and jazz trumpeter Wynton Marsalis. They discussed the need for marquee names to call attention to the '06 Jazz Fest. Marsalis sent a letter to Springsteen's reps, urging that he perform.

That effort continued in Los Angeles in early February during rehearsals for the Grammy Awards. Davis first befriended Ken Ehrlich, the telecast's producer, when touring with Longhair in the 1970s; he and Ehrlich collaborated on the 2006 Grammy tribute to New Orleans featuring Springsteen, Toussaint, Thomas, Dr. John and Costello. During rehearsals, Davis introduced himself to Springsteen and personally invited him to the festival. Ehrlich also lobbied the superstar's management on Jazz Fest's behalf.

Given the size of Springsteen Inc., it was not simply a matter of the Boss tossing an acoustic guitar in his trunk and driving on down to the Big Easy. Weeks of intensive logistical discussions ensued, as Team Springsteen weighed the pros and cons. His representatives peppered Davis and his staff with queries, from the potential number of festival attendees to what, exactly, would Springsteen see from the stage?

The final hurdle was beyond Davis's control: Would Springsteen's new Seeger Sessions Band be ready in time? Columbia Records was scheduled to release *We Shall Overcome: The Seeger Sessions*, a new Springsteen collection of songs by folk music legend Pete Seeger, on April 25, three days before the fest opened. If he could whip a band into shape, Jazz Fest, with its saturation media coverage and overriding theme of triumph over adversity, would serve as the perfect launching pad for the album's promotional campaign.

Additionally, Big Easy musical references abound on *We Shall Overcome*, from the joyous trumpet solo and saloon piano of "O Mary Don't You Weep" to the tailgate trombone throughout. Inadvertently, certain lyrics could refer to Katrina. "'My Oklahoma Home' jokes about this guy's woman being carried away by a twister," Springsteen told the New York *Daily News*. "It's light. But it's really a song about losing everything—and in New Orleans today we have our biggest natural disaster since the Dust Bowl. That's the way our lives tie into old folk music. It's why songs like this last."

In early March, Davis received word that Springsteen was in. He broke the news on March 8, less than two months before the gates would open at the Fair Grounds. Pete Seeger founded the Newport Folk Festival, perhaps the first outdoor, multistage American roots music festival; Newport was among the models George Wein used for his own festivals, including 1970's inaugural New Orleans Jazz & Heritage Festival. "If George Wein is the father of Jazz Fest," Davis said, "then Pete Seeger is the grandfather."

Seeger's soundtrack to the civil rights movement—"If I Had a Hammer," "We Shall Overcome"—would resonate in post-Katrina

New Orleans. "The basic theme of Pete Seeger's music is determination and defiance, triumph of the human spirit over adversity," Davis said. "Well, we are a people in a struggle for our city and our way of life. For someone to preach that sermon at this festival, Rev. Springsteen is pretty good."

On the morning of Friday, April 28, 2006, Davis and his staff anxiously awaited their audience. Around 100,000 advance tickets had been sold for the six days of the festival, but many more walk-up sales were needed to break even.

To everyone's tremendous relief, a line stretched from the Fair Grounds entrance at Sauvage Street down Fortin to Mystery Street, then turned back toward Esplanade Avenue—a distance of several blocks. "We'd never seen that before, so we were all wondering what was going on," Davis said. "And then we start getting calls from police that people are coming from every direction. When we announced that we were opening the gates, people cheered. I will never forget that morning. Ever."

Early arrivals streamed onto a restored Fair Grounds. The entire infield had been rewired. Tons of gypsum had absorbed the salt deposited by floodwaters. Acres of fast-growing rye grass had been planted (it would be torn out after the festival and replaced with the slower-growing Bermuda grass required for the fall horse-racing season). With the infield's subterranean sprinkler system still in shambles, the New Orleans Fire Department lent an old truck from its training facility to water the grass.

Katrina was unavoidable. From the Gospel Tent, blue tarps were visible on the damaged roofs of homes just outside the Fair Grounds fence. FEMA trailers and flooded-out bungalows greeted attendees who approached the Fair Grounds from De Saix Boulevard. The infamous "dirty bathtub ring" floodwater residue still marked homes and businesses along nearby North Broad Street. The Fair Grounds grandstand, traditionally the setting for intimate performances and respite from the sun and dust, remained closed.

Every year, Jazz Fest staffers Nicole Williamson and Laura Bell decorated the golf cart on which they zipped around the vast site. The 2006 model mimicked a scrapbook, plastered with photographic tributes to the late Gatemouth Brown, longtime Jazz Fest electrician "Mr. Eddie," and Joyce Wein, the late wife of George Wein. In a nod to gallows humor, the cart also featured a blue tarp roof, "waves" along the running boards, a toy helicopter engaged in a rescue, and inflatable floaties "in case the levee breaks during the festival," Williamson said. "I thought it would cheer people up. You've got to poke fun of yourself. You can't ignore the storm. Obviously, this is a very different year."

The festival's on-site record tent was downsized. Mark Samuels, founder of the local Basin Street Records, agreed to manage the tent; the usual vendor, the Virgin Megastore, had not reopened its downtown New Orleans store. The Record Tent's first weekend was rocky. All but one cash register supplied by the festival—relics from K&B, a defunct local drugstore chain—broke down. Inventory was low.

By the second weekend, Samuels had acquired functioning cash registers and sufficient product. Sales were brisk; one customer bought $700 worth of local music. All 240 copies of Fats Domino's new *Alive and Kickin'* CD sold out, with proceeds benefiting the Tipitina's Foundation's philanthropic efforts. "People wanted to spend money and be supportive," Samuels said. On record sales, "Jazz Fest did better than expected, given the circumstances."

Katrina sat in at many stages. Randy Newman's "Louisiana 1927" has long been a Jazz Fest staple; one year Newman sang the "they're trying to wash us away" refrain in a driving rain. That line, and song, resonated more directly in '06. At the WWOZ Jazz Tent, jazz-soul singer John Boutte altered the lyrics. Instead of "six feet of water in the streets of Evangeline," he mourned a flood that consumed the Lower Nine. In Newman's original, President Coolidge comes down in a railroad train to examine "this poor cracker's land." Boutte sang, "Bush flew over in his airplane with six fat men with martinis in their hand/Bush said, 'Fat man, great job . . . look what the river has done to this poor Creole's land.'"

Afterward, a woman informed Boutte that scores of listeners had fled the tent. "I thought I had pissed somebody off, getting on my soapbox," Boutte said. "But they were running out crying. They weren't just crying—they were heaving. They were leaving to get their composure." He expects such dramatic reactions. "If they don't carry them out, I didn't do my best."

During bassist Roland Guerin's set at the Jazz Tent, he recalled his first emotional post-Katrina gig at Snug Harbor; fans thanked him for coming back to the city. "Ya'll being here today," he said as applause rippled through the tent, "is just about the same thing." Alto saxophonist Donald Harrison Jr. transformed from suit-and-tie modern jazzman into the feathered, buck-jumping chief of the Congo Nation Mardi Gras Indian tribe. The audience responded in kind, surging into the aisles, dancing, chanting, roaring, celebrating.

U2 guitarist The Edge had co-founded Music Rising, a fund to replace instruments destroyed by Katrina. On one of his earliest post-storm visits to the city, he dined at the tony Restaurant August with Davis, who inquired about U2 performing at Jazz Fest. His pitch was one-quarter successful: The Edge popped up at the Fair Grounds during the first weekend, sitting in with the New Birth Brass Band and the Dave Matthews Band.

Matthews posted a $1.5 million "challenge grant" to help fund construction of Habitat for Humanity's Musicians' Village in the 9th Ward. "Don't think for a moment that we shouldn't be doing anything we can to get this city back on its feet," he declared at the Acura Stage. Given the federal government's distractions, "we've got to do it ourselves." The devil-may-care refrain of "Tripping Billies"—"eat, drink, and be merry, for tomorrow we die"—hit home in ways Matthews likely never intended.

To better understand the context for his performance, Bruce Springsteen visited the site of the Industrial Canal levee breach that erased much of the Lower 9th Ward. He shook hands with volunteers and left behind a fortune in donations; the New Orleans Musicians Clinic, which provides free medical care to musicians, received $80,000.

Save four "open rehearsal" charity concerts in New Jersey, Jazz Fest would be his Seeger Sessions Band's official debut. As he led the sprawling band onto the Acura Stage at five P.M. on Sunday, April 30, he confessed a hint of trepidation: "It's our first gig. Let's hope it goes well."

Moments later, he encountered a "technical problem" with his pants. Grinning and embarrassed, he turned his back to the vast audience and made the necessary adjustments. "It's not just a new band," he explained, "but a new belt."

That was his first, and final, glitch. For two glorious hours, Springsteen and the Seeger Sessions ensemble—six horns, a banjo, accordion, pedal steel guitar, fiddles, piano—invigorated vintage folk and protest songs. Few others in popular music could craft a show that spoke so eloquently to the city's struggles, both welcome distraction and poignant reminder.

The opening "O Mary Don't You Weep" set the tone. Springsteen led as the full ensemble swung in behind him. A muted trumpet, trombone and saloon piano all took solos. The Boss, as usual, heaved himself into the material at hand. The gravel in his voice stamped a ragged glory on "John Henry" over banjos and accordion. "Old Dan Tucker" and "Open All Night" were a hoot. Big horn swells lit up a gritty "Jesse James." In the timeless Irish antiwar ballad "Mrs. McGrath," a cannonball claims her son's "two fine legs"; transcend time and that cannonball could be an improvised explosive device.

Locals in search of relevant lyrics found them: "There'll be better times by and by." "God gave Noah a rainbow sign, no more water, but fire next time." "The only thing we did right was the day we started to fight." And it was easy to imagine "Louisiana" swapped into the lyrics to "My Oklahoma Home," which was "blown away" in a natural disaster.

In his most overtly political statement, Springsteen recounted the previous afternoon's visit to the 9th Ward. "I saw some sights I never thought I'd see in an American city. The criminal ineptitude makes you furious." In response, he adapted Blind Alfred Reed's "How Can a Poor Man Stand Such Times and Live" with new lyrics dedicated to "President Bystander": "My old school pals had some high times there/What happened to you folks is too bad," he sang, mocking how George W. Bush, in the early days after Katrina, reminisced about his collegiate hijinks in New Orleans.

Eyes closed, Springsteen rededicated "My City of Ruins," originally written as a eulogy for Asbury Park, New Jersey, to New Orleans. To a hushed, riveted audience, he described scenes of desolation that sounded all too familiar: "The rain is falling down . . . the boarded-up windows, the hustlers and the thieves . . . now tell me how do I begin again?" And then the refrain: "Come on, rise up! Rise up!"

Thousands of weary New Orleanians let the lyrics wash over them like a baptism. The personal pronoun of the title gave them voice: *My city of ruins*. Those in need of someone to express the anger, frustration, grief and resolve expended over the previous eight months had found their man. Fists were raised and tears were shed as Springsteen delivered a Jazz Fest moment for the ages.

Just as quickly, he kicked back into good-time mode with "Buffalo Gals" and an accordion/rubboard zydeco reimagining of "You Can Look (But You Better Not Touch)," from his 1980 album *The River*. A tuba, improbably enough, ushered Springsteen off the stage. In the encore, he noted that "a hundred bands in New Orleans" could play this last song better than he. But he thought two lesser-known verses might be appropriate. With that, he unspooled "When the Saints Go Marching In" not as a boisterous, high-kicking second-line parade, but as an acoustic prayer delivered in a desperate hour. Face clenched, he sought the promised land: "Now some say this world of trouble is the only world we'll ever see/But I'm waiting for that moment when the new world is revealed."

No other artist could have spoken to, and for, the city of New Orleans more purposefully, passionately and effectively than Bruce Springsteen and the Seeger Sessions Band. Years later, people still talk about it. "They should talk about that forever," Davis said. "I thought it was one of the most extraordinary things I've ever seen, and I've seen thousands of shows. Reverend Springsteen held church, and ministered to a flock."

Dave Malone, the guitarist and vocalist for veteran New Orleans roots rock/funk/R&B jam band the Radiators, had never experienced Springsteen live before Jazz Fest. "The cynical part of me thought it would be hokey—some Pete Seeger stuff can be dated. But that guy has some kind of magnetism I can't explain. His delivery and band were incredible. It was one of the best things I've ever seen in my life. I was sitting there crying like a third-grader."

After the drama, uncertainty, sponsorships and sacrifices, the story of the 2006 Jazz Fest nearly boiled down to weather. Three times over two weekends, severe thunderstorms threatened to shut down the Fair Grounds and deliver a brutal economic and psychic blow. The first weekend, a deluge threaded the needle between Saturday evening's Dave Matthews set and Sunday morning. The second Friday, rain skirted just north of the festival during Keith Urban's late-afternoon show.

The worst was yet to come.

Jimmy Buffett piloted his own plane to New Orleans' Lakefront Airport, on the shores of Lake Pontchartrain. As his party drove through devastated Gentilly, he narrated a disaster tour, reminding his friends that the entire neighborhood was submerged. Based on the forecast for Saturday, May 6, the streets of Gentilly were in danger of flooding again. A severe lightning and hail storm bearing down from the west was due to arrive in late afternoon—about when Buffett would close the Acura Stage. "It didn't look good," he said later. "We were out there putting scenarios together with thunderstorms. If we lose power, what do we do?"

As an aviator, Buffett is a better-than-average meteorologist. As his set time drew near, he consulted a weather map and the "lifted index," which measures atmospheric stability. Based on the readings, Buffett made a prediction: "I think this [storm] is going to break in half in the middle, and may go north and south of the lake."

An even higher power than the lifted index intervened on his behalf. In a Fair Grounds parking lot, he encountered Sister Jane Remson, of the New Orleans Artists Against Hunger and Homelessness charitable organization, and Sister Blaise Fernando. They assured Buffett that he would remain dry. Between the nuns and the forecast, he "went to work pretty positive."

The storm, as predicted, split in two around the Fair Grounds. As Buffett bounded onstage, barefoot, in aquamarine shorts and a bright yellow Bob Marley T-shirt, the sun burned through the clouds. "You start like that, you don't have to go far with emotions," he said. "And I was already emotionally amped . . . I believe a lot of it is still magic. It certainly exhibited itself to me that day."

He opened with "City of New Orleans," a song he'd last performed on September 5, 2005, a week after Katrina brutalized his beloved Gulf Coast. That night, he fought through his emotions to headline the first-ever concert at Chicago's Wrigley Field; he concluded by dedicating "City of New Orleans" to its namesake. Months later, as he pondered his Jazz Fest set list with his daughter, they decided that he should complete the circle at the Fair Grounds. "That fit my sense of connection. And how do you musically get to people about something that devastating, and still not preach to 'em? Some people choose to preach. I choose not to."

As he gazed out over thousands of smiling faces at Jazz Fest, Buffett choked up during the first verse of "City of New Orleans," but quickly recovered. Changes in latitude and attitude are his stock in trade. If Springsteen was the preacher delivering the eulogy, Buffett was the grinning uncle who cracked open the whiskey after the wake. He reaffirmed his ties to the region, singing about gumbo and crawfish pie. He slipped a reference to FEMA trailers into "Son of a Son of a Sailor." "I tried to gear it for New Orleans and do some things that would mean a little something there. I also had to be the realist. It wasn't the place to go down an energy level. I wanted to keep 'em up."

As Buffett bid farewell, Davis, clearly relieved that the rain spared the Fair Grounds, addressed a sea of veteran and newly converted Parrotheads. "Somebody wanted us to have a good time today. It's good to be alive in New Orleans."

Buffett's sway over the weather gods did not extend to his friends. On the final Sunday, he had lunch with Paul Simon and planned to catch Simon's show later that afternoon. But as Buffett pulled up to the Fair Grounds in a driving rain, he changed his mind and headed to the airport. Following a twenty-five-minute downpour, Irma Thomas opened her set on the Acura Stage with "It's Raining."

As the day progressed, Jazz Fest staffers faced a far greater crisis than the weather. When the Neville Brothers decided to sit out 2006, Davis realized he needed an equally prominent local act to close the fest and send 'em home happy. As the greatest living icon of New Orleans music, Fats Domino fit the bill. The infrequency of his performances qualified each as an event.

Booking Domino was not without risk. In his seventies, his performance anxiety had grown more acute, his memory less sharp. He declined an offer to play the 2005 Jazz Fest, and had not performed at all since the trauma of his Katrina rescue. It was not inconceivable that he would cancel at the last minute. But surely, Davis and his team reassured themselves, Fats wouldn't bail this time; he was even featured on the souvenir Jazz Fest poster.

Domino's inner circle wasn't so sure. At noon on Sunday, May 7, less than six hours before showtime, a contingent of friends arrived at Domino's handsome stucco home in Harvey, across the Mississippi River from downtown New Orleans. Eric Paulsen, longtime anchor of local CBS affiliate WWL-TV's morning show, retired federal judge Steve Ellis, and Ellis's wife Haydee intended to offer moral support and accompany Domino to the Fair Grounds.

But he claimed he did not feel well, and wanted to go to a hospital instead. Knowing he has a history of heart trouble, his friends bundled him into Paulsen's black Jeep and drove to Ochsner Medical Center, along the Mississippi on the New Orleans side. Doctors ran tests, which came back negative, but Domino insisted he did not feel well enough to perform. "No one knows how you feel except you," he told Paulsen.

Around one P.M., word reached Jazz Fest staffers that Fats was waffling. Ninety minutes later, they concluded that he would, in fact, bail. They glumly posted signs around the Fair Grounds announcing the cancellation.

When Domino left Ochsner, he thought he was headed home. Instead, Paulsen surreptitiously steered his Jeep toward the Fair Grounds. The Jeep pulled into the Mystery Street musicians' entrance at 4:30, setting off a minor frenzy as friends and fans clamored to take pictures, shake his hand and welcome Domino. He quickly retreated to a backstage trailer behind the Acura Stage.

His musicians trickled in to discover the gig was off. "It's a pity that this happened," said saxophonist Herb Hardesty, a Domino sideman since the 1950s. "But that's the way life is sometimes." "We were playing, then we weren't," baritone saxophonist Roger Lewis said. "You can never tell with Fats. He can bounce back in a minute."

Not this time. However, Domino agreed to address his disappointed fans from the Acura Stage. Davis introduced him; the enormous crowd cheered. Domino waved, doffed his captain's cap, and stepped to the microphone. "I'm sorry I'm not able to perform. I love you all, and always will. Thank you very much."

And that was all fans would hear from Fats Domino. As they

puzzled over the bizarre turn of events, festival staffers toyed with possible endgame scenarios. Two hours of silence was an unacceptable conclusion for the Acura Stage. Paul Simon was not prepared to play longer than scheduled. Lionel Richie, the former Commodores frontman with the thousand-watt smile and deep catalog of R&B hits, was slated to close the big stage on the Gentilly Boulevard end of the Fair Grounds. Davis considered bumping back Simon to the closing 5:30 P.M. slot at Acura and putting Richie on the same stage before him. But that wouldn't work: If Richie performed ninety minutes ahead of schedule, fans showing up at the original time would miss him.

The solution? Extend soul singer Sam Moore's penultimate set on the Gentilly stage and swap Richie to Acura *after* Paul Simon. Thus, Lionel "All Night Long" Richie would be the culmination of the most important Jazz Fest in history.

By standard cultural calculus, this made little sense. Given his legacy with Simon & Garfunkel and the world music explorations of his solo catalog, Simon was the more "important" artist and logical closer. But Davis was confident in Richie's ability to deliver; he had previously booked him for the Essence Music Festival. "We knew what was going to happen. Lionel was good enough to jump in that spot. He's a superstar in every sense of the word."

In what was likely the only time Paul Simon will ever open for Lionel Richie, the pairing worked to perfection. Simon applied a healing balm with "Slip Sliding Away," "Me and Julio Down By the Schoolyard," "Still Crazy After All These Years," "Loves Me Like a Rock" and a delightful "Cecilia." For the zydeco treatise "That Was Your Mother," Stanley "Buckwheat Zydeco" Dural sat in on accordion. New Orleans legend Allen Toussaint led Simon's band on "There's A Party Going On," an unrecorded Toussaint composition. During a joyous swing through the *Graceland* title track, he underscored such lyrics as "there is a girl in New York City who calls herself the human trampoline" with bouts of boogie-woogie piano. Irma Thomas sang lead on "Bridge Over Troubled Water," building slowly and methodically to an inspired finale. Simon, Thomas, Dural and Toussaint gathered at center stage, arm in arm, an affirmation of Louisiana's musical bounty by a star who is more than happy to celebrate it.

Moments later, Richie emerged from his backstage trailer with the air of a hero about to save the day. En route to the stage, he paused for a brief photo op with Domino and New Orleans Mayor Ray Nagin. He and his airtight band proceeded to slay skeptics with a nonstop singalong—and really, what's not to love about "Brick House"?—framed by an "Easy," self-deprecating banter. Newly minted fans sang along and danced on sodden grass. "It was such an important moment and time to have something energized happen, and work," Davis said. Richie, the producer correctly concluded, put on one of the best shows of the festival.

Total attendance over six days of the 2006 Jazz Fest topped 300,000; the daily average was not much less than in 2005. Food and merchandise vendors reported strong sales; some ran out of stock by the final afternoon.

Jazz Fest did not fix anyone's roof or expedite insurance checks or replace a ruined wedding album. But it was a marker on the road to recovery, a shot in the collective arm, an indication that the funky heart of New Orleans was still beating.

The tall flag pole at the center of the Fair Grounds traditionally serves as a rendezvous point for friends. The entire 2006 Jazz Fest fulfilled the same purpose for a populace scattered across the whole of the United States. "Everybody from the musicians to the carpenters to the food vendors came and made sure it happened," Davis said. "So did all the people who live here, who used to live here, who drove in, who flew in, who came in staggering numbers, day after day."

Jimmy Buffett got the sense that people who traveled to New Orleans "were so glad that they made the effort. They were angry at what they saw in terms of the devastation, but glad they experienced the fun that still is there. Everybody needs a couple days off; that's as much a part of recovery as anything. People left going, 'Wow, that was nice. Now let's go back to work.' A little sense of renewal—I felt that, for sure. And I think saving the musical culture and the soul of America is a very worthwhile endeavor."

To Davis, statistics don't tell the full story. "Intellectually, you have to get beyond equating 'great' with 'big.' Festivals go back to medieval times. They're rites, when tribes come together annually and restore something in their lives and souls. Well, this was that. It was a shared catharsis.

"The festival was strong enough to power two weekends; even Mardi Gras was relatively abbreviated, compared to what this was. That says something about what the New Orleans Jazz and Heritage Festival has become within the life and culture of New Orleans.

"And it's a metaphor for what New Orleans means to America."

Chapter Four

Allen Toussaint Comes Alive

On the first night of 1998, Allen Toussaint attended a benefit concert for veteran New Orleans rhythm-and-blues singer Oliver "Who Shot the LaLa" Morgan. Impeccably attired in a dark, double-breasted suit, spottled tie and matching pocket square, he moved among the tables, warmly greeting Morgan and other old friends.

From the stage, the ever-campy Frankie Ford, of "Sea Cruise" fame, couldn't resist tweaking Toussaint, who produced Ford's "I Can't Face Tomorrow" in 1966. Ford introduced "Rockin' Pneumonia" with, "This song is from when McDonald's had only sold six hamburgers, Dolly Parton was in a training bra, and Allen Toussaint was still poor."

Toussaint smiled, unflappable as always. In the years that I've known him, I've never seen him sweat—including on ninety-degree days at Jazz Fest. He typically navigates the fest in leather sandals and perfectly pressed cotton pants; I've never noticed him wrinkled, either.

His gentlemanly comportment is in keeping with his work ethic. For most of his decades-long career, Toussaint was content to be the man behind the curtain, writing and producing songs for other artists, handsomely compensated for his troubles. But a post-Katrina collaboration with Elvis Costello prodded him to step out front. Moreso than ever, he's found the stage to his liking.

But even under the spotlights, he still doesn't sweat.

On a dreary afternoon in December 2005, Allen Toussaint and Elvis Costello sat astride a grand piano, equally dapper, eminently inspired.

Four months after Katrina, they were ensconced in Piety Street Recording in New Orleans' working-class Bywater neighborhood, literally across the tracks from the French Quarter. Ostensibly, they were posing for a photographer, but with the tools of their trade so close at hand, they couldn't resist.

At Costello's request, Toussaint laid his hands upon the keys and conjured a spooky, minor-key variation on the Professor Longhair classic "Tipitina." Soon Costello joined in. He preached a sermon of queens in waiting and people pleading and no birds singing—alternate lyrics he titled "Ascension Day."

"We'll all be together," he sang, emoting for an audience of two, "come Ascension Day."

The final note drifted away. A long, pregnant pause followed, until Costello broke the silence.

"That was pretty, wasn't it?"

Yes, it was. Toussaint smiled, pleased.

He and Costello hail from different worlds. The genteel Toussaint is an icon of New Orleans music, a Rock and Roll Hall of Fame pianist, songwriter and producer. The brash, British-born Costello first made a name for himself as a scrappy, New Wave songwriter with Buddy Holly glasses, outsized ambitions and a chip on his shoulder.

But each possesses an innate gift for plumbing the emotional depths of lyric and melody. And together, they forged a simpatico partnership.

Costello had long admired Toussaint from afar. In Hurricane Katrina's aftermath, they shared stages at a series of benefit concerts in New York. Costello subsequently resolved to record an album with Toussaint, consisting of classics, long-forgotten gems, and fresh collaborations.

Like "Ascension Day," the overall project synthesized their sensibilities. Costello chose much of the material; Toussaint arranged it. Steve Nieve, the keyboardist in Costello's band, the Imposters, played organ; Toussaint handled the piano. The Imposters rhythm section backed the Toussaint horn section. Costello soloed over a foundation laid down by Anthony Brown, Toussaint's guitarist.

They commenced at Hollywood's Sunset Studio in late November 2005, then moved to Piety Street—a converted post office that narrowly escaped Katrina's floodwaters—for a week in December. Verve

Records would release the finished album, *The River in Reverse*, the following June.

"Elvis is a scholar of the music," Toussaint said at the time. "He loves New Orleans music, as well as music from everywhere. This will be New Orleans flavor, on an Elvis Costello CD."

Both Toussaint and Costello have orchestrated prolific careers across the spectrum of popular music.

Toussaint is New Orleans music's renaissance man, the golden boy in the golden age of rhythm and blues. He grew up the youngest of three children and learned piano on his family's upright, soaking up the music of Professor Longhair and Ray Charles from the radio. Barely thirteen, he joined the Flamingos, a rhythm-and-blues band that also included future guitar great Snooks Eaglin.

He dropped out of high school in favor of a music career, and was soon being hired as a pianist on recording sessions; often he was required to mimic the styles of Charles, Fats Domino, and other marquee players. "That initiated some of my writing ability. Many times, the artist wouldn't have but three songs, and the talent scout maybe wanted four. So they would take a break and I would write that fourth song in the studio—ever so humble, but a song it would be.

"So I became known as one who could readily do that. People began coming to me before we got to the studio for songs. That nudged me on to be a much more prolific writer."

Soon he was conducting the sessions himself, and the hits poured forth. He, Irma Thomas, Aaron Neville, Ernie K-Doe and Benny Spellman would gather in his parents' living room, making music for its own sake. He wrote and produced K-Doe's national No. 1 song "Mother-In-Law," Art Neville's "All These Things," Spellman's "Fortune Teller" and "Lipstick Traces," Lee Dorsey's "Ride Your Pony," Thomas's "It's Raining." Thomas has described "It's Raining" as "the New Orleans national anthem. It was written in Allen Toussaint's bathroom."

After the mid-1960s British invasion killed off much of the market for New Orleans–style rhythm and blues, Toussaint was able to stay in the game as a hot-handed producer, working out of Sea-Saint Studios, the bunker-like Gentilly facility he and business partner

Marshall Sehorn founded. A producer is the equivalent of a movie's director, overseeing the recording session and working as a creative partner with the artist. The Meters cut their seminal recordings, cornerstones of funk, on Toussaint's watch. He is as proud of his production work on Labelle's "Lady Marmalade," a No. 1 hit in 1975, and Dr. John's *In the Right Place* and *Desitively Bonnaro* albums as he is of an obscure record by vocalist William Smith.

"Early Irma Thomas, I feel very good about now," Toussaint told me in 1998. "Even though I never hear the recordings [anymore], I remember the feel. I had great fun with Lee Dorsey, a high-spirited individual. The early works with Aaron Neville were very good. And Chris Kenner—I had a ball with Chris Kenner on 'I Like It Like That' [which hit No. 2 nationally].

"Patti LaBelle, the most refined works came out of that. The other things were more fun and a bit more innocent. Working with Patti was definitely fun, but it was much more grown-up than some of the earlier works. Of course, time marches on."

More so than his productions, Toussaint's compositions made an impact throughout the 1970s. After he cast them upon the waters, they did indeed come back to him a hundredfold. Of the dozens of covers of Toussaint songs, some are especially memorable to their creator.

"Dobie Gray did 'Performance' and it just knocked me out. It wasn't a hit, but he did such a fine job. Herb Alpert and 'Whipped Cream,' I thought that was really fine [it became the theme music to the original *Dating Game*]. And of course, Al Hirt just really nailed 'Java' to the wall [and hit No. 4].

"Glen Campbell surprised me so much with 'Southern Nights'—he picked the tempo up. I considered my version of 'Southern Nights' as a message in the trees, along with the breeze, and that whole Southern night feeling, just a nice, mild, soft, message. Glen and that bunch stomped it off, 'one, two, one, two, three . . .' I thought that that was really fine, that they were innovative enough to do that to it. They heard another drummer."

So did early-1980s New Wave band Devo. They covered the Lee Dorsey hit "Working in a Coal Mine" for the animated science-fiction fantasy film *Heavy Metal*. ("Very interesting movie," notes Toussaint. "But then, Devo was very interesting, too.")

Later, mother/daughter country duo The Judds also did "Working in a Coal Mine," making it one of Toussaint's most lucrative creations. Estimates of his annual songwriting royalties run to six figures; he could live comfortably for the rest of his life on them.

Along the way, Toussaint has formed partnerships with business minds, freeing him to concentrate on the creative. "I've been fortunate that I've been surrounded by other good people, who allowed me to have the sandbox with all the artists and musicians to play around in. In the early days of Minit Records, it was Larry McKinley and Joe Banashak. Later on my partner was Marshall Sehorn, who provided the haven for what we did in Sea-Saint Studios. I got the musicians to record in the studio; he got them from there to the world."

Though many consider him as important a practitioner of New Orleans piano as Professor Longhair, his own recording career is spotty at best. His first album came out under the name "Tousan," because the label feared customers wouldn't be able to navigate "Toussaint" phonetically.

After Katrina, he found fresh purpose in making records for himself.

In the late 1970s, Elvis Costello, heart on his sleeve and devil may care, delivered urgent, literate dispatches with punkish attitude. He evolved into a versatile, tireless and much-loved performer and songwriter, writing with everyone from his wife, jazz singer Diana Krall, to 1960s pop composer Burt Bacharach and Sir Paul McCartney.

New Orleans has occasionally factored into Costello's creative process. The Dirty Dozen Brass Band guested on his 1989 album *Spike*. He dubbed his 2005 tour *The Monkey Speaks His Mind*, after a song by Dave Bartholomew, Fats Domino's producer and co-writer. And a young Costello admired Toussaint's songwriting, if unwittingly.

"I now know that I knew a lot of Allen's songs, but I didn't know he'd written them," said Costello in 2005, nattily attired in a jacket, tie, scarf, and sunglasses, during a break at Piety Street. "I didn't know he'd written 'Fortune Teller' and many staples of the beat groups in England when I was a kid. The first records that he produced that really struck me and I got curious about were the Lee Dorsey records, because they sounded so unique. Then the legend of who this person was grew up: Oh, he's the person who wrote that song and that one and that one, and did the arrangements, and produced them. As you get more curious, you get deeper into it."

Toussaint, New Orleans chic in blazer, slacks and sandals, confessed to not being as familiar with Costello's catalog.

"I'm sorry to say I wasn't. I have gotten familiar since, and let me tell you, he has been very busy. Very busy. He's going to be very tired when he gets to heaven. And it's quality stuff. He's a very high-quality person, and a very heart-filled person. And he's so wide awake."

Were it not for Katrina, Toussaint might not have discovered just how wide awake.

For many years prior to the storm, Toussaint lived on a nondescript street in the Gentilly neighborhood. His home was usually flanked on one side by a two-toned 1974 Rolls-Royce (license plate: "Piano") and on the other by a newer Mercedes (license plate: "Songs").

Divorced and living alone, his children grown, he added a second-story camelback to the house and acquired an adjacent property, giving him a spacious yard that spread out from his pool. The interior was done in retro bachelor chic; the front room was dominated by a billiards table and matching decor, including a lamp emblazoned with his name. Few tokens of his career were on display.

But many of his latter-day compositions first took flight in his first-floor music room. A glistening grand piano was surrounded by studio control boards, audio tapes and other gear. Alongside the piano, a stack of sophisticated recording equipment went mostly unused; Toussaint preferred the cheap cassette player perched on a nearby stool.

He collects scraps of songs at any time of the day—standing in line at the hardware store, waiting at a red light. He says he "tries to remain as open as I can for inspiration all the time," but prefers late-night composing. "I especially like the wee hours of the morning, like three. It's quiet. The air is different. I like that time of night for anything."

Toussaint is a disciplined songwriter who generally writes with a particular artist in mind. Songs call to him regardless. "They keep coming and saying, 'What about me?' I need to do this. There's something that makes us who we are. When you wake up, you have to do something. You just can't wake up and be—you have to do. What do I do? I do this.

"Some streak of fate puts us in the position that we're in, how we come about being a diamond cutter, a musician, this, that, or the other. Fortunately, I'm in this artistic garden, which I love so much. I have to do what those plants do."

As Katrina approached, he wisely chose not to remain in Gentilly. Instead, he embarked on a "vertical evacuation"—checking into a high-rise hotel, a time-honored hurricane tradition. He rode out Katrina alone in the Astor Crowne Plaza on Bourbon Street.

Costello was in Vancouver, receiving storm updates from a friend at the New Orleans Windsor Court, several blocks from Toussaint. After the levees gave way and the city began to flood, Toussaint boarded a commandeered school bus bound for Baton Rouge, then caught a flight to New York City. The Big Apple would be his extended-stay home in exile; his house in Gentilly was destroyed by floodwater.

Six days after Katrina, Costello performed Toussaint's "Freedom for the Stallion" at the Bumbershoot festival in Seattle, "just because I felt like it." He closed the set with another Toussaint composition, "All These Things."

A few days later, Wynton Marsalis invited Costello to a benefit concert at Lincoln Center. Costello in turn asked Toussaint to join him on "Freedom for the Stallion." Afterward, the musicians retired to Dizzy's Club Coca-Cola, a small venue within the Jazz at Lincoln Center complex.

"It was just like an after-hours session that you read about in books but you rarely see with musicians of that caliber," Costello said. "Ellis Marsalis and Marcus Roberts taking turns on a piano stool. Wynton would play a chorus, then Cassandra Wilson would get up and sing. Robin Williams improvised a song called 'Red Beans and Condoleezza Rice.' We were there until four in the morning, just watching."

The next afternoon, Costello saw Toussaint perform at Joe's Pub, a Manhattan club. "About halfway through the show," Costello said, "I thought, 'It's time to do this [record with Toussaint].'"

He was even more convinced after the September 20 *From the Big Apple to the Big Easy* benefit at Madison Square Garden, when Toussaint and his band backed a succession of stars, including Costello. The following Saturday, they shared a bill at a benefit sponsored by *The New Yorker*. Costello debuted a song he'd written that afternoon, "The River in Reverse."

Days later, Costello received a call from a Verve Records executive, proposing a joint album with Toussaint. "So I wasn't the only one thinking this was a good idea."

Costello and Toussaint blocked out time in early December 2005. Costello enlisted Joe Henry to produce the project. The avant-punk singer-songwriter's successful second career as a producer won a Grammy for soul singer Solomon Burke's acclaimed 2002 comeback album, *Don't Give Up On Me*. In 2005, Henry gathered together Toussaint, Irma Thomas, Ann Peebles, Billy Preston and Mavis Staples for *I Believe to My Soul*, a contemporary record that taps into the spirit of classic soul.

Costello and Toussaint framed their recording as a "meeting," Costello said during a break at Piety Street. "It is a dialogue between people from different parts of the world. At this moment, even the New Orleans people don't live in New Orleans."

The blueprint would not mimic *Painted From Memory*, Costello's 1998 collaboration with Burt Bacharach. "We were commissioned to write one song up front, and we liked that so much, we wrote eleven more," Costello said of the Bacharach project. "With this, I began with the thought that in the fifties, Ella Fitzgerald, for example, would do a songbook record. It was not unusual in those days, because very few performers wrote their own songs. I thought, 'Why can't that exist today?'"

The lesser-known songs in the Toussaint catalog appealed to Costello. "I wouldn't perhaps choose 'Southern Nights' or 'Working in a Coal Mine.' They're great songs, and they certainly don't need to be sung again by me. The songs that I love, some are more off the beaten track. Even Allen expressed surprise at a couple of my choices. That doesn't mean they shouldn't be heard again. And when you hear the record, you'll understand why."

Toussaint trusted Costello's instincts. "He always asked my opinion: Did I think he could do this one or that one well? With his nature, he could do any of them well, to be perfectly frank. I never would have thought of things like 'Wonder Woman,' something I wrote for Lee Dorsey so many years ago. Or 'Tears, Tears and More Tears.'"

For his part, Costello respected Toussaint's arrangements. "The horn arrangements and background voices are all part of the composition. They're not just things that have been added on, the way they sometimes are in recordings. If you take those building blocks away, you don't have as much. Every element fits together. That gives you strength."

What set their new renditions apart, Costello said, "is my voice and the personalities of the players on the record."

Those personalities included the horns. Toussaint said he "has to have New Orleans horns all the time." To that end, he recruited Brian "Breeze" Cayolle and Amadee Castenell on tenor saxophones, "Big" Sam Williams on trombone—who, Toussaint said, "is extremely impressive to everyone"—and trumpeter Joe Foxx, formerly of 1970s funk ensemble Chocolate Milk.

"He lives in Birmingham now," Toussaint said, "but he is definitely one of us. He has that New Orleans-ism."

Writing together deepened Costello and Toussaint's connection.

"When you co-write songs, you try and open up a conversation," Costello said. "On 'Where Is the Love,' I made the opening statement, then Allen responded. On another one, we literally wrote, change by change, how it should resolve; I had the opening but couldn't seem to close it.

"On another one, Allen came in with a whole piece of music that was already finished and didn't need anything musically from me. So I was the lyricist. We went from never having written together to trying out all the different ways you might collaborate."

Toussaint was impressed with his new partner's work ethic and skills.

"He has such a mind for the music, and he's always about what he does. If we were collaborating on something, the next day he would have loads to bring to the table. He's always working on so many things. And not just scraps—he takes things to their completion. He has covered continents, such a wide range. And he's welcome in so many areas."

Toussaint's minor-key "Tipitina," showcased on the Katrina benefit CD *Our New Orleans*, inspired Costello to write fresh lyrics. And so "Ascension Day" was born.

"That's the way music goes," Costello said. "In classical music days, they used to do variations on a theme. As Allen would say, Professor Longhair is the Bach of New Orleans music. 'Ascension Day' isn't better than the original, it's just a variation on the original for the present moment."

Costello said his new compositions "live in the present moment. Which inevitably means they reflect things that have occurred, or what you might feel about those things."

So were they informed by Katrina?

"As Allen said, very wisely, you want to leave space in the material for other people's imaginations. You try to make a song, not a speech."

Still, subtle changes convey much. "When I wanted to sing 'On the Way Down,' I asked Allen, 'Is it all right if I leave out the word "girl" in the second verse?' Because I'm not meaning it about a girl who's left her neighborhood behind.

"It's pretty clear what I mean. There are promises that need to be kept here [in New Orleans]. And if there was ever a moment for a song about dignity, like 'Freedom for the Stallion,' it's now. It's a timeless song. Other songs, like 'Who's Going to Help Brother Get Further,' sound like they could have been written yesterday.

"It's not for me to assume that I have the definitive rendition, but I can take it to some people that haven't heard it."

After he arrived in New Orleans, Costello drove through the 9th Ward, reinforcing the decision to record some of *The River In Reverse* in New Orleans.

"It felt right. Although I didn't write any of the material here, to have certain things that you felt or imagined confirmed . . . That drive confirmed it.

"This was always a welcoming city. But I've never known people so ready to talk about their own experience, inevitably because it was catastrophic. People will open up and tell you a lot of history. I've had a lot of interesting conversations just wandering around."

His conversation with Toussaint intrigued fans of both. "This has been a concentrated collaboration," Toussaint said, "and I'm glad it happened. It's been quite enriching."

The recording of *The River In Reverse*, a dramatization of which would appear in David Simon's HBO series *Treme*—with Toussaint and Costello playing themselves—invigorated the pianist. In the summer of 2006, he and Costello embarked on a successful five-week North American tour—the most extensive tour of Toussaint's career. Katrina, it seems, was the best booking agent he ever had.

That tour concluded on July 18, 2006, at the New Orleans House of Blues with a marathon, three-hour show. With Toussaint's guitarist and horn section grafted to Costello's Imposters, they rendered most of *The River in Reverse*. They also recast Costello chestnuts with intriguing new arrangements by Toussaint. "Allen has written 450,000 songs," Costello joked. "I'm catching up with him. I've written 350,000, including seventeen since we arrived here this afternoon."

In the first encore, Toussaint delivered a solo piano discourse on "Tipitina," imagining the Professor Longhair classic in multiple settings. In the night's emotional climax, he rested his hands on his heart to sing Paul Simon's "American Tune" against a soft cushion of Steve Nieve's Hammond B-3 organ and Costello's acoustic guitar: "I don't know a soul who's not been battered . . . I don't know a dream that's not been shattered or driven to its knees . . ."

In 2009, after even more shows with Costello, Toussaint released *The Bright Mississippi*, his first album solely under his own name in more than a decade. He worked once again with producer Joe Henry. Henry challenged Toussaint with a program of unfamiliar songs and prevailed on him to record in New York with such modern jazz allstars as clarinetist Don Byron, guitarist Marc Ribot, and trumpeter Nicholas Payton, the only other New Orleanian involved. The sublime result cast Toussaint's piano in an elegant setting of classic compositions by the likes of Jelly Roll Morton, Sidney Bechet and Thelonious Monk.

The Bright Mississippi was even nominated for a Grammy as best jazz instrumental album, individual or group. Alas, it did not earn Toussaint his first gold Gramophone. Still, he was pleased to be nominated. "My forte has been producing and behind-the-scenes. To be recognized right up front is quite an honor."

Chapter Five

Fats Domino's Excellent Adventure

My wife, Mary, worked on a 1999 concert series celebrating the opening of Harrah's Casino New Orleans. Fats Domino headlined; Mary's duties included driving the legend from an outdoor stage along the Mississippi River to his dressing room trailer a block away.

After his show, Domino hustled aboard a golf cart alongside my wife as a scrum of photographers and fans engulfed them. From the rear bench, hulking drummer Herman Ernest shouted for Mary to take off. As cameras flashed, she punched the accelerator. Much to everyone's surprise, the golf cart lurched backward into the crowd. Domino's eyes went wide as he pitched forward, stunned. Ernest piped up from the backseat: "Wrong way, baby. Wrong way." Mary shifted into the correct gear and sped to safety. Domino, unfazed, tipped her fifty dollars. He was probably relieved to survive unscathed.

Despite international acclaim, Fats Domino remained at heart an eccentric, dyed-in-the-wool New Orleanian. He was happiest amongst friends, family and neighbors, which endeared him to locals all the more. When my brothers and I were boys, our father occasionally drove us past Domino's house, the local Graceland. Unlike Graceland, it never passed into the public domain. It remained Domino's private retreat until a most unwelcome guest came calling.

On a cold, battleship gray Saturday in November 2007, a short, stout man in a black leather jacket and crisp white captain's cap paused at the corner of West 45th Street and Broadway, then plunged into Times Square. Anonymous amidst the bustle of New York City's neon canyon, he sang cheerfully to himself: *"On Broadway . . ."*

Had anyone stopped to listen, his sunny Creole cadence may have struck a familiar chord. Two blocks and fifty years from where he stood, Antoine "Fats" Domino triggered pandemonium. In 1957, he headlined promoter Alan Freed's multinight *Holiday Show of Stars* at the old New York Paramount. The Paramount held 3,400; thousands more clamored to get in. In a scene described in Rick Coleman's award-winning 2006 biography *Blue Monday: Fats Domino and the Lost Dawn of Rock 'n' Roll*, Fats and his band required a police escort from their hotel to the theater.

Five decades later almost to the day, Domino caused no such commotion in Times Square. He quietly absorbed the sensory overload, posed for pictures with his companions, then slipped away to a limousine idling around the corner near picketing Broadway stage hands. The limo whisked this most reluctant and reclusive superstar through the Lincoln Tunnel to Newark's Liberty International Airport, where he boarded a nonstop flight home.

Improbably enough, Domino spent the previous three days where no one expected to find him in 2007: someplace other than New Orleans.

Antoine Domino was born in New Orleans on February 26, 1928, to a family of modest means. The piano, an early obsession, proved to be his passport to the world. Guided by visionary producer, songwriter, trumpeter and Imperial Records talent scout Dave Bartholomew, Domino reportedly moved more vinyl in the 1950s than anyone except Elvis Presley. He facilitated rhythm and blues' transition to rock and roll. If there is ever a rock-and-roll Mount Rushmore, his face will be on it. Among New Orleanians, only Louis Armstrong's impact on popular music is greater.

But unlike fellow rock-and-roll founding fathers Little Richard, Chuck Berry and Jerry Lee Lewis, Domino quit globetrotting long ago. His last tour was a rocky three-week European jaunt in 1995 plagued by illness. For the next decade, Domino rarely strayed outside Orleans Parish save for the occasional gig at a Mississippi Gulf

Coast casino; he limited hometown shows to one or two annually. He preferred to cook and hang out with his "podnas" at his home on the corner of Caffin Avenue and Marais Street in the hardscrabble Lower 9th Ward. It was not unusual to find him padding around the house in a bathrobe, slippers and hair net.

Over the decades, the unholy trinity of drugs, poverty and crime decimated his neighborhood. With his old songs still generating six-figure royalties annually, he could afford to live anywhere, but he stayed put in the spacious split-level he built in 1960 as a sleek, modern mansion of blond brick. His wife, Rosemary, and various relatives occupied the two-story main house, with its pink and yellow trim and fence of wrought-iron roses. The far smaller adjacent house served as Domino's hideaway. In 1998, he famously declined President Bill Clinton's invitation to collect a National Medal of Arts at the White House, but stated, in all sincerity, that Clinton was more than welcome to drop it off in the 9th Ward. (His oldest daughter, Antoinette, traveled to D.C. in his place.)

Domino was an immovable object until confronted with Hurricane Katrina's irresistible force. Like many elderly residents, he refused to evacuate ahead of the storm, a decision that nearly proved fatal. Early on the morning of August 29, 2005, a retaining wall blocks from Domino's dwelling ruptured along the eastern side of the Industrial Canal, a shipping channel connecting Lake Pontchartrain to the Mississippi River. The resulting bulldozer of a torrent wrenched nearby houses from their foundations and inundated most of the Lower 9th Ward. Fats and his family retreated to the second floor of the main house, marooned by eight feet of water.

That night, a Harbor Police boat searching for stranded survivors docked at Domino's second-story balcony; he and his family clamored aboard. In the coming days, rumors that Domino had perished circulated; someone spray-painted "R.I.P. Fats You Will Be Missed" in bright red across the exterior balcony from which he'd been rescued. After the waters receded, a photographer visiting the abandoned house found a folded shirt on the bed of the upstairs master bedroom, a jar of pickled pigs' lips on a nightstand, and a small keyboard nearby. If you ignored the ransacked ruins downstairs, it was as if Domino had been snatched up by Revelations' Rapture.

But he was safe. After the boat deposited the Domino clan at the

St. Claude Avenue overpass, they were transported to the Super-dome, and then Baton Rouge. Domino and his brood stayed briefly at the Baton Rouge apartment of a granddaughter's boyfriend, LSU quarterback Jamarcus Russell; from there, they continued to Ft. Worth, Texas. To a then-seventy-seven-year-old creature of habit so adverse to travel, the upheaval was especially traumatic; after the storm, friends confide, Domino's short-term memory wasn't as sharp.

Still, he was determined to return as soon as possible. With the Lower 9th Ward still a ghost town, he bought a handsome stucco house in a gated subdivision in Harvey, across the Mississippi River from New Orleans. And he agreed to close out the 2006 New Orleans Jazz & Heritage Festival Presented by Shell. For that year's commemorative Jazz Fest poster, New Orleans artist James Michalopoulos painted a young, grinning, flat-topped Domino pounding a piano parked on a French Quarter street; the numbered edition quickly sold out. Domino's triumphant return would cap Jazz Fest's triumphant return.

But the booking wound up symbolizing something much different than organizers intended. Domino's performance anxiety may have gotten the best of him; the morning of the show, he said he had chest pains. Friends drove him to a hospital, where tests were negative. He still insisted he could not perform, leaving many fans deeply disappointed.

Not surprisingly, skepticism greeted the announcement a year later that Domino would headline a hometown concert at Tipitina's on May 19, 2007. Domino counts Tipitina's owner Roland Von Kurnatowski among his closest confidants. Von Kurnatowski oversees a rental property empire that stretches across the southeast; before Katrina, Domino consulted him on home renovation projects. The May 19 show would benefit the club's affiliated nonprofit, the Tipitina's Foundation. Among other initiatives, the foundation has purchased hundreds of thousands of dollars' worth of instruments for school marching bands—the mainstays of Mardi Gras parades and the proving grounds for many musicians who go on to professional careers.

When Domino first suggested headlining a benefit at Tipitina's, Von Kurnatowski "didn't bite too hard, because I didn't know if he was serious. We knew that there would be anxiety about it." As show day approached, a fully engaged Domino called the Tip's office daily. Still, memories of his 2006 Jazz Fest debacle lingered. "We knew it was a gamble from the start," recalled Bill Taylor, former executive director of the Tipitina's Foundation. "There were a lot of variables. But I thought we had to go for it, even if there was a chance it wouldn't happen."

Forty-eight hours out, Domino practiced with two musicians from his band at his home in Harvey. But the next day, he skipped an afternoon rehearsal with the full band at Tipitina's. The frazzled Tip's staff devised a contingency plan in case of a no-show: They would refund tickets and hustle local blues/funk/soul guitarist Walter "Wolfman" Washington and his Roadmasters onstage as a substitute.

Fans filing into Tipitina's on May 19 buzzed with uncertainty and anticipation. Decorating the stage was Domino's famous pink Cadillac couch, which had been salvaged from his flooded home and restored. The Professor Longhair banner above the stage and a bronze Longhair bust near the door wore Domino-style captain's caps. Two hundred VIP ticket-holders filled the club's balcony; sales of general admission floor tickets were limited to 300, to accommodate a documentary film crew's cameras. The audience included Jazz Fest producer/director Quint Davis and Neville Brothers founding father Art Neville.

When Domino arrived, dapper in a checkered, cream-colored sport coat, shiny chocolate-brown shirt, and his trademark bling, he was immediately sequestered in an Annunciation Street house around the corner from the club. Longtime friends Eric Paulsen, a news anchor at local CBS affiliate WWL-TV, and retired judge Steve Ellis and his wife Haydee were on hand to provide moral support. "We felt like we had to insulate him," Von Kurnatowski said of stashing Domino away. "Why add to his anxiety right before he stepped on stage?"

Domino's stage fright stems in part from doubts about his own abilities. "Fats doesn't ever want to give a substandard show," Von Kurnatowski said. "He seems to be absolutely focused on that. His anxiety going in is that he won't perform up to standards."

Shortly after nine P.M., Reggie Hall, Domino's brother-in-law and a respected R&B hitmaker in his own right, opened the show. Backstage, no one knew if Domino would actually perform—not even Domino. Von Kurnatowski "didn't want to prod him to get on that stage if he really didn't want to. Fats has a very keen sense of what's right for him, and what's going to work. If in his gut he thought, 'I better not do this,' then my job would be to say, 'OK, I understand,' and not in any way pressure him. Because then, if it doesn't go well, I put him in that position."

As his preshow jitters peaked, Domino expressed surprise at the expectation that he would perform. "He was just so nervous," Haydee Ellis said. "He may have been trying to figure out if he really had to do it." Von Kurnatowski thought Domino "was messing with me. That's when Eric Paulsen started talking to him. I was pretty proud of Fats when he finally stood up and said, 'OK, let's go get this over with.'"

In Tipitina's, Paulsen met him at the side of the stage. "I was going to stick on him like white on rice. I wasn't going to let him not sing." The newscaster draped a reassuring arm around Domino's shoulders: "Once you get up there, it'll be like the old days. You'll be fine. Start with 'I'm Walkin' and it will go from there."

The pep talk worked. To a huge cheer, Domino settled in at the baby grand piano on the overcrowded Tipitina's stage and launched into "I'm Walkin'." His five-piece horn section featured Herb Hardesty—a Domino sideman since the 1940s—and Dirty Dozen Brass Band baritone saxophonist Roger Lewis. They swung in as Domino, his voice as sunny as ever, tore off trademark triplets and trills. As he barreled through "Blueberry Hill," "My Girl Josephine" and "I'm in Love Again," he grew more confident. After each song, Hall whispered the next title in Domino's ear. Domino pumped them out like a human jukebox. Perhaps sensing the end of an era was at hand, even Hardesty snapped pictures from the bandstand.

Domino reeled off four songs in ten minutes, and bolted for the exit. Von Kurnatowski thought maybe "he got confused as to the sequence of songs, and thought he was on his last song." Fortunately, Paulsen intercepted him at the side of the stage and gently explained that folks would like to hear a few more. Paulsen suggested the first title that came to mind: "Blue Monday." So the reluctant star returned to the piano with "Blue Monday."

Beaming, Domino leaned into the microphone at his side, rolling his shoulders as he worked the keys. Warmed up, he played hard, showing off, finishing "I'm Ready" with a flourish. In the audience, Honduran-born vocalist Fredy Omar, experiencing his first Fat Man concert, was thrilled. "Can you believe this? His voice is so strong. It hasn't changed."

Domino cruised through "Ain't That a Shame," "Shake Rattle and Roll," "Valley of Tears" and "Jambalaya." "So Long" detoured into "Natural Born Lover," a modest hit from 1960, then came back around to its farewell: "So long, I'm all packed up and on my way." With that, having squeezed eleven songs into thirty-two minutes, Domino stood up and made his way offstage. Paulsen pleaded for one more song: "I asked, 'Will you sing "The Fat Man" for me?' He said, 'Eric, I'm too tired.'"

Having witnessed history—in all likelihood, Fats Domino's final performance—fans snapped up ten-dollar commemorative posters on the way out. The next afternoon, an exhausted but relieved Bill Taylor insisted the extraordinary effort to pull off the show was worth it. Cameras captured a half hour of performance footage, just enough to anchor a documentary, *Fats Domino: Walkin' Back to New Orleans*, that would air on hundreds of PBS stations. "Fats is as natural a performer as you'll ever find," Taylor said, echoing the opinion of most who have seen the footage. "He still has it, in a big way."

Emboldened, Taylor hatched an even more ambitious plan: Escorting Domino to New York to promote *Goin' Home: A Tribute to Fats Domino*, a double-disc Tipitina's Foundation benefit CD on which Paul McCartney, Elton John, Norah Jones, Robert Plant, Neil Young, B. B. King, and other A-list stars remade Fat Man classics.

Over beers in the bedroom of Domino's house in Harvey, Taylor proposed he make his first trip to New York since the early nineties. To Taylor's surprise and delight, Domino said yes. Given his stature, his infrequent travel and the "Katrina effect"—a heightened interest in all things New Orleans—opportunities for promotional appearances abounded. Taylor assembled an ambitious schedule. Over three days and nights in the Big Apple, Domino was slated to sing "My Blue Heaven" with Norah Jones on *The Late Show With David Letterman*; appear at a tribute concert; perform on *The Today Show*; and sign autographs at a bookstore.

The campaign hit its first snag before it began: A strike by the Writers Guild of America scuttled all scheduled tapings of the Letterman show. Was Taylor confident the rest of the trip would proceed according to plan? "Confident? No. I'm hopeful."

Twenty-four hours before departure, Fats bought new luggage—a positive sign. To everyone's relief, on the morning of November 7 he rolled up to Louis Armstrong International Airport an hour before flight time, accompanied by his buddy Walter Miles, a cab driver. Domino tapped Miles to accompany him to New York as his valet, caretaker and subject of good-natured ribbing.

In a black leather jacket, black slacks, black Nike sneakers and a white captain's cap, Domino was upbeat. Von Kurnatowski arranged a private security screening and a golf cart to whisk Domino through Concourse D to a secluded lounge—no one wanted to risk an on-slaught of well-meaning fans spooking him at the last minute. Safely stowed in the lounge, he cracked open his first Heineken of the day. It was 9:30 A.M.

Twenty minutes later, most passengers had boarded. As gate attendants issued a last call, Taylor signaled for Fats to be brought up from the lounge. The man of the hour boarded a golf cart, then disembarked and disappeared into a Hudson News outlet. He had chosen this moment to buy sunglasses. As minutes ticked by, Taylor got nervous. Finally Fats and Miles made their way to the gate and ambled down the jetway three minutes before departure. Literally the last passengers on board, they took their seats in first class among the Tipitina's party, which included Taylor, Von Kurnatowski, executive assistant Lauren Cangelosi, and Dean Dupuy, a longtime friend and business partner of Von Kurnatowski's.

At the back of the plane, Glenn Denning spotted my copy of *Blue Monday: Fats Domino and the Lost Dawn of Rock 'n Roll*. Denning spent the previous day with Columbia University professor Jeffrey Sachs and contemporary R&B star John Legend at a Tulane University seminar on poverty. Denning also accompanied Legend on a tour of the 9th Ward that included a pilgrimage to Fats' gutted, vacant home. "So is Fats on the plane?" Denning asked.

Against all odds, he was.

Three hours later, Continental Flight 617 descended into New Jersey. As he deplaned at Newark's Liberty International Airport, Domino was as sunny as the air was cold. A man called out, "Nice meetin' ya, Fats"; Fats immediately replied, "Same here."

Traversing the terminal on a golf cart, he skirted a bank of floor-to-ceiling windows that frame the distant Manhattan skyline. *"New York City, here I come,"* he sang to himself. On the escalator to baggage claim, Lauren Cangelosi—whom Domino referred to as "Blondie"—asked if he was excited. "I'm too old to be excited."

Riffing on one of his most popular songs, he observed to no one in particular, "I'm walkin' . . . to New York." As he waited for his luggage, a scruffy dude in a KEITH RICHARDS FOR PRESIDENT T-shirt approached. "I'm a big fan," he said. "Could you sign these albums?"

The guy presented a dozen vintage Domino albums and a Sharpie pen. He claimed he knew Domino was coming to New York for the tribute concert, figured he'd be on one of the few direct flights from New Orleans, and staked out the airport. Will the show include any special guests?

"Yeah," Domino said, establishing a theme for the journey. "Some Heineken beer."

Cangelosi examined images of the smiling young star on the album jackets. "Fats, you still look the same," she said sweetly.

"You don't wear glasses, do you?" Domino quipped.

As a second guy approached with a stack of albums, it was clear he and his companion were professional autograph stalkers. The albums still bore price tags from used record stores; with signatures, their value increased exponentially. Believing these are genuine fans, Domino patiently inscribed every item. One guy snapped pictures, establishing provenance. Domino, posing with his ever-present brown leather briefcase, sang a line from the New Orleans Carnival classic "Go To the Mardi Gras": *"Got my suitcase in my hand. . . ."*

The photographer stopped shooting at Taylor's request. But moments later, as Fats headed outside to a limousine, he circled like a shark and popped off flashes.

"Can you stop please?" Taylor demanded, more forcefully. The paparazzo ignored him. Taylor apologized to Domino, who was unperturbed: "It's good that they still know."

Domino was disappointed, however, to learn the limo was devoid of Heineken. During the thirty-minute ride into Manhattan, Von Kurnatowski previewed upcoming events. Billionaire New York Mayor Michael Bloomberg was scheduled to present Fats with a Key to the

City at the November 8 tribute; previous recipients include Mother Teresa, Nelson Mandela and Muhammad Ali.

Von Kurnatowski began, "So Fats, the Mayor of New York . . ."

Domino cut him off: "Tell him I said hello," dispensing with the request before it is made. Earlier, Von Kurnatowski noted that Domino was "always on edge about what he's going to be asked to do."

Exiting the New Jersey Turnpike, Domino inquired about the status of the Apollo Theater. Taylor was on his cell phone, fielding yet another possible schedule addition. "We don't want to be too adventurous," he said.

Walter Miles tells a story about how he and Domino got lost in the rock-and-roll legend's new neighborhood. They drove in circles until an exterminator who had serviced Domino's old Lower 9th Ward residence directed them to the correct house.

As the limo traversed Hell's Kitchen, Cangelosi noted that the first six hours of the trip had gone smoothly: "I'm floored. I was paranoid." Earlier, Domino had confided to her that he'd rather be home, but "I've got work to do."

The car glided east on 57th Street toward the heart of the Theater District. Outside Le Parker Meridien, a chic high-rise hotel half a block from Carnegie Hall in midtown Manhattan, Domino donned the wraparound sunglasses he bought at the New Orleans airport. Soaring marble arches frame the austere, ultra-contemporary lobby. At the front desk, he presented his driver's license to the receptionist. The young woman, like her colleagues, wore a purple cotton smock. She gave no indication that the name on the Louisiana license meant anything to her beyond its affiliation with the newly arrived hotel guest. Fats and Miles disappeared into an elevator, bound for adjoining rooms on the eighteenth floor.

By that afternoon, it was clear that Fats would not partake of New York's attractions, culinary or otherwise. He intended to order spaghetti from room service and rehearse on a rented electric keyboard. "He told Roland he's looking forward to playing," Taylor said. "That's a positive sign."

During dinner at the famed Carnegie Deli on Seventh Avenue, Von Kurnatowski received a call from Domino, who didn't much care for the hotel's spaghetti. (Neither did he enjoy the steak he ordered one morning for breakfast. The problem? The fat was trimmed off.

Fats loves his fat.) Suitably spicy soul food is hard to come by on the road. In the old days, Domino traveled with a hot plate, cooking gumbo, pig's feet, and red beans and rice in hotel rooms. He was not so equipped on this trip.

Von Kurnatowski offered to deliver a pastrami sandwich from the Carnegie. Before leaving, Taylor examined the framed celebrity photos that wallpaper the deli. Surely Fats Domino is of greater import than, say, Gavin "*Love Boat*" Macleod, Florence "Mrs. Brady" Henderson or a long-forgotten trio called Oui 3? Inspiration struck: Why not have Fats donate a signed picture the next morning? Taylor buttonholed a Carnegie Deli manager, explained that he's traveling with Fats Domino, and wouldn't it be great if . . .

The Egyptian-born manager stared blankly. He's never heard of Fats Domino; "Blueberry Hill" apparently did not resonate as loudly in North Africa as the rest of the world. But Taylor persevered, and the manager said he would be happy to accommodate a Domino photo.

In his junior suite at Le Parker Meridien, Domino sat at the rented keyboard, nursing a minibar Amstel Light. Von Kurnatowski invited him to breakfast the next morning at Carnegie Deli. "I don't want to, but I will," said Domino, who was flabbergasted by the $200-a-day cost of renting a keyboard. "I could have brought my own piano."

"That's New York City," Taylor explained.

"I don't care whose city it is," Domino cracked.

Talk turned to what Domino would perform on the *Today* show. Miles suggested "As Time Goes By," the theme song from *Casablanca*: "He sounded real good playing that for me the other day." The Tipitina's folks exchanged nervous glances. For promotional purposes, they wanted Fats to showcase something from the *Goin' Home* CD.

Fats was ambivalent. He toyed with the piano, obviously uncomfortable with so many visitors in his room, not all of whom he recognized. (He repeatedly asked me who I was throughout the trip.) Taylor offered to go find a six-pack of Heineken, a more economical option than the minibar. With the *Today* show question still unanswered, Domino was left alone with his expensive keyboard in an expensive hotel in New York.

Ready or not, tomorrow he was to meet and greet the Big Apple.

Indicative of a neighborhood in transition, a stretch of West 27th Street in Chelsea is home to both a scrap metal processor and a Lamborghini dealership. Inside Crobar, a black-walled, 1,100-capacity dance club, an all-star New Orleans band rehearsed for that night's Domino tribute concert. Crobar would soon close; events director Lee Blumer liked the idea of a New Orleans–style send-off. As an eleven-year-old in 1957, her mind was blown by Domino at the Brooklyn Paramount. Twelve years later, she helped produce the original Woodstock. "What a way to go," Blumer said of the Domino bash. "This is an amazing event. My heart is expanding."

As club employees bustled about preparing the room for the show, former Meters guitarist Leo Nocentelli, DumpstaPhunk keyboardist Ivan Neville and bassist Nick Daniels, and modern jazz saxophonist and Mardi Gras Indian Big Chief Donald Harrison Jr. sought the essence of Stevie Wonder's "Higher Ground" onstage. Everyone hoped Domino would sing a song or two, but no one was counting on it. "You've got to expect the unexpected, and be prepared," said Neville, who, as a son of Aaron Neville and a veteran of Keith Richards's X-pensive Winos solo band, knew a thing or two about the unpredictability of a musician's life. "And this is a good band to do it."

As they trotted out the Meters classic "Looka Py-Py," Domino arrived with Miles and Von Kurnatowski. He disappeared through a passageway into the Pink Elephant, a swank nightclub adjacent to Crobar. Academy Award–winning documentary filmmaker Barbara Kopple followed with her crew. Thirty minutes later, Domino reemerged in Crobar. The musicians took a break to pay their respects. Most had never met, let alone performed with, this member of the Rock and Roll Hall of Fame's inaugural class.

No one was in much of a hurry to resume rehearsals; Taylor, the show's de facto executive producer, was getting anxious. Gradually, the musicians reassembled onstage to feel out "Blueberry Hill" as Domino observed silently. "We need Fats!" Nocentelli announced.

Tentatively, Domino laid his hands on a black Yamaha piano and confirmed the song's key, B-flat. He launched "Blueberry Hill" with Nocentilli serving as bandleader. Every camera and eye in the room was focused on the Fat Man as he reacquainted himself with the arrangement. After ten minutes, he got up and left. "That's all you gonna do?" Nocentelli asked, incredulous. The guitarist hoped to run through

"Ain't That a Shame" or maybe "I'm Walkin'." Ten minutes of "Blue-berry Hill," though, was better than nothing.

Back in the Theater District, Domino, Von Kurnatowski and Miles stopped at Carnegie Deli. Sprung from rehearsal, Domino was in a playful mood. To underscore his need for sustenance, he showed off the slack in the band of his gold wristwatch. He eyed a bowl of the Carnegie's signature bright-green pickles suspiciously, then spotted a mountain of tuna salad on a nearby diner's plate. That's what he wanted, to go.

But first, a star-struck Carnegie manager—not the Egyptian-born gentleman who failed to recognize Domino's name—asked to take a picture of him next to the big fake pickle near the door. "Rock and roll means Fats Domino, Chuck Berry, Little Richard and Bo Did-dley," Dennis Howard declared. "That's it. They invented it." How-ard waxed nostalgic about Domino in his prime at the Brooklyn and New York Paramount theaters. "He was the best. He played the pi-ano like a typewriter. Nobody else came close."

Outside the deli, Renee Dimarzo sat behind a card table, solicit-ing donations for the United Homeless Organization. Domino tucked twenty dollars into her tip jar, a five-gallon water jug. "I could be homeless one day," he said.

Von Kurnatowski couldn't resist name-dropping: He leaned to-ward Dimarzo and whispered, "That's Fats Domino." Her eyes went wide. "Fats Domino! You're awesome!" She hugged him, gushed, in-sisted on taking a photo beneath the Carnegie Deli awning. He was happy to oblige: "Thanks for asking!"

Dimarzo was smitten. "He's got a beautiful smile. And he's very sweet, very humble."

In good spirits, Domino moved on. He spied the generous buffet inside the 55th Street Deli. He loaded up on additional provisions: spaghetti and meatballs, boiled eggs, pound cake. "It's like this is my last meal," he joked.

Back on the street, his car and driver were nowhere to be found, so he headed up Seventh Avenue toward his hotel a block and a half away. "I'm walkin' now," Domino said, dodging a yellow taxi at the corner of 56th Street. The temperature hovered in the low forties; the sun had yet to make an appearance. He paused under heat lamps warming the entrance to the Park Central Hotel. "I'll see you all later," he said, grinning. Outside Carnegie Hall, he observed, "They made a lot of live records there. Not me."

Earlier, at Carnegie Deli, Howard the manager wanted to know: Does Fats still perform? New York would soon find out.

Fats Domino is Santa Claus: short, stout, and jovial, his mere presence makes people happy.

At 8:15 P.M., with the distant Empire State Building bathed in Mardi Gras purple, green and gold, he returned to Crobar. He looked like a million bucks: black double-breasted pinstripe suit, silver shirt, pink tie—the same tie he wore in 2006 to pick up a replacement for his National Medal of Arts at the White House—matching spangled pocket square, shiny gold hardware. Dozens of early arrivals milled around beneath Crobar's giant disco ball as the P.A. pumped prerecorded music.

Domino made his way to the balcony VIP section with Miles and Von Kurnatowski. As he settled onto a red velvet banquette, fans down below spotted him and applauded. Heads turned; the ovation rippled across the room. Fats stepped to the railing, smiled and waved. He lingered, and kept waving. It was a perfectly sweet, unscripted moment. The Santa Claus effect.

Unfortunately, no one thought to establish a security perimeter around his booth. Soon he was mobbed by autograph seekers, photographers, the documentary film crew, musicians, friends-of-friends. An incessant guy in a denim jacket secured an autograph on an acoustic guitar, then piled on oversize posters, albums and a closet's worth of memorabilia. The normally even-tempered Von Kurnatowski was pissed; Domino looked overwhelmed and cornered.

Bouncers in suits and earpieces arrived, and order was restored. Fats relaxed. He spotted the documentary crew's boom microphone hovering over his head, looked into the camera, and hoisted a bottle of Heineken.

The all-star band fired up. Nocentelli, Neville, Daniels and Harrison were joined by Soulive guitarist Eric Krasno and hip-hop, funk and pop drummer Adam Deitch. The Meters' "Look-a Py-Py" was far more cohesive than at the afternoon rehearsal. Nocentelli embarked on an extended guitar solo in the Meters' "People Say."

Lost in the moment, he didn't notice Taylor signaling him to stop: Mayor Bloomberg had arrived. The guitarist finally powered down and Bloomberg bounded onstage. He worked "ain't that a shame" into a joke that flopped, then introduced Domino as a "favorite son of New Orleans, an American legend and, as of five minutes ago, my good friend." Bloomberg riffed about their respective ages. "When were we born, Fats? How many years ago?"

Without missing a beat, Domino shot back, "I don't remember," stealing the mayor's laughs and demoting one of the wealthiest men in the nation to straight man.

Bloomberg presented the Key to the City. Domino seemed genuinely thrilled to receive it; the key would later reside in his omnipresent brown leather briefcase alongside his medications. "You've supported me all my life," he said to the audience. "I can't thank you enough."

With that, he attempted an escape. But Nocentelli and a soundman steered him toward the piano. Domino sat down and counted off "Blueberry Hill." His playing and singing were unsteady; after ninety seconds, he tapered off and stood up. The band puzzled on without him—Neville was right about the need to "expect the unexpected"—and Fats appeared finished for the night.

But on his way offstage he encountered Lloyd Price, a native of Kenner, Louisiana, a fellow rhythm-and-blues survivor and a successful businessman now based in New York. Price invited Domino to play piano on "Lawdy Miss Clawdy," just as he did on Price's original hit recording in 1952. So Domino returned to the piano. No longer the center of attention, he came alive. He pumped the keys, mouthed the words, hunched his shoulders and grinned at the audience as he tacked on a final flourish. It was the moment everyone hoped for.

Safe once again on the balcony, Fats found his booth occupied. Toots Hibbert of reggae band Toots & the Maytals, along with his entourage, had taken up residency; Hibbert flew to New York from Jamaica to be part of the show. Toots scooted over, and was obviously thrilled to shake Domino's hand. Price stopped by to say he and Domino last shared a stage at a New Orleans nightclub in the 1950s.

Downstairs, avant-jazzman Olu Dara and Donald Harrison reprised their spoken-word take on "When I See You," from the *Goin' Home* CD. Allen Toussaint, in New York en route to Europe, mimicked

Domino's voice and piano on "I'm Walkin'" and "I'm in Love Again." Fats gamely greeted bigwigs and potential donors to the Tipitina's Foundation.

By 9:30, he was done. Outside in the bitter cold, a half-dozen fans stationed near his car besieged him. "You were bigger than Elvis in Florida," said one.

"Elvis was my man," Fats responded. He climbed into the car, bound for his hotel.

Back inside, the show rolled on. Harrison and Neville took turns leading the requisite "Hey Pocky Way" and "Big Chief." People shook their rumps, drank and cheered. Uptown New Orleans was briefly transposed on downtown Manhattan, even though Fats Domino had left the building.

Twelve hours later in midtown Manhattan's NBC Studios, Nocentelli, arguably the most influential guitarist in the history of New Orleans music, fired up a boombox in a basement men's room.

Before he backed Domino on the *Today* show, he wanted to preview a new Mardi Gras song for Harrison; the first available electrical outlet he found happened to be on the bathroom's counter. Nocentelli cued up "Hey Now Hey," air-guitaring bass lines and mouthing lyrics about Mardi Gras Indians. Harrison, an actual Mardi Gras Indian, nodded his head and hooted in approval. Nocentelli cranked it up; funk echoed off bathroom walls. Inspired, Harrison popped in a CD of *his* new Mardi Gras song. A game of funk one-upmanship ensued.

"I need you on this," said Harrison, grooving, recruiting Nocentelli to contribute to the recording.

"We're on the same page," said the guitarist, also grooving.

NBC security guards, pages and staffers filed in and out of the bathroom, unsure what to make of this New Orleans moment. Bill Taylor stumbled upon the scene, and didn't bat an eye. "Four minutes until we're on, guys."

Today co-host Hoda Kotb mingled with the musicians who had taken over the green room. She spent several years at WWL-TV in New Orleans, so was acquainted with many faces in the room. Warmed up and ready to go, Nocentelli, Harrison and the rest of the band—

Neville, Daniels, Deitch and Hibbert—made their way upstairs to the show's ground-floor studio. Across 49th Street, a crane hoisted the eighty-foot Rockefeller Center Christmas tree; gawkers peered through the studio's glass walls.

Domino was well rested thanks to his early departure from the tribute concert. Walter Miles asked if he wanted to wear his leather jacket during the show. He did—but first he removed a banana from an inside pocket. (Lauren Cangelosi eventually prevailed on him to eat it; Adonica, one of Domino's daughters, had entrusted her with assuring Fats ate well on the trip.) He was determined to atone for his aborted stab at "Blueberry Hill" the previous night.

The musicians taped a truncated "teaser" to preview the full performance later in the broadcast. Domino was not satisfied with the run-through. He consulted Nocentelli—whom he addressed as "Guitar Man"—on the closing chord.

With the live broadcast thirty minutes away, the musicians drifted off. Domino fidgeted in a tiny dressing room adjacent to the studio. His own worst critic, he wanted to rehearse more. "Is there another piano around here?"

He glanced at a playback of the teaser on a dressing room monitor. "I haven't been playing for six months," he said, apologizing for what he perceived as rusty chops.

Cangelosi reassured him: "You sound good."

Fats wasn't buying it. "I wish I saw it like that. If you think about it too much, you mess up."

Back in the empty *Today* show studio, Cangelosi—young, blonde and pretty—rested her elbows on the piano, switching modes from mother hen to muse. Fats' fingers reeled off samples of his deep catalog: "Whole Lotta Lovin'," "I Want to Walk You Home," "I'm Walkin'." "I got lucky with those songs," he said.

He asked Cangelosi to find another musician, any musician, to consult on chord changes. Left alone with his insecurities, Domino caressed the piano keys and hummed "Blueberry Hill," relearning the bridge of a song he'd performed thousands of times. Cangelosi returned with Nick Daniels; the other musicians soon followed, and they made another practice run up "Blueberry Hill." By the third try, Domino was cooking. He improvised lyrics: "Give me my beer/cause the time is near."

He laughed and gleefully jerked his head. "Give me my lunch," he said, reaching for the green bottle discretely stashed behind a leg of the piano.

It was nearly go time. "The moment of truth," Taylor said, holding his breath.

Twenty seconds before the "on air" sign illuminated, Fats, a bundle of nerves, pulled the trigger on "Blueberry Hill" prematurely. Realizing his mistake, he stopped, squinted into the bright studio lights and, near panic, searched for a producer to cue him: "I can't see you, bruh!"

But there's no stopping now. Kotb and co-host Natalie Morales were already addressing the nation. They plugged the *Goin' Home* CD, introduced Domino, and it was all on his shoulders.

He laid his hands on the keys, and they found the correct notes. Seconds later, he paused just long enough to uncork the opening lyric mimicked by everyone from *Happy Days* hero Richie Cunningham to former Russian Federation president Vladimir Putin: "*I found my thrill on Blueberry Hill . . .*" He navigated the bridge flawlessly and locked in with Nocentelli's guitar for a spot-on ending.

He nailed it, and knew it. The show cut to a commercial and Kotb bounded over to plant a congratulatory kiss on his cheek.

"Who's better than you?" she gushed.

"You!" Domino countered.

Back on the air, Kotb requested another song, and Fats froze. He grabbed her wrist, serenaded her with the line, "*I want to hold your hand,*" and suggested they reprise "Blueberry Hill." Why not?

The credits rolled; the *Today* show was finished, but Fats was not. With the cameras and pressure off, he picked up steam on the strongest version of "Blueberry Hill" yet. Dozens of NBC staffers crowded the studio, clapping, cheering, swaying and swooning; Kotb and Morales boogied alongside former New York Giants running back Tiki Barber and an NBC cafeteria lady. Fats beamed, electrifying the room with rock-and-roll magic. Decades dropped away and the clock turned back, however briefly, to the New York Paramount circa 1957.

"Blueberry Hill" concluded with a thunderous ovation; more than one onlooker dabbed at misty eyes, overwhelmed by the Domino effect. Fats, having fun now, immediately uncorked the lickety-split opening of "I'm Ready." As the other musicians jumped in, he laughed and cut himself off.

"I want to kiss Fats!" Morales enthused.

"Here I am!" Fats replied, eager to collect the unexpected dividend. So what happened? Why did he finally come alive?

"Fats got comfortable," Ivan Neville surmised. "The ladies were talking to him. He was like a youngster."

It was raining and cold outside NBC Studios as Domino's handlers shepherded him through an especially aggressive pack of autograph hounds. During a luncheon at the tony Michael's, he declined the lobster but consented to take a picture with director Mel Brooks. He briefly sat at the head of a reserved table among potential donors to the Tipitina's Foundation, but soon joined Miles and Cangelosi at the restaurant's bar. She noticed that Fats was "fading."

Back at Le Parker Meridien, the pace caught up with him. His fingers swelled so badly that he couldn't remove his bulky, star-shaped gold ring. Von Kurnatowski borrowed bolt cutters from a member of the hotel's maintenance staff, who made it clear that he wouldn't assume liability for some of the most valuable fingers in rock and roll. Von Kurnatowski snipped off the ring; the Fat Man's fingers remained unscathed.

Exhausted, Domino went to bed for a "nap." At seven P.M., he was due to sign autographs at the Borders bookstore on the second floor of the Time Warner Center at Columbus Circle. At the appointed hour, he did not answer his phone. Mindful of Domino's health, Taylor did not want to push him: "When is it too much? After what he did this morning, I don't want to put him in a position where he's unhappy. He hit it out of the park this morning."

Reluctantly, the Tipitina's team decided to let Domino sleep. At Borders, they faced 100 fans waiting in line. Von Kurnatowski explained that Domino was not well, and would not appear. Some fans expressed their disappointment less graciously than others.

Days earlier, Domino had pre-signed 200 copies of the *Goin' Home* CD booklet, in order to save time at the actual New York signing. Taylor, Von Kurnatowski and Cangelosi distributed these as consolation prizes. Some fans signed get-well cards; others left gifts.

Domino simply had nothing left to give.

———

At 3:30 the next afternoon, Domino materialized in the Le Parker Meridien lobby, packed, rested and ready to go home. He sang the "rollin', rollin', rollin'" theme from the 1960s Western television series *Rawhide* and was none the worse for wear after yesterday's ring-cutting incident.

On the way out of Manhattan, Von Kurnatowski directed the limo driver to stop near Times Square. Domino wanted to take pictures and see a Broadway street sign—the first time he had shown any interest in playing tourist on this trip. Mission accomplished, he bundled back into the limo.

On the curb at Newark's airport, he ran another gauntlet of autograph entrepreneurs. He finally reached the safety of the private Continental Club lounge above the terminal gates, where the leather chairs are plush, the apples are crisp and delicious, and the drinks are free. One problem: the draft beer wasn't Heineken. "I'd rather be down there," Domino said, gesturing toward the gates, "where I can get what I want."

He was antsy and eager to board, as if all flights to New Orleans might suddenly be cancelled. I asked if he enjoyed himself in New York. "As long as Roland was satisfied, it don't make me no difference. But I hope it went all right, you know? I ain't played in quite a while."

His fans undoubtedly enjoyed hearing him. "As long as they're satisfied, I'm alright."

Would he return to New York? "I guess so. If they want me to come up."

What was his favorite part of the trip? He grinned. "Right now." Going home.

Whatever the limits of his short-term memory—or is he crazy like a fox?—Domino's mischievous wit was still sharp. And as the off-air *Today Show* encore demonstrated, he could still rock and roll with much of the same purpose and drive as fifty years ago. New York invigorated him. "Maybe I'll start working again," he said. "I feel better."

In contrast to his lackadaisical pace through the New Orleans airport three days earlier, he moved briskly to the gate in Newark. Continental Flight 810 touched down at precisely eight P.M. Central Standard Time at Louis Armstrong International Airport.

The reception awaiting Domino in New Orleans was much different than the one in Newark. There were no limos, or photographers, or autograph bandits in baggage claim. Instead, Von Kurnatowski's three-year-old daughter, Mary Grace, bounded over and grabbed Domino's leg as if he were her long-lost grandfather. "Ain't that something?" Domino said, laughing. "She remembers me!"

So did Lorene and Dwayne Billiot, a couple from Cut Off, Louisiana, a tiny bayou town south of New Orleans. They were on the same flight, returning from a twentieth wedding anniversary trip to Niagara Falls. "We were worried about you after Katrina," Lorene said.

"Oh, thank you," Domino replied.

Outside, Miles's son waited in a well-worn gray sedan considerably less luxurious than a long black limo. Domino piled into the backseat, smiling, waving, basking in the humid air.

"It's always good to be home," he declared. "There's no place like home."

Contrary to his prediction in the New Jersey airport, Domino did not start working again. The death of his wife, Rosemary, in March 2008 dealt another significant blow to his constitution.

But family and friends occasionally coaxed him out of the house. On May 30, 2009, he attended *The Domino Effect*, a poorly conceived and executed tribute/benefit concert staged at the New Orleans Arena by promoters from Austin, Texas. Neither Domino nor his associates were involved in the planning, but he was persuaded to make an appearance. He waved to the small crowd from the balcony of a luxury suite, greeted B. B. King and Saints quarterback Drew Brees, and joined Little Richard for a dressing room prayer. The sly Richard pitched Domino on co-headlining some shows, but already knew the answer: the Fat Man didn't even perform at his own tribute.

In November 2010, the Rock and Roll Hall of Fame and Museum in Cleveland celebrated Domino and Dave Bartholomew as the subjects of its prestigious American Music Masters series. The eighty-nine-year-old Bartholomew traveled to Ohio to participate in the weeklong series' culminating concert.

Domino stayed home.

Chapter Six

Terence Blanchard and a Muse Named Katrina

Trumpeter Terence Blanchard was among the cadre of Louisiana musicians enlisted to perform during the 2008 Democratic National Convention in Denver, Colorado. The Serious Jazz Guy mask he often wears is not artifice. He takes his craft seriously, and carries himself with dignity and style. He is extremely sharp and works extremely hard.

But one night during the convention, having fulfilled his obligations for the evening, he held court at the corner of a hotel bar. Details of the after-hours, decidedly off-the-record session are hazy, but Blanchard was on fire, telling stories, doing impressions, cracking jokes, cutting up. In the dozen-plus years I've covered him, it was the loosest I'd ever seen him.

His 2007 CD A Tale of God's Will (A Requiem for Katrina) *remains, for my money, the most intelligent, articulate and elegant musical expression of the tragic events and aftermath of August 29, 2005. To say* A Tale of God's Will *was inspired by the storm doesn't sound quite right. But it was certainly inspired.*

Once-familiar suburban streets are foreign and deserted. Formerly tidy yards are piled high with debris. Green grass, trees and bushes are gray, brown and dead. From inside the van, the little old lady calmly absorbs the nightmare. It is December 5, 2005, her first viewing of the body that was New Orleans' Pontchartrain Park subdivision.

She already knew Katrina devastated her neighborhood. But *knowing* is not the same as *seeing* the ruin in person, touching it, smelling it, breathing in the rot and mold. "I'm telling you, nothing but destruction everywhere you look," she says, peering out a window, composed but wary. "This is so strange."

The van stops at a modest ranch-style house of blond brick. Her house. The house where she and her husband proudly raised their only child, a son, in a community built by and for middle-class African-Americans unwelcome elsewhere. The house where that son mastered the trumpet, the instrument that carried him around the world and blessed him to a degree his parents could scarcely imagine.

The son supports his mother as she steps down from the van. For a final moment, she is blissfully unaware. Still strong, still in charge, she reasserts her matriarchal authority. "Leave that in there," she snaps, directing that a canvas bag remain in the van. Silently, her son obeys.

They turn toward the house. "Now take your time," he cautions.

Wind catches her coiffed white curls as the first gut-punch of grief takes her breath away. Instinctively, her left hand moves to her mouth. She weeps. The son leans in, pressing his head against hers, rubbing her shoulders. She steadies herself.

"You doing OK?" the son asks.

"I'll be OK."

"You're OK. This is all stuff that can be rebuilt."

As they approach the front door, detritus offends her sense of order: "What is all of this?" They open the door. Burglar bars were powerless against this intruder. Water brutalized the home's contents, upending furniture, melting books and photographs, invading every privacy and memory. Black mold crawls up walls. This is more sinister than a flood. This is a perversion.

Her son, an entertainer, is accustomed to cameras. Aware that their words, actions and emotions are being recorded, he struggles to maintain his composure. Or maybe he's being strong for his mother.

She, by contrast, holds nothing back. "Look," she sobs. "This thing's way over here."

"What is that?"

"That's the thing you gave me. It was over here." She is disturbed wherever she looks. "What is that over there?"

"What is what?"

"That."

"That's a . . . uh . . . that looks like your china closet."

"The china closet don't have any business being over here."

The son takes her hand and leads her to another room. She has still not accepted the totality of the destruction. "Is Susan's picture still up on the wall?" she asks, hoping some little piece of personal history survived.

"There's nothing on the wall."

"Oh, Lord have mercy."

"You can rebuild this."

"That's easier said than done."

She collapses against a door frame and buries her face in her son's shoulder, clutching the doorway for support. They stand there, raw and exposed, as the enormity of it all weighs heavily on them. She weeps through the gauze shielding her nose and mouth. "Oh, Lord have mercy. I knew it was devastation but I didn't think it was this bad. It's unbelievable."

"I didn't know how bad it was," the son says quietly, as if apologizing for not better preparing her.

Later, he will face the camera alone in an attempt to contextualize the day's events. "Today when we went into the house, that was really hard because, you know . . . it's like I can't go home. You know what I mean? It's . . . it . . ."

Finally, he breaks down. He looks away, covers his mouth, touches a finger to the bridge of his nose, unable to continue. "I'm sorry."

In the coming weeks, director Spike Lee would edit footage of the mother and son into *When the Levees Broke*, his four-hour HBO documentary about Katrina and its aftermath.

It fell to the son, Terence Blanchard, to translate his mother's grief into music.

After his 1981 graduation from the New Orleans Center for the Creative Arts, the city's acclaimed arts magnet school, Terence Blanchard set out for New York to seek his fortune in jazz. He worshipped at the altar of bebop—Miles Davis, Clifford Brown, Freddie Hubbard, Woody Shaw—but first and foremost considered himself a descendant of the Louis Armstrong lineage. As a music student at Rutgers University in New Jersey, he gigged with vibraphonist Lionel Hampton's band on weekends. He and saxophonist Donald Harrison Jr., a fellow New Orleans expatriate, joined Art Blakey's Jazz Messengers, a launching pad for young musicians; Blanchard replaced Wynton Marsalis in the Messengers roster. After four years, Blanchard and Harrison left to form their own quintet; they released five albums for the Concord and Columbia labels. Before stepping out with his self-titled Columbia Records solo debut in 1991, Blanchard took a hiatus from performing to reconstruct his embouchure, a painstaking and laborious process.

He read an *Elle* magazine profile of fellow Brooklyn resident Spike Lee, whose 1986 full-length feature debut, *She's Gotta Have It*, established him as a promising new director. Blanchard dreamed of collaborating with Lee. "I've always wanted to work with people who are creative but not necessarily musicians or jazz musicians, so they could make me break out of the jazz world and expand my thing. Next thing you know, I'm working with him."

Blanchard was hired as a trumpeter for the score of Lee's 1988 film *School Daze*. He was asked back for *Do the Right Thing* and the 1990 jazz saga *Mo' Better Blues*. The director's father, jazz bassist Bill Lee, scored all three. In *Mo' Better Blues*, Blanchard, Harrison and Branford Marsalis overdubbed musical passages for the actors. When Denzel Washington "plays" trumpet on screen, viewers actually hear Blanchard's horn.

In but one example of Blanchard making his own breaks, he sat down at the studio's piano during the *Mo' Better Blues* recording session and showcased a short harmonic piece he'd composed. Lee liked it and decided to include it in the film. Originally, Lee intended to use it as a solo trumpet piece in a scene on the Brooklyn Bridge. Later, as Lee edited the film, he asked Blanchard to add a string arrangement. "I had never done one before. I called Roger Dickerson, my composition teacher at NOCCA, and said, 'Hey, man, I've got this project. What the hell do I do?' He said, 'Just trust your training.' I'll never forget that. So I wrote it."

As the studio orchestra prepared to record Blanchard's first string arrangement, Bill Lee pointed him toward the podium. "He said, 'You wrote it, you conduct it,'" Blanchard recalled, laughing. "I had never conducted an orchestra before. There I am, standing up there waving my hands. It was a big thrill, to stand in front of a sixty-piece orchestra and have them looking at me and playing something I'd written."

Still, a career as a film composer seemed far-fetched. "I was just happy for that opportunity. Spike walked up to me afterward and said, 'It sounds great. You've got a future in this business.' I still didn't think anything of it. I just thought he was trying to encourage me."

Lee did more than encourage him: He hired the young trumpeter to score 1991's *Jungle Fever.* Blanchard assumed his relative lack of experience would prevent him from working on Lee's next project, the big-budget *Malcolm X.* "I figured that he would get somebody from Hollywood, some big composer."

Instead, Lee gave the job to Blanchard. Creating an appropriate musical theme was a struggle. "We couldn't find anything that really fit," Blanchard said. "When I finally honed in on it, I just trusted my own relationship to Malcolm. [Lee] dug that. That made me trust myself.

"I've been blessed. My second film was *Malcolm X.* For a cat like me to have that be the second film I worked on, with Lee's vision and that acting, that set the tone for the relationship."

From the outset, Lee afforded him considerable artistic license. "He had free rein, because I'm not a composer," Lee said. "I respect musicians. I think they're the greatest artists of all. Painters and novelists and sculptors and photographers—they're all great. But musicians are the best." Even though Blanchard's music must suit Lee's vision, the director trusts the trumpeter's instincts. "Terence has a great gift for seeing what's on the screen," Lee said, "and transcribing that to music."

For his part, Blanchard feels an affinity for Lee's movies. "I remember seeing *School Daze* and *She's Gotta Have It*, and I related to those movies in a way that I didn't relate to other movies. There was a connection. You can go watch *Star Wars* and it's a great movie and you can relate to it on a certain level. But being African-American, when you see a movie like *She's Gotta Have It* and you see my man going, 'Baby, baby, please . . .' we all can relate to that in some form or fashion."

In 1995, Blanchard moved back to New Orleans and bought a stately, pre–Civil War mansion along an old-money stretch of Prytania Street. He missed his two young children, who lived in the city with their mother, and found that the frenetic pace of New York City no longer suited him. "It was rough. I was spending all my off-time in

New Orleans. That was the thing that helped me realize that it was time to move. I always knew that I was going to move back; it was just a matter of when. And then when I started to see how much I was spending on airline tickets and rental cars, I said, 'I need to move home.'"

His motivations were not only pragmatic. "Whenever I would come to New Orleans and hear guys play, that reminded me of why I got in the music industry—because I had fun playing music. Living in New York, it started to become a business for me after a while. Even though the artistic side of it was always there, you start to get caught up in the pace of everything, the whole thing of you can't see the forest for the trees.

"I was [into it]. I was always active. But the funny part about it is even when you're in that mode, you're always looking for the day when you can just slow down and be glad. Coming back to New Orleans really helped me to refocus myself. A lot of it didn't have anything to do with the music industry. It's just that the city itself is a nice place to be."

As it turned out, restoring his 504 area code did not hinder his film career. He has scored movies and TV shows for various directors, some more enthusiastically than others. "If the film is horrible, then the music is extremely hard to write. You sit there and go, 'There's nothing I can do to make this any better.'" His association with Lee remains his most fruitful. Their collaborations include *Crooklyn* (1994), *Clockers* (1995), a documentary about the Ku Klux Klan's 1963 bombing of an Alabama church titled *4 Little Girls* (1997), *Summer of Sam* (1999), *Jim Brown: All American* (2002), *25th Hour* (2002), *She Hate Me* (2004), *Sucker Free City* (2004), *Inside Man* (2006), and *Miracle at St. Anna* (2008).

Scoring films is far more lucrative than fronting a jazz band. It is the sort of second career that enables a jazz bandleader to park his Porsche in neighborhoods not typically populated by musicians. It can feed revenue streams beyond the six-figure composer's fees. A tour built around Blanchard's compositions for Lee films, augmented by special guests, did big business on the road. More than 8,000 fans paid to hear Blanchard at the Hollywood Bowl with Chaka Khan, jazz singer Dianne Reeves, and members of Public Enemy.

Blanchard was in Los Angeles as Katrina threatened New Orleans.

He caught a red-eye back to the city, landing at four A.M. He quickly boarded up his house on Prytania, then drove to Atlanta with his wife/manager, Robin Burgess, and their kids. When it became clear New Orleans would be inhospitable for some time, they settled into Blanchard's Los Angeles apartment for what turned out to be a six-month exile.

Lee joined him in L.A. to score *Inside Man*, a big-budget bank caper starring Denzel Washington, Jodie Foster and Clive Owen. "Spike didn't even say hello," Blanchard recalled of their first meeting in L.A. "The first thing he said was, 'I want to do a documentary on those levees.' He was going to use his notoriety and his fame to help. You've got to give this cat credit for even doing it. It speaks volumes about how we've got to take responsibility and act. We can't sit on the sidelines. He was doing his part, and he's not even from here."

Blanchard had already attempted to address the storm through music. "But I was drawing a blank. I couldn't think of anything. And the vastness of the devastation was so crazy, I couldn't assimilate it. I couldn't put it in context."

As he and Lee discussed what became *When the Levees Broke: A Requiem in Four Acts*, a four-hour chronicle of Katrina's human toll and aftermath, Blanchard concluded that his entire career had led up to that moment. "I didn't want to write New Orleans–style music—I wanted to write music that was more universal. Because in my mind, this was a universal story of tragedy, hope, despair. I tried to find melodic themes related directly to those emotions."

On a hot afternoon in July 2006, Blanchard and Lee holed up in New Orleans' Lower Garden District to fine-tune their soundtrack to a disaster. Three days earlier, Blanchard viewed a rough cut of *When the Levees Broke*. The trumpeter spent the next frantic forty-eight hours composing the score for the film's first segment.

Lee flew in from New York to hear the results at the Music Shed, a recording studio and rehearsal space fashioned from an old warehouse. Clad in white with matching sneakers, the director peered at a TV monitor occupying his entire field of vision. Blanchard slumped in a chair nearby, resting his weary head in his hands. A dozen musicians and assistants arrayed behind them watched silently. The mood was calm, but focused. Fifteen years into their creative partnership, Blanchard was well-acquainted with Lee's tastes. Of the first twenty *Levees* musical cues, Lee requested retakes on only three. Robin Burgess breathed a sigh of relief. "To only have three redos out of twenty, that's fantastic. We're like, 'Phew!'"

When he tapped Blanchard to score *When the Levees Broke*, it made little difference to Lee that the trumpeter was a New Orleanian. "Terence does my scores," Lee said, "so it was not even a question."

But to Blanchard, it made all the difference in the world. As he composed, he could not remove himself from the subject matter. "I drive around the city, and I'm stepping into what I saw [in the film]: 'That's the Circle Foods store. That's the gas station on Napoleon.' I can't get a break emotionally."

Blanchard and Lee deployed a seventy-piece orchestra for the *Inside Man* score. But practical and artistic considerations often dictate much smaller ensembles. "We have to adapt to the budget and the stories," Lee said. "*Levees* is very similar to *4 Little Girls*, which was tragedy on a much smaller scale, but still a tragedy nonetheless. That was a small ensemble piece. Even if we had the money, I don't think seventy pieces would be appropriate for *Levees*."

Instead, Blanchard featured his horn alongside members of his band: saxophonist Brice Winston, bassist Derrick Hodge and pianist Aaron Parks. Veteran New Orleans drummers Adonis Rose, Shannon Powell and the Meters' Zigaboo Modeliste also contributed, as did jazz banjoist Don Vappie. Lee prefers long, lyrical passages, and *When the Levees Broke* would be no exception.

When the documentary expanded from two to four hours, Blanchard's workload also doubled. And given the compressed timeframe—HBO planned the premiere for August 2006, on the first anniversary of the storm—he would have even less time than usual.

To make *Levees* as current as possible, Lee tinkered with additional footage until the last minute. While screening the score at the Music Shed, less than four weeks before the premiere, he dispatched an assistant to track down footage of a recent news conference with Louisiana governor Kathleen Blanco. Already, Blanchard planned to stay up all night composing the second hour of music. "What makes this so extraordinary," said Burgess, "is that this is like the never-ending documentary."

The extraordinarily tight deadline necessitated shortcuts. Typically, each musical "cue" has its own title. But with *Levees*, "we didn't have time to name them," said Burgess, who tracked the recording session's ever-changing road map on a laptop. "We're calling all of them "Levees" and identifying them by cue numbers."

In Blanchard's view, *When the Levees Broke* was not only a chronicle of the darkest chapter in his hometown's history, but an unusually accurate and honest representation of the city's distinct personality and dialect. "My wife and I watched the first cut together, and we were blown away. Not only in terms of the story, but in terms of capturing the city's culture. Because people come down here and . . . they always want to put these things on us that really don't apply to New Orleans, that just apply in tourists' minds.

"The thing about this that got me was that it's all local people talking, from all walks of life, but who are from here. I can relate to all of that. It was the first time, I'm sad to say, where you see [a film about New Orleans] and you go, 'Wow, I'm proud of my city's heritage, because somebody got it right.'"

The authenticity shone through on multiple levels. "Having worked on it, looking at it every day, it's rough," Blanchard said. "It's really rough. You see the angst in these people who stayed here and survived all this stuff. What's deep about all of it is that everybody in the piece wants to come back. They have a desire to rebuild the city.

"We've always had a love-hate relationship with this city. Always. We love the culture, but we hate some of the political stuff. We love what we've done in terms of art, but we hate all this other stuff in terms of race relationships. But throughout all of it, we don't leave. To me, that's really profound. You can't put that into words. I can't even put that into music."

Watching a rough cut of *Levees* "sparked a whole other type of inspiration. I realized the music can't get in the way of these stories, but had to bring those elements together. The music had to be the glue that brings you back to a reflective frame of mind."

Lee has always encouraged his composer to write music that could stand on its own. "He wants people to walk away from the theaters humming the melodies," Blanchard said.

For *When the Levees Broke*, he sketched elegant, somber themes. The story of a seventy-two-year-old trumpeter stuck on a roof with two elderly women inspired the song "Levees"; the trumpet solo is their unanswered cry for help. For the foreboding "The Water," Blanchard drew on his own boyhood experiences when Hurricane Betsy flooded his Lower 9th Ward neighborhood in 1965. "It must have been traumatic, for me to remember as much as I did. I remember stepping out on the porch. The water wasn't that high, only two or three feet, but to me it seemed like the ocean. There are big, dramatic moments in the arrangement, because I kept thinking about these kids here during Katrina. If I was traumatized from Betsy, and Betsy was nothing compared to Katrina, what are these kids going through?"

His "Funeral Dirge" is a dignified repast for extremely undignified deaths, for a parade of bloated bodies, tearful testimonials and despair: slow tempos, spacious arrangements, haunting melodies, elegant, sustained trumpet lines, and solitary piano notes shadowed by an upright bass. "When you look at those city streets, places that you've been and areas that you know, and you see dead bodies . . . it's hard. Because you say to yourself, 'This isn't a war zone. This is New Orleans. This is my hometown.' I wanted to write an arrangement that would pay respect to the dead and give them a proper burial, at least in the documentary."

Like a journalist who unwittingly becomes part of the story, Blanchard appears in one of the most poignant and devastating scenes from *When the Levees Broke*. He wasn't present when Lee pitched Wilhelmina Blanchard on the idea of filming her first visit to her devastated home in Pontchartrain Park. Blanchard later asked her, "'Do you realize what you agreed to?' And she said, 'People need to see what we're going through.' I was really proud of my mom." Weeks later, Lee remained outside as a lone cameraman accompanied Wilhelmina and Terence inside.

Terence first relived the episode at a *When the Levees Broke* screening in New York. More than 10,000 New Orleanians would empathize with Wilhelmina at the documentary's local premiere at the New Orleans Arena on August 16, 2006; millions more watched on HBO. "It's hard watching anybody you love go through something like that," Blanchard said. "When I travel, people ask me about my mom. I say, 'She's fine, thank you for asking. But if you cried for my mom, you've got to multiply that amount of emotion by at least 100,000 people.

Because that's how many people went through the exact same thing. It wasn't just my mom.'

"That's what blows me away. If people around the world were that affected by my mom in that one little scene . . . that should give you an understanding of the massive amount of destruction and heartache that people have gone through."

In the 1990s, Blanchard crafted a series of concept albums: *In My Solitude: The Billie Holiday Songbook*; *Jazz in Film*, on which he remade such scores as Duke Ellington's *Anatomy of a Murder*, Jerry Goldsmith's *Chinatown*, Quincy Jones's *The Pawnbroker* and Alex North's *A Streetcar Named Desire*; and *Let's Get Lost*, a collection of Jimmy McHugh compositions sung by prominent female jazz vocalists. But after the release of *Let's Get Lost*, he left Sony Classical in part because he no longer wanted to make themed albums. However lucrative, they are by definition confining. In search of greater latitude to write and record with his band, he signed with Blue Note Records and released the adventurous *Bounce* in 2003, followed by the even more ambitious *Flow* in June 2005.

Even as he wrote the score for *When the Levees Broke*, he considered repurposing some cues for an album of his own. He knew his Katrina album, whatever it turned out to be, would have a home on Blue Note. Before Lee came to him with the documentary footage, he'd been stymied by the daunting task of addressing such a massive, complex subject as Katrina via music—where to begin? Lee's footage gave him direction and focus; after more than a decade of composing scores, Blanchard was adept at writing music to match moments on film.

He selected four compositions from *When the Levees Broke*—"The Water," "Levees," "Wading Through" and "Funeral Dirge"—to rework for his own album. But rather than rehash the entire soundtrack, he and his quintet, augmented by a forty-piece orchestra, expanded on and embellished its themes. Divorced from Lee's footage, the compositions, arrangements and performances must paint the necessary mental pictures—and translate the scope of the disaster and its human toll—on their own. "Frankly, I was going on faith," Blanchard said. "Generally, when you do an album, you think about the songs, the tempos, the moods, how you can fit them into some kind of structure that makes sense and makes for an enjoyable listening experience. With this, we didn't have a clue as to what it was going to be. We just needed to do it."

In the process, they discovered that when words won't suffice, sometimes a trumpet will. *A Tale of God's Will (A Requiem for Katrina)* is a coherent, vivid modern jazz meditation on the storm, one that does not pander to obvious extremes or sentimentality. The rhythm section steps out on the opening "Ghost of Congo Square," setting the stage with the disc's least congruous track. Uptempo, elastic and heavily percussive, it is the only cut with vocals—a chant that repeats the album's title. The strings of "Levees" ease in, followed by Blanchard's burnished horn, hinting at what's to come. Viewers of *When the Levees Broke* will recognize the core "Levees" melody, as well as that of "Wading Through." Blanchard and his bandmates spin what were accents to Lee's documentary images into full-blown statements with extensive solos and changing moods, as in the piano, bass and woodwinds that stitch together the delicate intro of "Wading Through."

Just as Art Blakey once encouraged a young Blanchard to write original compositions, Blanchard encourages his musicians to do the same. Thus, *A Tale of God's Will* is a group effort. Drummer Kendrick Scott intended his "Mantra" as a "mantra for healing and renewal"; it builds to a full-bodied, full-band climax with heavy drums before resolving itself. Bassist Derrick Hodge's lush, lovely "Over There," written before Katrina, nonetheless fit the CD's theme; sadness and hope coexist. Saxophonist Brice Winston wrote "In Time of Need" after moving with his family from New Orleans to Tucson, Arizona. Pianist Aaron Parks contributed the achingly beautiful "Ashé" as a benediction; the opening strings, especially when paired with Blanchard's understated trumpet, reduce Katrina to its most basic level: Grief, personal and intimate, multiplied by tens of thousands. The foreboding slow-crawl of "The Water" magnifies the theme. Scott taps out a somber snare drum march to open the Blanchard composition "Funeral Dirge," another holdover from *When the Levees Broke*. Ominous piano chords follow, until Blanchard's majestic horn finally breaks like the first rays of the dawn, or the first glimmer of rebirth.

The final track on *A Tale of God's Will*, "Dear Mom," moves beyond the moment in *When the Levees Broke* when Blanchard escorts his mother through her ruined home. As strings wrap around long, lush trumpet notes, the trumpeter salutes Wilhelmina Blanchard's courage and class, even as she mourns her tremendous loss. In this song, and throughout *A Tale of God's Will*, there is sadness, despair and quiet desperation in spades, but also strength and hope. That is the ultimate requiem for Katrina.

Blue Note released *A Tale of God's Will (A Requiem for Katrina)* on August 14, 2007. It won Blanchard his first Grammy as a leader, for best large jazz ensemble album, and placed No. 2 on *JazzTimes'* list of the best albums of 2007. During the summer of '07, Blanchard and his quintet performed selections from *When the Levees Broke* at European concerts devoted to Spike Lee's film music. During a weeklong stand in New York, the quintet showcased much of *A Tale of God's Will*. "Everybody was just exhausted," Blanchard said. "It's very emotional stuff that we're dealing with."

They performed *A Tale of God's Will* in its entirety for the first time on September 22, 2007, at the Monterey Jazz Festival in northern California. Thousands of miles and two years removed from the events that inspired it, the music still resonated with listeners. "It is a universal story of tragedy," Blanchard said. "Human loss, human suffering, the human spirit. People could relate to it on that level. People told me they cried during certain parts of the concert. They were profoundly affected by what happened here. We brought a little bit of this world out there."

Three weeks later, a cool morning in New Orleans found Blanchard traversing the wood floors of his Prytania Street home in bare feet. Most rooms were empty. He and his family would soon move to an even more impressive manse on grand oak-lined St. Charles Avenue. Even before Katrina, he had outgrown his home studio on Prytania. His wife found the St. Charles property while Blanchard was on the road. In high school, while commuting from Pontchartrain Park to a summer music camp at Loyola University via multiple bus and streetcar lines, he passed the mansions of St. Charles Avenue. "He couldn't believe that he'd be living in one of those houses," Burgess said. "He was blown away."

The new place required renovations before it could be occupied. On one of Blanchard's visits to check the progress, a Dumpster occupied the driveway. So he parked his beloved 2007 Porsche 911 Carrera S—the one he spent three glorious days driving by himself from Los Angeles to New Orleans—on a side street. Rainwater from a sudden deluge backed up and pooled along the curb just deep enough to breach the Porsche and swamp computer circuitry under the driver's seat. "The water came up so quick," Blanchard said. He shook his head. "That's why we have insurance."

Thus, for the first time in two years, Katrina was not the foremost flood on his mind. But he would soon return to it. On November 3, 2007, Blanchard and his quintet, backed by conductor Rebecca Miller and the Louisiana Philharmonic Orchestra, staged the New Orleans premiere of *A Tale of God's Will (A Requiem for Katrina)* at Dixon Hall on the Tulane University campus. It would be only the second performance of the entire album.

"I'm trying not to think about it," Blanchard said days before the show. "I mean, it's here in New Orleans. I don't know how other people feel, but some part of me doesn't want to revisit that issue that way. I really want to move on. But one of the things we've understood as a band is that this music, unlike any other CD that I've done, has been meaningful for people to experience. So we understand the responsibility as artists to play this music. But it takes us to some dark places emotionally."

A capacity crowd filled Dixon Hall. The music's grand swirl swept up an audience populated by people who had lived with Katrina and its aftermath for more than two years—including Blanchard's mother. The storm still intruded on her life, often unexpectedly. One evening as she discussed her late husband, she stood up to retrieve her wedding photos. "She stopped and realized they don't exist anymore," her son recalled. "And that's months after the damn hurricane."

That night in Dixon Hall, tears of sorrow were also a release. Blanchard, serving as the evening's emcee as well as lead trumpeter, struck the proper balance between reverence for the work and the circumstances that inspired it, and putting folks at ease. He was, after all, amongst his people. The evening concluded with a standing ovation. Blanchard was relieved.

In the years since Katrina, he has emerged as a far more visible and active advocate for his city. He entered the fray of post-storm politics by supporting Louisiana lieutenant governor Mitch Landrieu's unsuccessful bid to unseat incumbent mayor Ray Nagin in 2006. (Four years later, the term-limited Nagin left office deeply unpopular, with the city's finances in tatters; Landrieu ran again, and won.) "I quickly learned that politics is not the route for me," Blanchard said after the '06 race. "The quickest way is not to try to hit a home run, but to try to get on base with what I do. I can't do everything. But if everybody does whatever they can, we'll be fine."

For years, he had served as an instructor at the Thelonious Monk Institute of Jazz, an intensive, graduate-level jazz program based at the University of Southern California. When the Institute announced plans to move, Blanchard and others lobbied successfully for New Orleans. In the fall of 2008, the Institute opened at Loyola University, where Blanchard himself once attended summer music camps. The Monk students, two dozen exceptional young jazz musicians from all over the world, conducted clinics at New Orleans schools and gigged at Snug Harbor, welcome additions to the city's jazz community. Previously, Blanchard commuted each month to L.A. to teach at the Institute; now he could walk from his home on St. Charles Avenue.

He had mixed emotions about leaving Prytania Street; he and Burgess's two daughters grew up there. Though he may change addresses, he insists he will never leave his hometown again, whatever the demands of his vocation. After Katrina, he "never thought about not coming back to New Orleans. I had the mind-set that if it took me and some friends building a house . . . it would have been the most lopsided house, but it would have been standing."

Returning to New Orleans from New York in 1995 "rejuvenated me. Coming back reminded me why I got in the business of music to begin with. To think that there could be a time when this place didn't exist was not on my radar. It would have to totally be destroyed, impossible for me to physically be here, for me not to think about coming back."

Soon after the conclusion of his six months of post-Katrina exile, he dined at Brigtsen's, a new New Orleans classic restaurant. He ordered a spinach salad; it arrived topped with a fried oyster. "Man, I bit into that fried oyster and I stopped. It's kind of embarrassing to admit . . . a tear came down my face. That flavor was something that I hadn't had in my mouth for six months. When I came back and tasted that, I was like, 'Thank you, Jesus.'

"I know that sounds silly, but it blew me away. It was confirmation that it was time to get to work and make this city better than it was before."

Chapter Seven

Alex Chilton Undercover

In the spring of 1995, a mutual friend arranged for me to interview Alex Chilton. The former Box Tops and Big Star frontman had recently released a new CD and was booked at the upcoming New Orleans Jazz & Heritage Festival; our conversation would run as a lengthy Q&A in OffBeat magazine's Jazz Fest preview issue. He selected the setting: The lunch counter of the F. W. Woolworth five-and-dime near the corner of Canal and North Rampart streets, on the frayed edge of downtown New Orleans.

Woolworth was long past its prime, but Chilton was a regular. He arrived aboard his bicycle, dressed down in a white T-shirt, blue pullover, plum-colored shorts and battered leather moccasins. He rarely granted interviews, and I'd been warned about his prickly demeanor. But as he munched a grilled cheese sandwich, sipped Diet Coke and smoked Camels, he answered all he was asked. Unpretentious, matter-of-fact and well-spoken, he even cracked a wry smile or two.

For the next fifteen years, he kept a low profile around town, but was hardly a J. D. Salinger–style recluse. Our paths crossed occasionally at music clubs and restaurants. He was consistently cordial, clearly comfortable in his own skin. A license to live as he pleased was New Orleans' gift to Alex Chilton. The city is a little less interesting without him.

Alex Chilton assumed he was right. In the waning days of August 2005, the sum total of his knowledge and experience convinced him to ride out Hurricane Katrina at home in Tremé, the historically black neighborhood north of the French Quarter he'd grown to love since moving to New Orleans in 1982.

Thousands of residents made a similar choice for various reasons: A belief that the storm would be less destructive than forecast. A desire to protect property. A lack of the means or wherewithal to evacuate. Chilton had the means, but no intention, to leave. He treasured his house, humble as it was. The ancient, anonymous Creole cottage sagged under the weight of time. Paint peeled. Boards blocked dormer windows. At times, a vine sprouted from the roof's peak. But to Chilton, one of rock's great enigmas, the cottage, like New Orleans, was not just home. It was a refuge.

As fellow citizens fled in the face of the approaching cataclysm, he hunkered down, alone. Confident in his decision, he loaned his well-worn Volvo to a former girlfriend for her own evacuation. But after monstrous winds nearly pried an exterior wall from the house and floodwater fouled the street and lapped at his door, he reassessed: No electricity. No gas. No running water. Limited supplies. No means to communicate with the outside world. Gunshots ringing out across the city as looting spread like a cancer and neighborly decorum gave way to desperate need and criminal intent.

Friends familiar with the intensely private Chilton's laid-back, laissez-faire lifestyle would not describe him as a man of action. But days after the storm, as conditions rapidly deteriorated, he realized his most trusted authority in all matters—himself—had miscalculated. It was time to get the hell out.

And so one of the most celebrated songwriters of his generation stepped outside and hailed a helicopter as casually as a cab. The chopper lowered a rescue basket and hoisted him heavenward. As his beloved, battered cottage receded from view, Chilton knew he would return to New Orleans as soon as possible. Because there was no place on earth he'd rather be.

William Alexander Chilton was born in Memphis, Tennessee, in 1950, the youngest of four children. In 1967, as the teenage singer of the Box Tops, his preternaturally gritty, blue-eyed soul bark of a voice mailed "The Letter"—"gimme a ticket for an aeroplane, ain't got time to take a fast train . . .'cause my baby just a-wrote me a letter"—directly to the top of the pop charts. Four years later, after a New York sojourn, he co-founded Big Star. Named for a grocery store chain in Memphis, Big Star released three albums, all commercial failures plagued by poor distribution.

They are now hailed as indispensible power-pop touchstones and templates, thanks in large part to Chilton's deft singing, songwriting and guitar work. *Rolling Stone* enshrined all three albums in the magazine's Top 500 of all time. R.E.M., Wilco, the Replacements, the Bangles, Matthew Sweet, Jeff Buckley, Cheap Trick and many more have covered and/or borrowed from Big Star. In the ultimate affirmation of an enduring legacy, in 2009 Rhino Records issued *Keep an Eye on the Sky*, a lavish four-CD, ninety-eight-track Big Star box set with a 100-page booklet.

But in 1982, Chilton was just another underemployed musician with a checkered past and uncertain future. A second foray to New York had run its course; he had soured on the music business in general, and Memphis in particular. "It could be that I spent too much time there, and have a lot of bad memories," Chilton told me in 1995. "I got off on the wrong foot in that place." A failed marriage and substance abuse deepened his disillusionment. "About the mid-seventies, I wrote drugs off—they were too much for me. But somehow I developed this drinking problem without even knowing. That took five or six more years to stop."

Hoping a change of scenery would reinforce his sobriety, he resolved to start over in, of all places, New Orleans.

His history with the city was scant. As a boy, he occasionally stayed with relatives in McComb, Mississippi, a two hour drive away. In the early 1970s, New Orleans' City Park hosted one of only a dozen or so performances by the original Big Star (drummer Jody Stephens broke his bass drum on the first note of the first song). Chilton visited a friend in New Orleans in 1981, and returned early the following year for Mardi Gras. "When I went back to Memphis, it was so damn cold and horrible I just said, 'This is insane. I'm going back to New Orleans.' I was ready to go somewhere else, but New Orleans was like a dream come true."

Soon after his arrival, he met Nick Sanzenbach, a journeyman drummer and saxophonist whose lengthy Crescent City résumé includes such colorfully named ensembles as Sex Dog and Blood 'n'

Grits. In the early '80s, Sanzenbach drummed with the Blue Vipers, a rockabilly quartet fronted by guitarist and singer "Johnny J." Beninati. The Blue Vipers shared bills with pompadoured, pencil-mustached vocalist Tav Falco's Panther Burns. Chilton was an on-again, off-again member of Panther Burns, a semi-ironic garage rockabilly outfit forged in Memphis in 1979.

One night at Jimmy's—a brick box of a rock club in New Orleans' Carrollton neighborhood—Sanzenbach boasted that, as a boy, he had memorized the lyrics to "The Letter." Chilton was unimpressed; he often deployed a half-smirk, half-smile in such situations. "He said, 'Well, there's only like eight lines in the whole damn song,'" Sanzenbach said. "He could really brush you off. He had this whole attitude, an aristocratic approach that was really fascinating."

Nonetheless, Chilton and Sanzenbach hit it off. For several months, they rented rooms above a chiropractor's office in an old Victorian mansion at the corner of Prytania and Peniston streets Uptown. For Chilton, it was a period of intense focus and transition to sobriety; he immersed himself in the writings of Wilhelm Reich, the controversial Austrian-American psychoanalyst and psychiatrist. "He was searching," Sanzenbach said of his roommate. "He was really an artist, trying to figure it out, because he'd been handed this thing, and he was working it."

Many mornings, they rehearsed jazz standards as a guitar and drums duo. Sanzenbach would later find scraps of paper with notes Chilton wrote to himself: "Flat on the B." "A little sharp on the E." "He was continuously working on tunings," Sanzenbach said. In the tradition of Memphis country-blues guitarist Furry Lewis, in tune didn't necessarily mean *in tune*. During a recording session with Chilton and Sanzenbach, an engineer mentioned that a guitar was out of tune. "Alex snapped, 'Look, man, there's out of tune, and then there's *out of tune*,'" Sanzenbach said. "A lot of bands ruin themselves because they tune their guitars. Alex made me intensely observant of that, the whole primal element to how he played. He was into the primal act, the essence of what rock and roll was."

In December 1982, Chilton joined Sanzenbach at local rhythm-and-blues singer Jessie Hill's fiftieth birthday celebration at the Rose Tattoo, a neighborhood bar across Napoleon Avenue from Tipitina's. The Rose Tattoo catered to a mostly older, African American clientele.

Chilton found himself on stage with Hill—best known for the 1960 novelty hit "Ooh Poo Pah Doo"—and fabled keyboardist James Booker. Such encounters affirmed Chilton's love for his newly adopted hometown, where he was accepted into a community of musicians who didn't know, or care, about his past. "I think that's one of the reasons we clicked right away," said Rene Coman, a bassist who met Chilton through Sanzenbach. "I wasn't a drooling fanboy. I met him as just another musician."

In the fall of 1982, Chilton hired Coman for a gig at a friend's going-away party; their set included Michael Jackson's "Rock With You." Chilton found such anything-goes eclecticism refreshing. "He definitely had his fill of trying to push [his career], and feeling smothered," Coman said. "Some air was needed. He was looking to escape everything that had gone on in Memphis, and to be away from negative influences. He wanted a clean start."

Chilton eventually found the perfect hideaway: a 400-square-foot studio apartment behind a rambling old mansion on oak-lined Esplanade Avenue. Artist Bob Tannen bought the compound in 1974. The property spans an entire block, and is crowded with Tannen's sheet metal and cinder-block artwork, a Southern Gothic sculpture garden. In the '70s, New Orleans rhythm-and-blues piano legend Professor Longhair sometimes laid low in a house across the street; his robust, open-window rehearsals were audible inside the Tannen manse. Kinks frontman Ray Davies even convalesced in the mansion's upstairs apartment after taking a bullet in the leg during a 2004 armed robbery in the French Quarter.

An urban forest of naturally occurring flora cloaks the grounds: palms, oaks, camphors, banana, bamboo, figs, night jasmine, Virginia creepers, an ancient catalpa tree that Chilton particularly admired. He inhabited what was previously the detached kitchen of the main house. His space consisted of a bedroom, a combination kitchen/dining/living room, a bathroom and a storage loft. The deep green exterior melted into surrounding foliage. A garage topped by another apartment hid the cottage from Barracks Street, on the property's back side; the main house blocked the view from Esplanade. Free-ranging Catahoula hounds added another layer of security and privacy.

Chilton paid around $300 a month in rent, utilities included. He was an exceptionally low-maintenance tenant, unperturbed by his abode's dilapidated condition. "It was a disaster, but he didn't complain about it," Tannen said. "When I asked him if there was anything I could do to improve it, he said, 'I like it just the way it is.'" Tannen recalls only one maintenance request in Chilton's decade-long residency: that a broken air conditioner be fixed. Even that took him a while to mention.

The Esplanade property borders a rough-and-tumble section of Tremé. Chilton roamed around on foot and by bicycle. "He loved this neighborhood," Tannen said. "For Alex it was not a 'black neighborhood,' the typical white reaction. He clearly identified this neighborhood as home. He liked the history, the architecture, the people of Tremé. He was one of the first white people to hang out in this hood. You might call this 'gentrification,' but in his case it probably wasn't." One attraction was apparently the availability of Chilton's relaxant of choice. "He once told me that you never had to go more than a block to get a marijuana cigarette," Tannen said. "That may be one of the reasons why he loved this neighborhood as much as he did."

For music fans, New Orleans is a wonderland without end. Chilton plunged in, exploring the city's diverse offerings. His discoveries ranged from the Mistreaters, a country-blues band consisting of Tulane University students, to Big Al Carson, a 500-pound Bourbon Street blues and soul belter. In the French Quarter, he sought out the Preservation Hall Jazz Band; when he was a boy in Memphis, members of the legendary traditional jazz ensemble visited the Chilton home to jam with his father, Sidney, a jazz pianist. He thought of his father's Nancy Wilson records whenever soul-blues guitarist Walter "Wolfman" Washington sang "Save Your Love for Me."

He frequented Jimmy's, a popular destination for touring New Wave and rockabilly bands. In the late-1960s, proprietor Jimmy Anselmo owned a New Orleans bar called Co-Eds; patrons literally wore out the Box Tops' "The Letter" on the jukebox. Years later, Anselmo had no idea the voice behind "The Letter" was a Jimmy's regular. "I always thought he'd be a bigger guy," Anselmo said. "And he was so unassuming. I just thought he was one of the punks, one of the guys you see for all the shows, until someone pointed out, 'That's Alex Chilton.'"

In Chilton's tiny apartment, he and Rene Coman—who years later would anchor New Orleans roots rock/Latin/rhythm-and-blues combo the Iguanas—picked along to a thrift-store record player. "It took a long time before he played any Big Star stuff, or even mentioned it," Coman said. "Big Star was great, but that's not how Alex saw himself. To Alex, his work with Tav Falco's Panther Burns was as legitimate as anything else he did. Alex didn't feel like he had to be defined by [his past]. He was perfectly comfortable defining himself."

One night, Dave Catching, a guitarist friend from Memphis, rolled into town with his band. Their gig in the French Quarter was canceled when the venue's proprietor didn't show up to unlock. Chilton suggested they relocate Uptown to the Rose Tattoo, where the owner agreed to let this scruffy, white rock band play in exchange for an open tab. The lead singer was soon falling-down drunk; his bandmates deposited him in their van, feet protruding from the rear door. Chilton volunteered to fill in. After a few songs, the bar's owner had heard enough. "She said, 'I'll let you boys keep drinking, but you've got to stop playing. I like you all right, but you're scaring the regulars,'" Catching recalled, laughing. (Along the way, Chilton taught Catching open-G tuning, a favorite of the Rolling Stones. Decades later, Catching would deploy the open-G to great effect in uproariously irreverent rock band the Eagles of Death Metal.)

During those first few lean months and years in New Orleans, Chilton supported himself with a variety of odd jobs. He washed dishes at old-line French Quarter restaurant Louis XVI, scrubbing scraps of eggs Benedict from tourists' plates. He cleaned an Uptown bar called Tupelo's. Perched in a cherry-picker, he trimmed trees near power lines on River Road along the Mississippi River. He put those skills to use in the common yard on Esplanade Avenue. His landlord once discovered him high up an oak tree, suspended by ropes, pruning dead branches with a chain saw.

Eager to make money from music again, he recruited Coman for a revamped Panther Burns. Chilton and Coman also joined a Bourbon Street cover band called Scores. During five-hour gigs at Papa Joe's, patrons called out requests, mostly R&B standards, from printed song lists, unaware of the scrawny guitarist's infamy. "It was an adventure," Coman said. "It was like we were a human jukebox." Weeks into the job, they were fired.

With limited prospects, Chilton finally reached out to Frank Riley, the New York booking agent whose clients included Chilton's buddies in jangle-rock band the dB's. Riley booked a series of national tours that established Chilton as a solo act.

For those tours, he enlisted Memphis drummer Doug Garrison—who would, a decade later, join Coman in the Iguanas. After hearing Garrison perform at a Memphis art museum, Chilton invited him on the road. Garrison accepted "not fully knowing who he was. I'd heard the name, but at that point in my life I was strictly immersed in be-bop. I was not a rock and roller at all. I was completely ignorant of pop music on the radio." The drummer primarily knew Chilton as the son of Sidney Chilton, a "supercool older guy, one of the older guys who was not curmudgeonly, but took a shine to younger players. Sidney had some funny jokes, too."

Garrison first shared a stage with Chilton at Memphis's storied Antenna Club in late 1984. To prepare, the trio rehearsed once—the only formal rehearsal the drummer can recall during ten years with Chilton. At the gig, they covered Ray Charles, the Ronettes and Jackson's "Rock With You," which, in Garrison's estimation, Chilton "smoked." "We hit it off musically from beat one. I was superimpressed with his approach, sort of the embodiment of a Southern, Memphis guitar player and songwriter. Tav Falco, [producer] Jim Dickinson, people like that who were doing important stuff in Memphis, all have this relaxed attitude about music that's really cool. He oozed this vibe."

Chilton, Coman and Garrison barnstormed Europe, then crisscrossed America in a '73 Buick LeSabre with a missing driver's side window. Garrison logged multiple tours in the LeSabre. "For the first one, they pull up in front of my house, Alex pops the trunk open and says, 'All right, whatever you can fit in here is what you're taking.' We had three people plus all the gear in a sedan—it wasn't even a wagon."

The drummer downsized his kit to a bass, snare and floor tom. The last item stowed was Chilton's guitar, a borrowed Mosrite autographed by the Ventures, the '60s instrumental/surf rock band that created the *Hawaii Five-O* theme music. "Alex didn't have a case," Garrison said. "It was just the guitar with a strap on it. He would lay that on top of the gear and gently close the trunk. If it had been in a case, the trunk wouldn't close."

On the road, the trio shared one hotel room with two beds, taking turns on the prized single bed; every third night, someone got to sleep alone. They often crashed with friends; in Los Angeles, they bunked with Lux Interior and Poison Ivy of psychobilly band the Cramps, a Chilton production client. Venues ranged from the hipster Knitting Factory in New York to University of Alabama frat houses. The reception afforded Chilton impressed both Garrison and Coman. "There might not be many people in the club, but the R.E.M. guys would be there," Coman said. "The caliber of fans was much higher than the numbers."

Sets favored obscure covers and early Chilton solo recordings: "My Rival," "Rock Hard," "Bangkok." Few Big Star songs were showcased other than "In the Street" and "September Gurls." "At that period of time, Alex was annoyed when people wanted him to play Big Star stuff," Garrison said. "He considered that there were only three or four really good Big Star songs, so we did those. He was mostly interested in the stuff he was exploring at the moment. He was always trying to stay on the cutting edge."

His eclectic tastes tended toward the offbeat. On tour in Amsterdam, he and Garrison holed up in a hotel room with a cassette of the Reverend Fred Lane with Ron Pate's Debonairs. Lane was a performance artist based in Tuscaloosa, Alabama; his musicians swapped instruments for cacophonous, free-association takes on such big-band standards as "My Kind of Town" and "Volare." "They just butchered the hell out of it," Garrison said. "The first time you hear it, it's so freakin' funny. Alex and I were rolling on the floor. I thought Alex was going to stop breathing, he was laughing so hard."

Back in the yard on Esplanade Avenue, Chilton and his landlord engaged in long conversations about art and politics; Chilton was fluent in socialist, libertarian and anarchist philosophies. He relished the *New York Times*, especially columnist Paul Krugman. "Apart from his music and creativity, Alex was one of the most extraordinary people I've ever known," Tannen said. "He was an authentic person. He was a great admirer of Karl Marx. His political interests were not doctrinaire—he would never say he was a liberal or a socialist. His political interests were well-integrated with his personality. When we talked politics, he never used himself as an example for why he thought about certain things."

When Chilton received a royalty windfall or returned from a tour with cash, he paid several months of rent in advance. "He didn't like having money sitting around," Tannen said. "Money was not a thing he liked to have." (Chilton also rented the apartment over the property's garage for his brother Howard, an avid reader who died there of a heart attack.) When he rehearsed or recorded at home, alone or with other musicians, he turned down the volume in the evenings. "Not because we had shown any displeasure," Tannen said. "He felt that was the appropriate thing to do."

Occasionally, Chilton and Garrison recorded demos on a four-track; sometimes Chilton handled the guitar, bass and drum parts himself. "Thing for You," a song on the 1987 release *High Priest*, was "one of the few tunes we ever recorded where he said, 'I want you to play the drums exactly like this,'" Garrison said. "He had composed the tune with the drum part. It was simple, but the bass drum was not on one."

Chilton's restless nature and meandering career path led him to a variety of projects, the more primitive, the better. He cut a Panther Burns record at a small studio in New Orleans' Mid-City neighborhood behind a movie house that served pitchers of beer. He produced 1990's *I Know You Fine, But How You Doin'*, the second album by Detroit garage rock trio the Gories. In the summer of 1990 at Easley Studios in Memphis, he produced *Shocked & Amazed* by Koolkings, an ensemble fronted by Kristof Hahn. Hahn, a former member of bleak New York post-punk band Swans, had served a boozy tenure as a Chilton tour manager in Europe. "By the time he was our tour manager, he was pretty much a wreck," Garrison said. "But he's not a bad singer and songwriter."

Chilton played keyboards and bass on *Shocked & Amazed* and devised an unconventional approach to the recording session. "He insisted that everybody get drunk," Garrison said. "Alex was not drinking at that point, but he went so far as to suggest, or demand, that everyone else start drinking. That was Alex's idea for cutting the record. I guess he wanted to capture a certain vibe."

Throughout the '90s, Chilton booked occasional gigs in his adopted hometown. On Valentine's Day 1998, he shared a bill with blind R&B guitarist Snooks Eaglin, the "Human Jukebox," at a Warehouse District rock club called the Howlin' Wolf. One night at the Wolf, he delivered an entire set of jazz tunes with Garrison on drums and James Singleton of long-running New Orleans modern jazz ensemble Astral

Project on bass. "The Howlin' Wolf likes to have me play there a few times a year," Chilton said in 1995. "And that's OK with me. Generally two or three times a year in the same town is too much—it's something I don't like to do. But when they call, I hardly see enough reason to say no."

Garrison moved from Memphis to New Orleans in 1993 to join the Iguanas full-time. His schedule no longer allowed him to tour with Chilton, but they continued to work together locally. Chilton contributed Beach Boys–style backing vocals to "Rock Star," a tongue-in-cheek tale of a crack addict on the Iguanas' 1996 album *Super Ball*. For a time, Garrison and Chilton backed keyboardist/vocalist Davis Rogan—the inspiration for the Steve Zahn character in David Simon's HBO series *Treme*—for "oyster happy hour" gigs at Le Bon Temps Roule, an Uptown roadhouse on Magazine Street. Chilton played bass, refused to sing and, in keeping with his desire to be just another guy in the band, insisted on using an alias; Rogan introduced him as "Norman Desmond."

At the tiny Circle Bar, he broke his "no singing" rule the night New Orleans rhythm-and-blues icon Ernie K-Doe wandered in; he sang K-Doe's 1961 hit "Te Ta Te Ta Ta" in tribute. "He loved the fact that the whole culture was based on this musical legacy," Garrison said. "If it was New Orleans music, he loved it. I don't think he would have ever lived anywhere else. He never looked back when he moved down here."

By the mid-1990s, Chilton's solo career had settled into a comfortable, steady groove. He issued two well-received albums via the reactivated Ardent Records, Big Star's old label. 1994's *Cliches*, recorded at Chez Flames studio in New Orleans, featured him alone with an acoustic guitar on a set of lovingly rendered big-band and jazz standards by the likes of Mel Tormé, Cole Porter, Slide Hampton and Ray Charles. For 1995's *A Man Called Destruction*, he and a horn-heavy band set up at Ardent Studios in Memphis. They chiseled new Chilton compositions alongside "Sick and Tired," a modest hit for Fats Domino in 1958. At the 1995 New Orleans Jazz & Heritage Festival, he covered the relentlessly optimistic "Got a Lot of Livin' to Do."

An unlikely Big Star reunion at a Midwestern university proved even more beneficial to his professional fortunes. As befitting his modus operandi, its genesis was essentially random. During Christmas break 1992, Mike Mulvihill, general manager of University of Missouri student radio station KCOU-FM, visited his parents in New Orleans. His college radio pedigree predisposed him to Big Star fandom; a KCOU countdown had even named "September Gurls" as the top indie/alternative song of all time. In New Orleans, he attended a Chilton gig at Tipitina's alone. He struck up a conversation with an acquaintance of Chilton's, who invited Mulvihill backstage to meet the singer after the show.

Back on the Mizzou campus in Columbia, Missouri, Mulvihill pondered possible bookings for KCOU's annual Springfest fundraiser. He suggested Chilton—and wouldn't it be cool to reunite him with Big Star drummer Jody Stephens, and maybe a famous Chilton acolyte like Matthew Sweet, Paul Westerberg, or R.E.M.'s Mike Mills?

Stephens, solicited at his job at Ardent Studios, signed on. Mulvihill then contacted his new buddy from Tipitina's and pried loose Chilton's home phone number. Screwing up his courage, he called with his modest proposal: Would you want to perform in Missouri on April 25? Jody Stephens will be there, and possibly some well-known Big Star fans. Play whatever you want. KCOU will cover your travel and lodging costs, but there's no money to pay you beyond that.

Chilton had spent nearly two decades trying to escape Big Star's shadow. "Anybody who was a music business professional or had had any past interaction with him would have said either A, he'll reject you out of hand, or B, he'll accept and then he won't show up," Mulvihill said. "I don't know what he heard in the way I pitched it, but he said, 'Sounds like fun. Let's do it.' He accepted right away, without hesitation. Why he agreed to it, and agreed to it so quickly, I'll never know."

With Chilton and Stephens confirmed, Mulvihill, KCOU promotions director Jeff Breeze, and other staffers met in the station's basement office to brainstorm collaborators. "I was twenty-one years old and didn't know what I was doing," Mulvihill said. "But I did know enough to pitch it to Alex as *not* a Big Star reunion, and pitch it to everybody else *as* a Big Star reunion."

A scheduling conflict prevented Matthew Sweet from participating. But Sweet tipped his record label, Zoo Entertainment, that a Big Star reunion was afoot. Zoo's Bud Scoppa stepped in and offered to fund a live album. Unlike KCOU, Zoo could actually pay the musicians.

"All these people were asking me, 'Gosh, I hear there's going to be a Big Star reunion,'" Chilton recalled two years later. "I said, 'Well, I hadn't heard about that. It was proposed to me as something different.' But then [Zoo] jumped in and said, 'If there's going to be a Big Star reunion, then we'd really like to record it. And here's this much money on the table about it.' And I said, 'There's going to be a Big Star reunion.'"

Sort of. Founding Big Star guitarist, vocalist and songwriter Chris Bell died in a 1978 car accident. Bassist Andy Hummel, entrenched in his nonmusical life as an engineer in Texas, was not interested. At Stephens's suggestion, they rounded out the group with Big Star disciples Jon Auer and Ken Stringfellow of Seattle power-pop band the Posies.

Chilton's demands, Mulvihill recalled, were minimal: He required a specific amplifier, which a St. Louis music store employee would drive to Columbia, Missouri. And he requested a bag of weed, which a deejay volunteered to supply.

As the event grew in stature—the makeshift quartet even rehearsed in Seattle—Mulvihill felt the pressure. Stephens, Auer and Stringfellow arrived in Columbia the day before the April 25 show, and rehearsed as a trio. Chilton was scheduled to fly from New Orleans to Columbia via St. Louis on show day, a Sunday. Mulvihill assigned the most reliable person he could think of—his mother, Jan—to pick him up in Tremé and drive him to the New Orleans airport. Hours before showtime, the KCOU deejay dispatched to collect Chilton from the Columbia airport returned empty-handed. Minutes later, the missing star materialized on campus—a fan had spotted him at the airport and offered a ride.

Inside a tent erected near the campus events center, Chilton and Big Star 2.0 cherry-picked the Big Star catalog—"September Gurls," "Back of a Car," "In the Street," "Ballad of El Goodo"—and tossed off T. Rex's "Baby Strange" and Todd Rundgren's "Slut." Chilton screened the live recording before agreeing to its release as an album; Zoo issued *Columbia: Live at Missouri University 4/25/93* later that year.

"Thinking back on it, it was exactly the right tone and the right atmosphere," said Mulvihill, who parlayed the reunion's notoriety into a Los Angeles internship and, later, a career in TV production. "It was so unprofessional and so loose and off the hinges. It really was college kids trying to hold their little festival together for one day. And that was about as loose as I ever saw Alex on stage."

The Missouri reconstitution of Big Star as Chilton, Stephens, Auer and Stringfellow stuck. They toured Japan and Europe and appeared on *The Tonight Show*. Additionally, Chilton participated in a handful of Box Tops reunions annually. "That's fun, getting together with all these old sixties bands," he said in 1995. "I get to play with Ronnie Spector and people like that."

With his past providing fresh capital, Chilton officially put down roots in New Orleans. In the spring of 1995, in keeping with his fondness for decrepit dwellings, he paid the princely sum of $9,500 for a crumbling, nineteenth-century center-hall cottage in Tremé, not far from his old apartment. He bought an adjacent lot for $3,600. Now he had his own modest Eden in a forgotten corner of New Orleans. (He also retained his apartment as a satellite guest house for musicians, friends and former and future girlfriends. Tannen, the landlord, believes he "wanted to maintain his privacy with his new home, and didn't want a lot of people hanging out there.")

Chilton was now all-in with New Orleans, moving amongst locals as one of them. Keith Keller, owner of Chez Flames recording studio, hosted a crawfish boil each spring during Jazz Fest; friends from various social circles gathered over tables of steaming crustaceans, the classic Big Easy culinary common ground. During one of Keller's boils, Alex McMurray, a versatile singer, songwriter and guitarist with his own finely tuned sense of the absurd, noticed a guy alone at a piano tinkering with the jazz standard "On the Sunny Side of the Street." McMurray guided him through the bridge, then introduced himself. "So *you're* the other Alex," Chilton replied.

McMurray wasn't familiar with Big Star's music. "I was aware that it was out there, but I didn't know what it was. I knew Keith Keller was friends with this guy Alex Chilton, who was in the Box Tops and had some other band in the seventies, and that people thought he's a big deal. But you can't really be that big of a deal down here." To the point, McMurray "had no idea what [Chilton] looked like. I wouldn't have known him from Adam. That probably made him like me. I didn't know who the hell he was."

Chilton invited McMurray to his house for an astrological chart reading. McMurray showed up to find Chilton, a dedicated sports fan, immersed in a Detroit Red Wings game. Thus began a casual friendship marked by a mutual appreciation for absurdist humor. Unexpected encounters around town—as when McMurray sang the national anthem prior to a Tulane University men's basketball game, and ran into Chilton in the gymnasium's lobby—gave rise to a running gag: "What are *you* doing here?" For a time, Chilton and McMurray dated roommates who lived on a street named North Alexander—Alex and Alex on Alexander. Once, Chilton, McMurray and music journalist Alex Rawls converged on Frenchmen Street. The three Alexes (Alexi?) "just looked at each other for five seconds, had a little chuckle, then walked away," McMurray said. "It was a pretty funny moment."

Chilton had married and divorced young. In New Orleans, he did not lack female companionship, romantic or platonic. He was drawn to smart, creative types who moved in the same informal, quasi-underground circles as he. Margaret Ann "Peggy" O'Neill, the drummer in Detroit garage rock band the Gories, eventually moved to New Orleans; she borrowed Chilton's Volvo for her Katrina evacuation with her husband. Aimee Toledano, who snapped the photos for Chilton's 1999 album *Set*, twirled flags in the Ninth Ward Marching Band, an independent, high school–style ensemble that avant-garde musician and inventor Mr. Quintron established to march in Mardi Gras parades.

After a post-Katrina odyssey that took him to Houston and McComb, Mississippi, Chilton settled back into his New Orleans routine, albeit with a fresh twist. He reconnected with Laura Kersting, a flutist, philosophy major and librarian who shared his love for baroque classical music. They met in the 1990s when he produced a record by her first husband's band, retro-rockers the Royal Pendletons. After the storm and the dissolution of her marriage, they grew closer. For a time, Kersting lived in Chilton's old apartment behind the mansion on Esplanade. They married in August 2009 in San Diego.

With Kersting at his side, the final chapter of Chilton's life was one of happy contentment in tune with a city nicknamed the Big Easy. Tremé especially agreed with him. He "identified with black people more than white people," Kersting told me in the spring of 2010. As her husband cut grass with a manual push mower, the couple's black neighbors "would sit on their stoop, silently watching, like we were a movie." He had little patience for sycophants and fools, but chatted amiably with strangers who strolled by the house. During long bicycle rides, he engaged people from across the New Orleans social strata. He regaled ragged "gutter punks" on Decatur Street with impromptu astrological readings. "Everyone was equal in his eyes," Kersting said. "He gave everyone a chance."

A high school dropout, Chilton was nonetheless well-read and well-spoken; given his casually elegant sartorial sense and gentlemanly air, he was occasionally mistaken for a college professor. He consulted an extensive collection of dictionaries, movie guides and other reference books, and debated philosophy.

Dining out was a nightly ritual for the couple. They frequented a Thai restaurant called Sukhothai in the Faubourg Marigny neighborhood, the Italian-style Maximo's and Angeli on Decatur Street, and a French bistro Uptown named La Crepe Nanou. Chilton loved the latter's roast chicken, Kersting said, because it reminded him of his mother's.

Back at Chez Chilton, he smoked cigarettes and pot and tuned in to deejay Joe Hastings on classical station WWNO 89.9 FM. Catlike, he observed no structured sleep schedule; he often stayed up all night watching television. *Walker, Texas Ranger* and *Touched by an Angel* fascinated him; he taught himself the *Walker* theme music on guitar.

After Katrina's winds damaged the room containing his piano—he loved to practice Scott Joplin rags—he abandoned the instrument and spent more time playing classical guitar. "It was very chill when you went to Alex's house," said Anthony Donado, a local drummer and acquaintance. "Maybe you'd play a little guitar, or watch college basketball."

He disdained pretention and artifice, and did not e-mail. When the spirit moved him, he collaborated with fellow Big Easy denizens regardless of stature, or lack thereof. Days after first hearing Donado's band Soupchain, Chilton bumped into him in a grocery store and offered to produce a Soupchain album. Incredulous, Donado asked if he was serious. "He's like, 'Yeah. I'll come to your house.' So Alex laid on my couch, pressed 'record,' and said, 'OK, boys, go.'"

Cristina Diettinger first met Chilton around 1999, her senior year at Tulane, through mutual friend Aimee Toledano. Unfamiliar with the Box Tops and Big Star, she took him to be "one of those veteran-musician, hanging-around-New Orleans kind of guys, just like anyone else."

They remained friends as she built a portfolio as a music journalist. Later, she moved to New York, learned ukulele and developed a side career as a songwriter under her married name, Cristina Black. Frustrated by the cost of recording in New York, she turned to a friend in New Orleans, Galactic saxophonist Ben Ellman, who offered use of the nouveau funk band's studio/rehearsal space. Finding musicians also proved easier in New Orleans. In New York, she "asked people, and they would want to know how much money was involved, or they wouldn't have time. In New Orleans, I called up my friends and they're like, 'Well, is there air-conditioning there?'"

She recruited guitarist Alex McMurray and keyboardist Brian Coogan, and made a "utilitarian" decision to solicit Chilton. "I thought, 'Who do I know in New Orleans that plays bass and knows pop music? Alex Chilton.'" She mailed him song demos, and was pleasantly surprised when he said yes. "I think he liked the project because it was low-profile. He liked doing out-of-the-way, weird gigs and recording projects that didn't have to do with the stuff he was famous for. He was in a place where he was like, 'I'm going to do what I want.'"

In September 2009, the musicians recorded five songs with Black over two days in Galactic's studio. Chilton sat in a corner of the high-ceilinged room, smoking and divining astrological charts between takes. "The last thing he would have wanted was to be the musical director of anything," McMurray said. "He liked hanging out being the bass player." Still, he offered opinions when asked. "He had this incredible musical mind," Black said. "We would finish a take and be like, 'Alex, what do you think about this?' He would say, 'There was something happening on that one. There was some magic there.' And that's the one we would keep."

Chilton had warned Black in advance that he "hadn't really played bass in a while, and that what he would do would be really rudimentary. Which to me was very attractive—that's what I wanted. I was trying to avoid fancy, jazzy, funky bass playing. At one point, he took me aside and he's like, 'If I'm not working out, it's OK. You can just tell me to get the hell out of here, and I won't be offended at all.'"

To the contrary, Black was thrilled with the result. Chilton's bass is prominently featured throughout her independent EP, *The Ditty Sessions*. "All the Alex Chilton completists who bought my record are really happy," she said. "They can hear exactly what he did."

In the weeks before his death, Chilton worked on recordings by former Blue Vipers guitarist and singer "Johnny J." Beninati; Chilton previously produced the Vipers' 1986 release *Nuclear Hayride*. "It took a long time to get to know him as a person," Beninati said. "He played things close to the vest. He was very reserved, and his sense of humor was very dry. But once you got to know him, he was very funny."

Chilton once loaned him five dollars to get his electricity reinstated. From then on, Beninati considered him a friend. He noticed a photo of early rock-and-roll singer Freddy Cannon hanging on a wall of Chilton's house. "Alex said, 'Freddy Cannon's shows always worked because he moved through life with ease.' That's exactly what Alex was like. He moved through life with ease."

Thanks to his low overhead, Chilton subsisted on periodic Big Star, Box Tops and solo gigs augmented by modest publishing income. Cheap Trick covered Big Star's "In the Street" as the theme music for the Fox sitcom *That '70s Show*, resulting in a steady stream of royalty checks for Chilton. In 2005, the latter-day Big Star released a new album, *In Space*, via Rykodisc.

But he completed few songs in the last five years of his life; songwriting for its own sake did not interest him. "He worked best under pressure," Kersting said. "He wouldn't write songs if a record deal wasn't in the works."

He saw little reason to hustle more than was necessary to make ends meet and travel, a favorite pursuit. He reminisced fondly about a Jazz Fest gig in the 1980s that was rained out: "I like it when they say, 'Here's a thousand bucks. Don't play, all right?' That's my favorite thing." McMurray still laughs at Chilton's response to Iguanas saxophonist Joe Cabral's invitation to join a new project: "Well, Joe, I'm not really into that." Kersting confirms that her husband "was kind of lazy. He took it very easy. He'd say, 'Why work when I don't have to?' He wanted a very simple life."

His attitude puzzled and frustrated some acquaintances. Greg Dulli, the former Afghan Whigs and current Twilight Singers frontman, is an unabashed Chilton fan. "He's one of the greatest pop songwriters who's ever lived. If you're going to call Brian Wilson a genius, you better call Alex Chilton a genius, too. There's no bigger fan of his early work than me." Dulli has lived in New Orleans off and on for years, and got to know Chilton in the '90s. He was thrilled when his hero contributed backing vocals to "Crazy," from the Afghan Whigs' 1998 album *1965*. "He nails the part. It's inimitably Alex Chilton singing the harmony."

The hyperkinetic Dulli occasionally confronted Chilton about his lack of ambition. "At the height of his art, he was untouchable. Alex Chilton could have been like Prince, or the very least, Todd Rundgren. When you see someone with that light, you want it to burn bright. I wanted him to be all he could be. And maybe that's why he and I used to scrap. I would ask him straight-up, 'Are you afraid of money and nice houses? You should be famous, dude. And the fact that you didn't get what you deserved when you deserved it doesn't mean you won't get it now.'"

Chilton's typical response to Dulli's lectures? "Go f—yourself. What do you know? Who do you think you are?" Ultimately, Dulli concedes, "people should be whatever they want to be. Alex did what he wanted to do. He wasn't living his life for me."

In the last years of his life, Chilton mostly limited his New Orleans performances to benefits. On December 2, 2007, he helped raise money for longtime La Crepe Nanou bar manager Robert Strong, who was injured in an armed robbery. "He wanted other people to have the slots at the clubs," Kersting said. "New Orleans was his oasis from his other life as the musician Alex Chilton. Here, he wanted to be a person, a New Orleanian. That's why he did benefits. He didn't want to gain from New Orleans—he wanted to give to New Orleans."

More than once, he appeared as an anonymous sideman at the Ponderosa Stomp, an annual revue of "lost" legends of soul, R&B and early rock-and-roll at the New Orleans House of Blues. Strumming guitar behind the likes of Brenton "The Oogum Boogum Song" Wood and Alabama singer Ralph "Soul" Jackson "wasn't about him making a superstar appearance," said Stomp founder Ira "Dr. Ike" Padnos. "It was the exact opposite. He didn't want anybody to know he was there. He didn't want to be a distraction. He loved to play for the music itself. The more raw, stripped-down, minimalist it was, the more he loved it."

Kersting often traveled with Chilton to gigs. In Paris, a favorite destination, they frequented neighborhoods with large African populations. In November 2009, the Box Tops appeared in Niagara Falls, New York, and Big Star headlined the Brooklyn Masonic Temple in New York City.

But the most memorable performance of the trip, according to Kersting, was at a bar called the Sportsmen's Tavern in Buffalo, her former hometown. At the urging of friends, Chilton briefly sat in with the country-leaning house band. Finding common ground was not easy; they finally settled on country singer Jimmy C. Newman's 1962 single "Alligator Man," which Chilton recorded for his 1979 album *Like Flies on Sherbert*. In a long-sleeved striped T-shirt, he gleefully strummed an acoustic guitar over the chugging drums and acoustic bass. Such an informal setting "was where he was most comfortable," Kersting said. "He was incredible that night. Finally I understood what the big deal is about him."

Chilton agreed to participate in a hastily organized benefit for Doctors Without Borders' earthquake relief efforts in Haiti on January 24, 2010. He and Kersting arrived at the Big Top, a funky downtown New Orleans art gallery/performance space, to discover he was expected to perform solo. Instead, Chilton enlisted Anthony Donado, a benefit organizer, to play drums. Trey Ledford wound up as the bassist. "Alex asked if the first bass player I had in mind could read music," Donado said. "He couldn't. Trey said, 'Well, I can kind of read.' So he got the job."

Not surprisingly, Chilton wouldn't discuss the set list in advance; they would "wing it." The impromptu trio banged out a ragged thirty minutes of early rock and roll and New Orleans rhythm and blues, including Chuck Berry's "Maybelline" and Ernie K-Doe's "Te Ta Te Ta Ta." As dozens of patrons looked on, Chilton called out songs and coached his backing band. More than once, Donado demonstrated different beats, in full view of the audience, until Chilton deemed one appropriate. "He'd scold me in his funny way. But we had fun. It was very fast and loose."

Her husband "thrived on that kind of stuff," Kersting said. "He didn't like glamour or fuss. He liked simple and spontaneous."

The guerrilla benefit would be his final performance.

As his wife would later recall, at least twice in the spring of 2010, Chilton experienced shortness of breath and chills while cutting grass. These warning signs followed years of heavy smoking, as well as his brother Howard's death from a heart attack. But he apparently did not seek medical attention. On the morning of March 17, Kersting went to work. Chilton called her after suffering another episode; she arrived home before the ambulance, and rushed him to Tulane Medical Center. He lost consciousness a block from the emergency room, after urging his wife to speed through a red light. He was fifty-nine.

Big Star had been scheduled to perform at the South by Southwest Music Conference in Austin, Texas, three days later, on March 20; the band was also the subject of a conference panel. Instead, attendees mourned Chilton's death, and the Big Star showcase at Antone's morphed into a musical wake.

Two weeks later, on Easter Sunday, friends and fellow musicians gathered on the grounds of the Esplanade Avenue property he once called home to swap stories, of which there were many. Tribute concerts in Memphis and New York followed. Myriad publications eulogized him; *Rolling Stone* devoted four full, ad-free pages to his life and career.

The health care debate dominated Washington, D.C., the week of his passing. Rep. Steve Cohen (D-Tenn.) memorialized Chilton from the floor of Congress, a gesture Kersting believes her husband, an avid C-SPAN viewer, would have appreciated. Far less amusing was the mercenary manner in which bloggers appropriated his death as an argument both for and against universal health care. (Chilton, his wife said, chose not to have health insurance, for various reasons.)

He was not particularly sentimental about death; his widow described his view as, essentially, "It happens. Move on." He had as much use for death, it seems, as celebrity.

In New Orleans, insulated from his international cult of fans, he was just another character in a city full of them. "A lot of people thought he still lived in Memphis," Kersting said. "But New Orleans was his home. His heart was here. He really cared about New Orleans houses and people."

Not surprisingly, his primary concern in his final months was his Tremé retreat. The foundation and latent Katrina damage required repairs. Like his cottage, his career had long subsisted on minimal maintenance as he sought to reconcile his past with his present. How to benefit from the past without being defined by it? How to, like Freddy Cannon, move through life with ease?

Alex Chilton ultimately struck an agreeable balance in the house, and city, he loved even more than himself.

Chapter Eight

Jeremy Davenport Makes a Record

So Paul McCartney and Heather Mills show up at jazz trumpeter Jeremy Davenport's weekly gig at the New Orleans Ritz-Carlton. During a break, the Beatle waves Davenport over, borrows his horn and riffs on "When the Saints Go Marching In." He later joins Davenport onstage to serenade Mills, his then-girlfriend and eventual ex-wife, with "The Very Thought of You." Before leaving, McCartney slips his cell phone number to his new buddy.

The trumpeter never called. What, he figured, am I going to say to Paul McCartney?

On one level, Davenport moves easily amongst the rich and famous, and wouldn't mind joining their ranks himself. Unlike some New Orleans musicians, he enjoys success, fine clothes and fancy cars, and actively engages the world beyond Louisiana.

But he's also a decent, grounded guy who doesn't fully believe he's all that. One Saturday in the Ritz-Carlton's Davenport Lounge, where mini-soap operas and dramas unfold with a new cast nightly, I watched him sneak out behind a bandmember's upright bass, hiding from a stunning young woman vying too aggressively for his attention.

This is the same, smooth Davenport who, exiting a coffee shop with a tall cup of joe and a newspaper, tripped, fell and banged his head on the fender of his Porsche. In the process, he dented the car, tore his jeans and rendered his left leg numb. Unable to operate the clutch, he sat behind the wheel, dazed, until the numbness subsided.

He's not as effortlessly cool as his music suggests. The fantasy does not always align with his reality. But sometimes, it comes close.

Jeremy Davenport resides in the Ritz-Carlton New Orleans, the posh downtown hotel that is also his place of employment. On weekends, the jazz trumpeter and crooner swings out sweet, sentimental and sad songs from the Great American Songbook in the third-floor lounge that bears his name.

He has welcomed the likes of Paul McCartney and Sting to his cozy stage, and pals around with celebrity chef Emeril Lagasse. *People* magazine deemed him one of "America's Top 50 Bachelors." He drives a Porsche and rocks nice suits with French-cuff shirts. The beautiful women who populate his workplace often cast an eye, and more, his way.

For all the advantages of his gilded cage, this is not how it was supposed to be.

Born in 1970, he grew up in St. Louis, Missouri, as the son of a symphony trombonist and a music educator who encouraged creative achievement. He studied trumpet and voice at University City High School; alumni include the playwright Tennessee Williams and the rapper Nelly. Davenport's father arranged for him to meet a future mentor, New Orleans jazz trumpeter Wynton Marsalis.

After graduation, Davenport enrolled in the classical program at New York's Manhattan School of Music. Marsalis introduced him to fellow New Orleanian Harry Connick Jr. around the time the *When Harry Met Sally* soundtrack catapulted the pianist to stardom. Connick and Marsalis encouraged Davenport to continue his studies with Wynton's father, jazz pianist Ellis Marsalis, at the University of New Orleans.

Davenport moved to New Orleans, but soon left school to join Connick's globetrotting big band. The young trumpeter reveled in his role as the wiseass kid and straight man. He developed a taste for the trappings of fame that were his by association.

Ultimately, he aspired to be a frontman, not a sideman. He left Connick's employ in 1996; the Rubicon moment was choosing his own gig at Snug Harbor Jazz Bistro in New Orleans over a Connick show at the Cannes Film Festival in France.

He developed his singing voice as part of a polished act inspired by Dizzy Gillespie, Count Basie and Connick: high-caliber musicianship served with a side of highly entertaining banter. His stylish brand of classic jazz—think Chet Baker minus the baggage—was spiked with a subversive, sharp wit and self-deprecating humor. He remained at heart the back-row schoolboy instigator who perpetuates mischief with a smile and impunity.

In New York, Davenport had met Mark Samuels, a former high school classmate of Wynton's from New Orleans. Samuels was thinking about getting into the music business, maybe starting a management/booking agency, or a record label. He offered to work with Davenport. The trumpeter declined, believing a more lucrative, major-label contract awaited.

But such a contract proved elusive. Instead, he released his self-titled 1996 debut and the 1998 follow-up, *Maybe in a Dream*, on Telarc, an independent label specializing in classical music. The albums, an agreeable mix of standards and like-minded original material, generated some flattering notices, but not the momentum needed to establish a national fan base or touring circuit.

So in 2000, Davenport hired on as the featured weekend entertainer at the Ritz, and moved in. Except for a nine-month Hurricane Katrina intermission, he's been there ever since.

As the years passed, he watched entertainers with comparable repertoires and styles strike it rich: Trumpeter Chris Botti, a friend from the sideman circuit. Vocalist and pianist Diana Krall, a former duet partner. Similarly irreverent crooner Michael Bublé.

In spite of himself, he sometimes got jealous. "I really thought it was my turn," Davenport once told me. "At least ten times a day, I get, 'Hey, we saw Michael Bublé on *Oprah*. Why aren't you on *Oprah*?' Oh . . . OK. That's helpful."

In the decade after *Maybe in a Dream*, his only new release was 2005's *Live at the Bistro*, a concert album recorded in St. Louis. Meanwhile, the record industry self-destructed. High-dollar deals, especially for jazz, went the way of the cassette tape.

Davenport did not immediately accept this reality. "In the back of my mind, I was waiting for some guy in a fancy suit to come along and sign me up for this big, planned-out adventure. It was Harry who sat me down and said, 'Bro, you're waiting for something that's never going to happen.' That's when I got off my ass and decided to do something else."

Closing in on forty with his boyish good looks still intact, he realized his window of opportunity would not remain open indefinitely. And whatever the record industry's ills, music must still be recorded. A new album excites fans, defines an artistic point of view, generates press coverage and, if properly budgeted and marketed, can even net some cash.

Davenport's friend and attorney Rob Konrad encouraged him to consider Mark Samuels' Basin Street Records. In the twenty years since the trumpeter spurned his initial overture, Samuels had grown Basin Street into a credible independent label; its catalog boasted New Orleans stalwarts Kermit Ruffins, Theresa Andersson, Michael White, Henry Butler, Jon Cleary, Jason Marsalis, Los Hombres Calientes, the Rebirth Brass Band, and Irvin Mayfield.

The time had come for Davenport to set aside unrealistic expectations and flesh out his embarrassingly thin body of work. He agreed to be the first new artist signed to Basin Street since Katrina. For three years after the storm, the company released only a five-song compilation from pop singer/violinist Theresa Andersson and a live Kermit Ruffins album. Davenport's Basin Street debut, then, would be a fresh start—for the label, and for him.

"Ten years ago, if you had said, 'You're going to sing in a lounge, and it's going to have your name on it,' I would have been like, 'No way.' And now that's what I'm doing. I'm a hotel lounge singer, and enjoying it. A few years ago, I couldn't admit that—it wouldn't be cool.

"But you have to understand—I want to be on TV. I want to travel the world. I still have those kinds of dreams."

To help chart his new album's course, Davenport enlisted veteran New Orleans jazz keyboardist, composer and arranger David Torkanowsky. Torkanowsky's father, Werner Torkanowsky, was a celebrated classical conductor who led the New Orleans Philharmonic Orchestra in the 1960s and '70s. Werner guest-conducted the St. Louis Symphony while Davenport's father was a member.

Intensely type-A, David anchored long-running New Orleans

modern jazz ensemble Astral Project for many years and compiled a diverse resume across the spectrum of New Orleans music and beyond. He and Davenport express their mutual admiration via good-natured jabs and insults.

Theresa Andersson recorded her acclaimed 2008 Basin Street release *Hummingbird, Go!* alone in the kitchen of her Algiers Point home. Davenport had no interest in a similarly unorthodox approach. He wanted to spend several days in an actual studio—preferably, with a string section.

Cognizant of slim profit margins and the limited audience for jazz, Basin Street budgeted $25,000 for studio rental, the backing musicians, and the engineer's and producers' fees. Given the additional tens of thousands of dollars in post-production costs—advertising, publicists, buying shelf space in retail outlets, photography and graphic design for the CD package, etc.—Davenport's CD would need to sell around 10,000 copies to break even.

There would be no string section.

In his Telarc days, Davenport insisted on recording without overdubs. He sang and played trumpet live alongside the other musicians, "thinking I was being some kind of hero. I would never do that again. It's too hard, and nobody cares."

Neither was he concerned about subjective ideals of "authentic" jazz. He hoped "to make a record that people who hear me at the hotel will like. Music that's not only artistically sound, but enjoyable. Music that makes people feel good, and that they can dance to. But I also want to absorb everything that I've established as a jazz artist, and figure out a way to filter a common aesthetic. Whatever that is, I want it in this record."

Additionally, he planned to "get neurotic" while recording his vocals and trumpet. Not that doing so would eliminate future doubts: "My recording career is like looking at pictures of myself—I can't stand it."

To establish a stylistic template, Torkanowsky suggested Davenport select a dozen songs "representative of the album you want to make." Wayne Newtown abuts Wayne Shorter on his iPod; he submitted a playlist ranging from Frank Sinatra to John Mayer, Jason Mraz to Justin Timberlake.

The recording session was tentatively booked for February 9–11,

2009, at the Music Shed, a studio and rehearsal complex in the Lower Garden District of New Orleans. The Dave Matthews Band had reserved Davenport's first-choice studio, Piety Street Recording, for the entire month.

Three weeks out, Davenport and Konrad met over lunch at Mandina's, a popular eatery on Canal Street several blocks north of the Ritz, to assess the project's progress. Nothing was finalized beyond the album's title, *We'll Dance 'Til Dawn*, the name of an original Davenport composition. It replaced the album's working title, *Hotel Jazz*.

They gradually assembled a team for the recording. Tracey Freeman would co-produce with Torkanowsky. Freeman attended Jesuit High School with Connick and is now his trusted musical confidant and producer. Instead of moving to New York or Los Angeles to pursue other marquee clients, Freeman opted to stay in New Orleans and produce records by Ruffins and other local favorites.

The primary drummer would be Troy Davis, a Baton Rouge, Louisiana, native who spent years with trumpeter Terence Blanchard's band. Rounding out the rhythm section was Roland Guerin, a forward-thinking jazz bassist who has collaborated with Allen Toussaint, jazz pianist Marcus Roberts and guitarist John Scofield, and crafted multiple albums of his own.

The week before the scheduled recording, Davenport flew to Miami to celebrate the fifth anniversary of an Emeril Lagasse restaurant. He returned to New Orleans for the February 5 grand opening of the Ritz-Carlton's newly rechristened Davenport Lounge and the premiere of its "Davenportini" cocktail.

On February 7, two days before he was due to enter the studio, he accepted an invitation to audition for a lucrative national TV commercial in New York—on February 9.

The recording had to be rescheduled.

But the next available block of time at the Music Shed wasn't until mid-March. The month-long delay meant *We'll Dance 'Til Dawn* likely wouldn't be out before the late-April opening of the New Orleans Jazz & Heritage Festival, thereby squandering a major promotional opportunity. And selling jazz is never easy.

Davenport allowed me to observe the recording of *We'll Dance 'Til Dawn*. The process was not nearly as tidy as the result. In the studio, wisecracks flew as fast as eighth notes; humor helped burn off anxiety.

The recording involved artistic debates, camaraderie, crisp musician-ship, psychological games, self-doubt, self-confidence, budgetary con-straints, tight timetables, unforeseen delays, merciless ribbing, sudden inspiration, Chinese takeout and a missing trumpeter.

From this, a jazz album emerged.

Monday, March 16, 2009

A well-groomed bundle of nervous energy, Jeremy Davenport is the first to arrive at the Music Shed. Keyboardist, co-producer and chief creative foil David Torkanowksy pulls into the unpaved parking lot minutes later, at 10:30 A.M.

"I don't want you to take our lateness," the keyboardist says, "as any sign of disrespect."

Davenport notes that he even beat Tracey Freeman.

"I figured you spent the night in the parking lot," Torkanowsky says. He clutches a sheaf of musical scores. "I pretty much memo-rized all this stuff. I just wanted to go over it."

The day's first complication: bassist Roland Guerin has mistakenly arrived with his girlfriend's cell phone, and must return it. He leaves; the vacuum is filled by a torrent of jokes at his expense.

Studio time is money; the goal is to finish five songs on the first day. "I'll show you how neurotic I am," Davenport says, producing a neatly typed recording schedule listing the songs in alphabetical order.

"I believe the jury has already adjudicated on that," Torkanowsky offers.

"Don't let me run the tunes alphabetically," Davenport continues. "That would show my OCD."

Yoga positions are discussed, along with the height and technique of drummer and Baton Rouge resident Troy Davis. Davenport wants a syncopated, New Orleans second-line beat on several songs. He doesn't want the "Baton Rouge version of a second-line."

"You mean the Red Stick Shuffle?" says Freeman ("Baton Rouge" translates as "Red Stick").

Davenport considers the diverse personalities at hand. "I've man-aged to assemble an odd team. Let's rehearse, in case Roland ever comes back."

The studio's bedroom-size control room is clutter-free. In place of the bulky mixing boards of old is a computer monitor, keyboard and mouse. With walls of overlapping wood tiles, wood floors and a dark brown leather sofa and chairs, the room feels like a chalet's study. One window overlooks the spacious main recording room, where the band will set up. Another peers into the "isolation room," where Davenport will toil. Tracks will be stored on the same hard drive used the previous week for a Kermit Ruffins session.

That morning, Davenport was struck by a 1940s-era jazz concert broadcast by WWOZ-FM. "When," he asks, "did jazz stop being fun?"

By eleven A.M., they've accomplished nothing; Davenport is getting antsy. "You want to call Roland and get his ETA?" he says to Torkanowsky, before discovering a text message: Guerin is on his way back.

A vibrating snare drum emits a low-frequency hum audible over the control room speakers. "That," Davenport says, "could drive me to the hospital."

Torkanowsky, tongue in cheek, suggests transposing every tune to that key.

Minutes tick by, and still no Guerin. Davenport wonders if his girlfriend lives in Tulsa.

The bassist finally reappears at 11:10 A.M. "Let's break for lunch," Davenport cracks, then adds, "I want the bass to be loud."

"It will be."

All four musicians wear blue jeans accessorized by their respective fashion sense. The diminutive Davis, his hair close-cropped and meticulously slicked, is in an oversize sweatshirt and tennis shoes with ankle socks. Guerin sports a leather cap and suede shoes. Torkanowsky may have snatched his untucked plaid shirt off a pile of clothes as he rushed out the door. Davenport, in black leather shoes and a tidy black pullover with a zippered turtleneck, looks like he stepped out of a casual-wear ad.

Freeman ducks out to smoke a cigarette. He returns as the musicians test sound levels.

"What are you feeling so far?" asks Chris Finney, the Music Shed's genial engineer.

Freeman: "It's too bright and stringy."

Davenport: "You want to run one?"

At 11:20 A.M., the band runs through "Almost Never," one of five compositions Davenport wrote for the album. Freeman doesn't like the sound of the microphones. "It's just so thin to me."

"They're just to catch those outer harmonics," Finney replies.

They start another take, then stop and reconsider.

"Right after Tork's solo, when I come back with the vocal, I want it to go back to the original feel," Davenport says. "Once we get through the logistics, I want the feel of it to be really bouncy. Troy, swing it out on the solos." He suggests Davis uses drumsticks instead of brushes.

Another take is cut short by a hideous squeal of feedback. A bad microphone cable is replaced. Davenport pops into the control room.

"Don't listen to anything I'm singing and playing," he tells Freeman, establishing a theme. "I'm just trying to get comfortable. I want to get through these tracks. I definitely want to get some of them livable."

Before returning to the isolation booth, he confides some misgivings about the sound of Guerin's bass. Freeman detects a strange rhythm underlying the music. "Is that Torkanowsky's *foot* hitting the floor?"

It is.

At noon, the musicians file into the control room and settle into leather chairs to screen "Almost Never." They immediately realize the tempo Davenport counts off is not sustained throughout the song; the drums drag slightly.

Rising to his own defense, Davis posits that Davenport is more comfortable playing trumpet at the faster tempo and singing at the slower tempo. The others chime in.

Torkanowsky: "It's not majority rules."

Davenport: "Oh, that's right, it's my record. Who wrote this piece of s—song anyway? Oh yeah, I wrote it."

He counsels Davis: "I don't want you to overthink it. Make it comfortable."

They return to their instruments. Davenport wants "Almost Never" to have "that Miles quartet kind of bounce."

Torkanowsky: "It's kind of disjointed to have half a chorus of piano and half a chorus of bass."

Davenport: "Why don't we give you a whole chorus and him a whole chorus?"

Back in the control room once again, Davenport says, "What am I thinking? I hate bass solos. But I'd like to give the cat a solo. This would be the best tune to do it."

Pause. "I hate bass solos."

They find the proper tempo. "You like everything you're hearing?" Freeman asks Davenport.

"Everything except the vocals and trumpet."

A quote from the previous night's episode of Fox's *Family Guy* is batted around. Freeman works his BlackBerry.

"What did you think?" Davenport says.

"We're getting close. You want to do one more, then move on?"

Guerin needs to rosin his bow to eliminate a slight squeak, but can't find his rosin.

"Let's move on," Davenport says. "We can revisit that. Because I know you can play a better bass solo."

The next song on his alphabetical list is "By the Time I Get to Phoenix." The classic ballad by legendary songwriter Jim Webb was a hit for Glen Campbell, among many others. Davenport first heard Frank Sinatra's version while driving to the airport one morning before dawn. "I had this weird emotional moment. It's a very sad song."

He compared different singers' takes on iTunes, searching for one best suited to his style. He settled on an arrangement he calls "New Orleans meets Brazil meets a country-and-western tune."

As they prepare to record, Finney asks, "Isn't Phoenix the kidnapping capital of the world?"

Davenport scans his song list. "Man, I've got a lot of breakup songs on here."

From the isolation booth, he says, "I want this to be superauthentic bossa nova. I don't want it to be jazzy bossa nova."

He stops the first take. "I don't like that groove. I want the bass on one and three, like on those bossa nova records. Am I saying that right? I want the groove harder. I don't want it so light."

Davis pipes up, "You've got to remember, I'm just laying a path. I'll come back later and lay the cajon," a boxlike, Afro-Peruvian hand percussion device.

"What's a cajon?" Davenport asks. "If I was on a real record label, I would have hired three Brazilian guys. Oh, wait, I *am* on a record label."

"Way to pump up morale," Torkanowsky says.

"He is a motivator," notes Rob Konrad, who has arrived at the session still wearing his day-job attorney's tie.

They go again. In the booth, Davenport sings, *"She'll probably stop for lunch and give me a call . . ."*

"The whore," someone interjects.

"Uh, Tork . . ."

"What? What?"

Davenport: "I want Tork to love his solo."

Torkanowsky: "I loved *that*."

The keyboardist suggests a "rising chord" might work better as a prelude to the chorus.

"So Jimmy Webb's chords weren't good enough?" Davenport replies, mock outraged. "How many hit songs do *you* have?"

Torkanowsky announces, "I have a question. So I can prepare myself, is every count-off going to be five minutes?"

Davenport jokes that a more appropriate title for Webb's song might be, "By the Time I Get to Metairie," a reference to the traffic-clogged burg on New Orleans' western border. For Freeman's benefit, he states, "I don't want Harry Connick Jr. doing this song. I discovered it."

"Could you tell Jeremy to quit hustling overdubs and come out and play?" Torkanowsky says.

At four P.M., Davenport realizes they skipped lunch. "So I guess we're not eating?"

They consult the studio's supply of restaurant menus. Torkanowsky assures the trumpeter that "we can send a runner to the Ritz, if you prefer that menu."

Freeman is charged with procuring sustenance. A nearby Chinese restaurant can deliver in forty minutes. Davenport checks his watch. Drummer Herman Ernest and bassist George Porter Jr. are scheduled to arrive at five P.M. to contribute to a song called "Mr. New Orleans." "They're going to be ready to work and the food will just be getting here."

Somebody suggests calling to see if they want anything. They don't.

While awaiting lunch, Davenport mulls how his perfectionist tendencies fuel multiple recordings of the same song. "You can do it a hundred and fifty times. There comes a time when you have to walk away from it."

That's why he surrounds himself with people like Torkanowsky and Freeman, who will tell him when it's time to move on. So, is anything recorded so far usable?

Torkanowsky: "The answer is yes. But that would be a question for Tracey."

Freeman: "It sounded good."

During a playback of "By the Time I Get to Phoenix," Davenport paces nervously. He can't stand the sound of his voice, especially on this "scratch," or practice, take.

"The first time I heard that, I threw up a little bit in my mouth."

Weeks earlier, as he lay awake obsessing over the upcoming recording, a song popped into his head. He leapt out of bed and worked out an arrangement on the piano in his room at the Ritz-Carlton, "which is very rare for me."

What became "Mr. New Orleans" was envisioned as a duet with Kermit Ruffins. Before Ruffins's weekly Thursday night gig at Vaughan's, a ramshackle roadhouse in the Bywater neighborhood, he usually turns up at the Ritz-Carlton to drink beer and sit in with Davenport. The "special combination" cited in the lyric may or may not refer to Ruffins's oft-stated fondness for both beer and marijuana.

Davenport outfitted "Mr. New Orleans" with a "real authentic New Orleans groove. No one can mess this song up. Even I can't mess this song up." He has not told Davis and Guerin that Porter and Ernest will replace them on "Mr. New Orleans." All they know is that they're done for the day.

In the parking lot, Guerin discovers the missing rosin in his car. He normally records and performs with a small, clip-on microphone. The large boom microphones stationed near his upright bass at the Music Shed distracted him; he was afraid he'd bump them if he extended his bow too far. "Mentally, that was holding me back." As a result, his playing was tentative; he's not pleased with his bass solo. "I'll delete the solo if I have to. Whatever makes the song better."

Back inside, Davenport and Torkanowsky strategize on how to coax the best performances from Porter and Ernest, titans of New Orleans funk. Should Porter read sheet music, or simply play by ear?

"He's one guy you don't want looking at paper," Torkanowsky says. "Show it to him verbally."

Fortuitous timing made Ernest and Porter available simultaneously. The drummer flew home to New Orleans the previous day from Las Vegas, where he concluded a six-week tour with Dr. John. Porter would fly to Denver the following day to launch a tour with his band PBS. He'd forgotten about the Davenport session; his wife reminded him earlier that afternoon.

Unfortunately, his two main bass guitars were already en route to Colorado aboard an equipment truck. He rustled up a spare instrument, and borrows a guitar strap at the Music Shed. Torkanowsky hazes him about the secondhand gear: "Does one of your basses have four strings?"

"I play on three strings," Porter deadpans. "The fourth string is extra money."

After a quick, late lunch of Chinese food, the musicians gather around the grand piano. Torkanowsky walks Porter through the arrangement of "Mr. New Orleans" as Davenport sings and plays trumpet behind them. Ernest wanders over, quietly mouthing potential drums parts.

Neither he nor Porter requires much instruction. Freeman chuckles: "They come in joking then get their game faces on, all serious."

Davenport encourages them to follow their instincts. "It's better that they don't look at the sheet music. I wrote it with that in mind."

Torkanowsky instructs Porter and Ernest to seek the song's "g-spot," then remembers a female photographer is in the room. He apologizes. She waves him off. "I'm just impressed you know where it is," she says, instantly earning one-of-the-guys status.

Finney verifies that Porter is almost ready. "Can he just plug in and be legendary? We cater to legends here."

At 5:10, game faces on, they rehearse "Mr. New Orleans." The first run-through sounds very close to a finished take.

Finney: "What do you think, Tracey?"

Freeman: "Sounds good."

From the studio, Torkanowsky addresses Finney: "Did you get any of that? Did you get *all* of that?"

Yes.

Torkanowsky: "We're done."

Davenport: "We would have been done if you hadn't f—up the intro."

Equipment and settings are adjusted. Davenport is eager to run another take. "Let's do this. It is exactly right."

They try again. Porter laughs as they crash-land: No one had considered how to conclude the song.

Torkanowsky: "What do you want to do for an ending?"

Davenport: "Not that."

They test various "tags." In the control room, Freeman and Finney marvel at Ernest's effortless groove. He records with his baseball cap on backward, headphones clamped on top.

"Herman could play a trash can and it would sound like that," Freeman says, with admiration.

"I don't understand what he's doing," Finney says. "It's like he's got a snare drum-in-your-pocket."

Torkanowksy wants to know if Finney can digitally insert the chosen "tag" on the end of the first rehearsal take. Freeman laughs. "Tork's obsessed with takes that people don't think are takes."

At 5:25, the keyboardist bounds into the control room. He insists the first "Mr. New Orleans" take should go on the album. "It was loose. It was natural as a m—f—."

Through the control room window, Porter and Ernest emphatically shake their heads no. Finney cuts off the playback as Torkanowsky protests.

Finney: "I'm not the producer. I'm just the engineer."

Torkanowsky: "And you're speaking why?"

Ernest, a hulking presence, materializes in the control room.

"You don't like it?" Torkanowsky asks.

"It's terrible."

Among other problems, the bass drum microphone was swapped midway through. Porter seconds the drummer's negative assessment.

Hoping to marshal support, Torkanowsky cites the similarly causal feel of Porter's classic Meters recordings: "Most of your records were takes like this."

Everyone laughs, but the keyboardist has persuaded no one.

Freeman: "I like the last take."

Porter: "The last take is great from first to last."

Davenport shakes his head and settles it: "Let's do one more."

As the musicians file out, Porter says, "Should I play like I know the song, or play like I don't?"

More laughter. They are loose and ready to roll. But "Mr. New Orleans" grinds to a halt after the first chorus; Ernest can't hear the other musicians through his headphones. Knobs are tweaked; they go again.

Torkanowsky declares the result "cool." They now have a solid foundation for "Mr. New Orleans." "All we need," Davenport says, "is to add a little Ruffins to the mix."

Ruffins is scheduled to come in Wednesday morning.

Torkanowsky marvels at the "Herman Ernest proprietary groove," something Ernest calls "diesel funk." "Herman can groove under a kazoo player and I'd like it."

Davenport is so pleased—"whatever that groove was you were playing, sign me up"—that he wants to re-record "By the Time I Get to Phoenix" with Ernest and Porter. If an additional session fee is required, Davenport says he'll pay it out of his own pocket, if necessary. "You got to do what you got to do. In the fourth quarter of the game, what are you going to do? You've got to win."

The Ernest/Porter foundation for "By the Time I Get to Phoenix" is very different. Porter's electric bass is much more prominent that Guerin's acoustic.

"Can you turn that vocal down?" Davenport says, again dismissive of his own singing. Otherwise, he likes the new "Phoenix."

"I hope you like it tomorrow," Torkanowsky says.

By six P.M., they are done for the day. "Thank you, gentlemen," Davenport says.

As they unwind, Torkanowsky receives a text from drummer Jaz Sawyer. Sawyer is in New York, and has just learned that the massive Virgin Megastore in Times Square has closed.

Coming in the middle of a recording session, the closing begs the question, Just where will the album they are working so hard to create be sold?

Davenport and Torkanowsky return to the more immediate question of "By the Time I Get to Phoenix."

Davenport: "So what do you think?"

Torkanowksy: "I don't think you'll like [the Porter/Ernest revision] tomorrow. I don't think it works for you."

Davenport: "It's a cool groove."

Torkanowsky: "It's distracting from the words."

They also reconsider "Mr. New Orleans."

Torkanowsky: "You ought to give [New Orleans keyboardist] Jon Cleary a whack at it."

Davenport: "What about Harry [Connick Jr.]?"

Torkanowsky: "I wouldn't know."

Davenport: "I liked the way you played it."

Torkanowsky: "If you keep me on there, I'd like another whack."

Davenport looks around the nearly empty control room. "Are we done? Who's producing this record?"

But he's ready to call it a night. They accomplished their goal of finishing basic tracks for five songs, nearly half the total.

"I think we got some good stuff, I really do," Davenport decides. "It'll be nice to sleep on it and revisit it tomorrow."

Tuesday, March 17, 2009

By 2:45, the musicians have consumed another meal of Chinese takeout and laid down instrumental "beds" for six more songs. Most clock in around three minutes. "They're all running short," Davenport says. "I like that. What's the shortest we can do a record?"

Someone suggests reclassifying *We'll Dance 'Til Dawn* as an EP instead of a full CD. To beef up the running time, Davenport briefly considers recording a trumpet/piano duet of a song by James Booker, the troubled-genius New Orleans piano wizard who tutored a young Harry Connick Jr.

In the control room, they scrutinize "Almost Never." For now, the second-to-last take is the favorite. Torkanowsky asks Finney to turn down the bass in the mix.

"If I turn down any more instruments," the engineer says, "we're not going to hear anything."

"Kinda makes you think, don't it?" Torkanowsky replies.

The musicians sit motionless, eyes closed, listening. On "I Could Hear Your Heartbeat"—recorded during a rare deviation from the alphabetized song list—Troy Davis mimics a heartbeat with his kick drum. "I think it would be funny to have it out of time," Davenport says.

"I don't," Torkanowsky counters. "Because it would highlight all the rest of the time we're out of time."

Davis suggests a boom-BOOM, boom-BOOM pattern would make more sense, as the lyric refers to not one, but two hearts.

"The heartbeats are perfect," Torkanowsky says. "Can I get a sample of these for my next Touro [hospital] commercial?"

More praise is heaped on Davis's rhythm. Feeling cocky, he says, "I didn't want to get too polyrhythmic for you guys."

Davenport considers this for a moment, then cuts the drummer down to size: "When do you have to give your wife her shoes back?"

Checking his song list, the bandleader believes Davis and Guerin may be finished with the session. "Do we need to recut anything else? I don't hear anything that was—"

He's interrupted by the Porter/Ernest "By the Time I Get To Phoenix" on the studio speakers. Davis and Guerin realize a substitute rhythm section came in after they left the previous day.

"We took your drum take and sampled it and did some stuff," Torkanowsky jokes. "See what you think."

The original, Davis/Guerin version is cued up. It is still Torkanowsky's favorite: "The rhythm section is saying what the words say."

"Mr. New Orleans" gets a listen, and Davenport considers adding an organ. Torkanowsky pronounces one take "too studio-clean."

"That's what people like," Davis says. "The stuff that we don't like, people like."

The rhythm section is dismissed. "Thank you," Davenport says. "Job well done."

At 3:15, Basin Street's Mark Samuels, the guy writing the checks, pays his first visit to the studio. Wearing a New Orleans Hornets

T-shirt, he shoulder-hugs Davenport and hands out copies of the up-coming Ruffins CD. Davenport engages Samuels in a discussion of how he wants his own CD package to differ from Ruffins's.

Davenport and Torkanowsky consider adding more instrumental-ists, possibly a percussionist. Names are bandied about, including Michael Skinkus, a local who has studied extensively in Cuba. One disadvantage of using Skinkus, Davenport jokes, is that would add up to more than three white musicians on the record, including himself and Torkanowsky. Despite his melanin deficiency, Skinkus gets the call.

Samuels is invited to weigh in on the "By the Time I Get to Phoe-nix" debate. Torkanowsky still prefers the Davis/Guerin groove and wants to play it for Samuels.

Davenport: "Do you think he cares about music?"

Samuels: "Let me ask you one question. Do you consider this a jazz record?"

The jazzier, Guerin/Davis take is cued up.

Freeman: "To me, that's the verse where you reach for the snooze button."

Davenport: "You need to think about the suburban housewife. That's our market."

Samuels votes for the funkier, Porter/Ernest take.

They move on to "When I Take My Sugar to Tea." Davenport tosses off a succession of trumpet solos, then addresses Finney: "Are you saving all this? 'Cause this could go on all night."

He knocks off another one. "Let's do one more. I've got to throw in some stuff for the trumpet students."

In the control room, he articulates his primary philosophical debate. "Sometimes I just want to play the melody on the trumpet. But I don't want to be so sparse that it sounds like I can't play. I've got to play enough trumpet to impress the jazz critics. It has to have enough trum-pet so it sounds like I did my homework, but not like a douche bag."

Samuels, joking, suggests he cover the notoriously difficult "Flight of the Bumblebee."

Freeman: "A bonus track."

Samuels: "Call it 'Jazz Critics.' Or 'For Jazz Critics Only.'"

Next up is the title track, "We'll Dance 'Til Dawn." Someone notes that this is another of Davenport's original compositions.

Freeman: "They're so well crafted . . ."

Samuels: ". . . they sound like they could have been written in the seventies."

Davenport: "That's what I wanted you to say."

At five P.M., he's still laying down trumpet intros, outros and solos, fretting over his arrangements. "This is what happens when you look at the music you wrote. In your mind it turns into a spaghetti mess."

And then: "I don't understand why I don't have more records made."

Skinkus is due in three hours. Davenport debates whether to continue recording until them. "I'm not tired, but I don't want to spin my wheels. I don't want to get to the point where I'm—"

Freeman: "Burnt out?"

Davenport: "I'm not even close to that. Let's do 'The Lady Is a Tramp.' That's fast. That will wear me out."

Instead, talk turns to the following day's session. As far as they know, Ruffins plans to record his duet in the morning. However, no one has been able to reach him to confirm.

"I don't want that to take three hours tomorrow," Davenport says. "With all my love for Kermit, I can't take all day."

Samuels volunteers to drop off a copy of the rough recording of "Mr. New Orleans" at Bullets, the nightclub where Ruffins is playing that night, so he can familiarize himself with the song. Samuels also requests the "We'll Dance 'Til Dawn" sheet music.

Freeman asks, tongue in cheek, if Samuels wants to make sure his name is on it. In the bad old days—and more recently—label executives and producers assigned themselves unearned songwriting credits. But Samuels only wants to photograph the sheet music for possible inclusion in the CD artwork.

A long discussion ensues on the state of the local and national music industry, with much dishing. Freeman proposes that "records would be better if everyone agreed to stop using technology."

Davenport has a request: "Can we finish my record first?"

Wednesday, March 18, 2009

Freeman finally reaches the elusive Ruffins at 9:15 A.M. Unfortunately, the trumpeter won't be coming to the Music Shed as planned.

Instead, he's bound for the set of *Treme*, the David Simon drama set in the world of New Orleans music. A second-line scene is being shot for the pilot episode, and Ruffins wants to be there.

Freeman, a veteran of numerous Ruffins sessions, vouches for the trumpeter's reliability. "Usually when he's got something to do in the studio, he's there before anybody else. Sometimes he'll be outside in his truck, waiting."

Davenport is unperturbed. Ruffins is "keeping it real. When we couldn't find him last night, I thought this might be the scenario."

Shifting gears, he decides to spend the morning on vocal and trumpet parts for other songs. Ruffins is rebooked for Friday.

But the two-day delay causes some consternation. Samuels wants to include "Mr. New Orleans" on a Basin Street promotional CD to be distributed at the massive 2009 SIGGRAPH computer graphics conference in New Orleans. The deadline is Friday—the same day as the rescheduled recording. And Freeman must still mix the track, balancing the relative volume of the voices, trumpets and backing instruments. The producer says he can finish the mix by Saturday; they'll have to hope for the best.

Davenport adds a song to his alphabetized list: "Come Rain or Come Shine," which he wants to record as a duet with Torkanowsky on piano. The additional four minutes will boost the CD's running time to nearly an hour, the target duration.

Torkanowsky learns about "Come Rain or Come Shine" when he arrives at the Music Shed. Years ago, he recorded it with the late rhythm-and-blues singer Johnny Adams. He spends an hour reacquainting himself with the sheet music.

At 11:30 A.M., only a skeleton crew is on hand. In the control room, Davenport paces, arms crossed, listening to a take. Torkanowsky reclines in an office chair. Freeman surfs online, an ear cocked toward the conversation.

Torkanowsky: "This is funkier so far."

Davenport: "I agree."

Torkanowsky: "I sound like an old black man with three fingers."

Davenport: "They call him Mittens."

Torkanowsky: "This is cool, I think."

Davenport: "Yeah. I like the ending."

More takes follow. In the isolation booth, Davenport deadpans a note-perfect Little Richard "ooo-ooo" and imitates classical-pop singer Josh Groban.

"Ready when you are, Lil' Josh," Finney says.

Hands in his pockets, head nodding ever so slightly, Davenport taps his left foot in time to the piano.

Satisfied, he and Torkanowsky both break for the control room. Davenport arrives first and anticipates the pianist's desire to tweak more: "Let's move on. We could be here all day. He's trying to beat the piano out of tune."

As if on cue, Torkanowsky enters with, "I have a suggestion. Before you go all half-cocked and pull the take, I suggest we listen to the first take. I could be wrong, but once again, I have no baseline reference."

Davenport agonizes over a trumpet solo: "Why don't I just play the melody?"

Both he and Torkanowsky are highly critical of their own work. "We're fraternal brothers in the fraternity of self-loathing," the keyboardist admits.

Recording is especially challenging for perfectionists: The result endures forever. With that in mind, Torkanowsky wants to re-record several piano passages.

Finney turns to Freeman: "Producer?"

Freeman defers to Davenport. "If he wants that on the record, no. If he doesn't, you can come back."

Torkanowsky lobbies Davenport: "I promise I won't mess with much. I want to take out two or three things."

"That's fine," Davenport says.

"That Old Black Magic" is under review. Davenport cues up Frank Sinatra's 1943 recording on iTunes, then contemplates his own voice. "It's amazing that I'm not gay. I did a duet with Diana Krall—we're in the same range. I played it for my dad. He said, 'It sounds like two middle-aged women.'"

He debates how best to phrase the lyrics of "That Old Black Magic." "This whole tune, people fake. People have bastardized the harmonies; jazz musicians had something to do with that. These are pop songs from the thirties and forties. I want to come back and capture the original magic of the songs. I want to try to get it."

Torkanowsky: "When these songs were written, they were written by people with almost classical chops. Classical music is principally about execution. Jazz is about intent."

Davenport: "The problem with all this is no one gives a s—."

Torkanowsky: "Your final arbiter as to absolute truth is the Harold Arlen songbook."

Davenport: "That book was given to me by Harry Connick Jr."

Torkanowsky: "The defense rests."

Davenport: "Where David gets his information is his iPhone."

Finney returns from the studio's kitchen with a muffin.

Torkanowsky: "I thought you said we couldn't eat in here."

Finney: "I meant musicians."

Back in the isolation booth, Davenport rips off a flurry of high notes. Torkanowsky is reminded of another New Orleans trumpeter, Irvin Mayfield: "Tell Mr. Mayfield to do it again."

Freeman picks up the thread: "What is he doing, auditioning for the New Orleans Jazz Orchestra?"

Davenport: "Part of me wants to play ultracool, understated, Chet Baker. But part of me wants to *play*."

Torkanowsky: "Either approach works."

Freeman: "I agree. I prefer mellower."

Davenport: "Me, too. But I like my tribute to Irvin. How funny is it that I'm mellow, then . . ."

Torkanowsky: "It's funny, but you're not doing a comedy record."

Back to the isolation booth; try again. "No one cares about the trumpet solo," Davenport announces. "Let's get the vocals."

At 1:30 P.M., Freeman orders two pizzas online; everyone needs a break from Chinese food.

In the isolation booth, Davenport sings, *"Forever is a long, long time . . ."* as the music eases in for a soft landing. He bounds into the control room with an extra spring in his step—he knows he nailed it.

"Is that food here yet? I'm hungry."

Friday, March 20, 2009

Granted a mulligan, Kermit Ruffins arrives on time for the rescheduled session. He and Davenport slap hands and embrace. Twelve hours earlier, Ruffins hung with Davenport at the Ritz-Carlton, before setting off for Vaughan's.

Davenport: "Whazzup, dude?"

Ruffins: "Had a good time last night, man."

Davenport: "Always, always."

Ruffins is as happy-go-lucky as Davenport is tightly wound. Davenport wants the whole world to know his name; for Ruffins, the only world that matters is Orleans Parish.

As Ruffins settles in, Davenport polishes off a trumpet solo for "Almost Never," the song destined to lead off the new album. Ruffins sizes up the task at hand. He limbers up his voice, and chuckles. The previous afternoon, he listened to the rough recording of "Mr. New Orleans" in his car. He examines a color-coded lyric sheet.

"You're red," Davenport says. "No, I'm red. You're yellow."

Will they record in the same room? No, Davenport says—he will be in the isolation booth, Ruffins in the main studio.

Ruffins: "It's all set up?"

Davenport: "Yep."

Ruffins and Davenport, simultaneously: "Let's do it."

In front of a microphone, Ruffins makes himself at home. He removes his fedora and clamps headphones over a bandanna festooned with a playing card design. He pours himself a Bud Light over ice— the first alcohol of any kind consumed during the session.

"All aboard!" Ruffins exclaims, his traditional prelude to any artistic endeavor.

He sips iced beer, then sings, *"Mr. St. Lou-eee/when you croon a tune, you say oo-oo-wee."*

Sips more. Positions his trumpet case on a stool. Extracts his horn. Blows it. Consults with Finney on the position of the microphone. Clears his throat. Laughs to himself. Coughs. Scats. Grins as Davenport, whose sense of humor Ruffins compares favorably to Jerry Lewis, clowns in the adjoining isolation booth: "Jeremy's a fool, yeah!"

Ruffins sings, *"I said, 'La de da da.'"*

In the isolation booth, Davenport locks his fingers behind his head and stretches. Under the watchful gaze of a Professor Longhair poster, the "tape"—actually just a computer's hard drive—rolls.

Davenport: *"I've got one question/How do you play those high notes?"*

Ruffins: *"Those high notes you've referred to . . ."*

Davenport: "RE-fer?"

Ruffins: " . . . *come to my secret combination.*"

Ruffins cracks up. "I like that—high notes you *reefer* to."

Davenport offers direction and good cheer: "You take the high road on the harmony, and I'll sing the low harmony. Let's give it a shot. Lovin' it! Lovin' it!"

Ruffins's voice is even more gravelly than usual; he clears his throat loudly, and often. Hands in his pockets, bouncing at the knees, he's getting into it. But he's still not sufficiently familiar with the lyrics; his delivery sounds deliberate. "*Let's stay together, make the people dance . . .*"

Davenport answers in his smooth croon, "*Let's sing together . . . ,*" then stops. "I keep f— it up."

"Me, too," Ruffins says.

They go again, and blow it again.

"One more time," Davenport exclaims. "That was perfect except I f— it up."

They reset and restart. Ruffins snaps his fingers and nods his head as Davenport delivers the "let's sing together, make the people dance" harmony.

Ruffins should answer him, but is silent. After a few seconds, he throws up his hands and shakes his head in frustration: "I started dancing and totally forgot to sing."

They reconsider Ruffins's pronunciation of "fancy pants" in the line "Look at you, Mr. Fancy Pants, let's sing together, make the people dance."

Between takes, Ruffins improvises, "I got one reefer . . ." He laughs at his modification. "I'd make that a beautiful reefer song."

They go again, the singsong lyrics flowing easier now.

Davenport: "*I got one question . . .*"

Ruffins: "Wait, what's that?"

Davenport: "*How do you play those high notes?*"

Ruffins: "Aw, I ain't gonna tell you too much!"

And again . . .

Ruffins: "*Hey, NOW . . . how 'bout you . . .*"

Cut.

Ruffins: "Aww, 'Mr. Fancy Pants' . . . I just totally lost that one."

He finally nails it, or at least thinks he does: "Awww, YEAH!"

Davenport tries to get his attention. "Actually, you know what . . ."

But Ruffins is still celebrating, still leading his own parade: "Pat me on my back and call me Shorty! Play that doghouse music! What'd you say, J?"

J wants another take. This time, they'll sing, "Let's play together and make the people dance," then trade two-bar trumpet solos. Ruffins hoists his horn, which emits a ragged squawk. "I haven't seen this horn in three days. I shoulda warmed up a little."

Stripped down to his long-sleeve T-shirt, he clears the mouthpiece. "All kinda s— . . . reefer, beer . . . from about a week ago."

He squeezes out a flurry of screeches—"that's my Irvin imitation"—and riffs on the possibility of Irvin Mayfield, his good-natured rival, running for mayor of New Orleans.

"I'd bring the whole damn 6th Ward to vote. We get Irvin in office, ooh, we're gonna have some fun in this city. I was going to run. I just wanted to put on my pajamas and show up the first day so they could fire me. You talk about partying . . . Free liquor for everybody in front City Hall. A big block party."

The detour into mayoral politics exhausted, they get back to work. They solo on either side of a thick pane of glass, listening to one another through headphones. There is a natural bounce and swing to their playing, a reflection of their easy rapport.

Davenport: "Let's do a couple more, just for fun."

Ruffins: "It feels good."

They revisit the lyrics. Davenport suggests changing "on top of Canal Street"—a reference to his gig at the Ritz-Carlton—to "in the Vieux Carre."

Ruffins still hopes to recast "Mr. New Orleans" as a "reefer song. If we didn't have Jeremy here, it'd be a whole other thing."

Davenport sings to Ruffins, *"You're always looking sharp in a sexy hat/You make the little ladies' hearts go pitter-pat."*

Ruffins replies, *"Look at you, Mr. Fancy Pants."*

They harmonize on, *"Let's sing together, make the people dance!"*

Davenport points out the twist in the final lyric: "Just remember, on the way out we'll say, 'Let's *play* together,' because that's into the trumpet solo."

Ruffins: "Sounds good."

Davenport: "You want to do one more pass just for safety and then—"

Ruffins: "Let's do it. All aboard!"

They take another swing, which is to everyone's satisfaction. Ruffins pulls on his button-down shirt and fedora. In barely an hour, they're done.

Ruffins: "That was some fun s—."

Davenport: "That was good stuff. Thank you. Appreciate it."

Ruffins: "Thank you."

Davenport: "It's going to be great. And we're going to leave all the good . . ."

Ruffins: "Laughter . . ."

Davenport: "Yeah. All that. That's good stuff. We're going to leave that all in there."

Five weeks after the recording session, Basin Street rushed copies of *We'll Dance 'Til Dawn*—with the Porter/Ernest "By the Time I Get to Phoenix"—to New Orleans stores in time for Jazz Fest. What one reviewer described as a "dry martini of an album" was released nationwide on July 21, 2009. It is also available in the New Orleans Ritz-Carlton's guest rooms, positioned next to the "intimacy kit." (Whether anyone using the intimacy kit has ever paused to contemplate Davenport's trumpet solos is unknown.)

The *All Music Guide* declared "Mr. New Orleans" a "joyous wink of a tune, the type of track that only performers confident in their personas can get away with."

As of December 2010, *We'll Dance 'Til Dawn* had sold 5,000 copies—not yet enough to recoup its cost, or make Davenport a star.

Undaunted, he continues to hold court each weekend at the Ritz. He sings classic jazz, takes requests, sends out birthday wishes, charms and cracks wise, all the while longing for brighter lights.

Chapter Nine

Mystikal Versus Michael Tyler

Michael "Mystikal" Tyler wore a half-scowl, half-smile on the June 1995 cover of OffBeat *magazine. I wrote the accompanying story, the first major profile of the ambitious local rapper. I was struck not only by his drive and discipline, but the contrast between his fierce image and actual personality. He was exceedingly charming, affable, open and upbeat, especially with the kids who buzzed around whenever he materialized on the streets of his old neighborhood.*

In 1998, after he graduated to the ranks of platinum-selling star, I visited Tyler and his mother at their home in a gated community in Baton Rouge. Once again, I came away convinced he was unlikely to court serious trouble—and stated as much in the pages of The Times-Picayune.

Two days after that story ran, news broke that police had busted Tyler with a joint and pistol in his car. Turns out he wasn't infallible after all. Four years later, he stood accused of far more serious charges stemming from a bizarre, sad incident that spoke directly to the corrupting influence of money, fame and power—and one very fallible human being's epic bad decision.

Tyler's mistake cost him six years, hundreds of thousands of dollars in legal fees and restitution, millions in lost income, and his reputation. Months after his release from prison, he and I convened for another lengthy interview. Once again I came away with a positive impression, hopeful—if cautiously so—that this time he would justify it.

In a discrete recording studio stashed near a busy highway in Baton Rouge, Louisiana, Michael "Mystikal" Tyler reduces six years of incarceration to three minutes of taut, rugged, hip-hop swagger. As a new Mystikal recording titled "Bitch I'm In Jail" booms from the studio's speakers, he pantomimes his own rapid-fire lyrics like a silent-film star on fast-forward: Hands cuffed behind his back. Sad farewell. Toiling in the prison garden. Parole denied.

The song represents where Tyler, rap's Rip Van Winkle, found himself in the summer of 2010: drawing inspiration from an episode that might have extinguished his career, in an effort to rekindle it.

Prior to his 2004 imprisonment for sexual battery, he was New Orleans' most formidable MC. Before Lil Wayne or Juvenile, he blazed a trail nationally for New Orleans rap. As the self-proclaimed Prince of the South, Mystikal sold millions of records in the late 1990s and early 2000s. But his high-flying life crashed overnight. Fame, fortune and the freedom to indulge every desire were replaced by three hots and a cot, courtesy of the Louisiana penal system.

Six years later, having served his time, he rejoined the free world with a far more restricted lifestyle. He faced years of probation. He must receive permission from parole officers to travel outside the Baton Rouge area, where he lives. And he is required to register as a sex offender.

Still, he was determined to reclaim his place in the pop music pantheon. Within weeks of his release, he and veteran New Orleans hip-hop producer KLC had sketched out a batch of new songs, including "Bitch I'm In Jail." Despite Tyler's unshakeable confidence, a successful comeback was not guaranteed. Fads come and go in six months; by that standard, six years is an eternity. When Tyler went to prison, Lil Wayne was little known and MySpace, Facebook, YouTube and Twitter had yet to revolutionize social media and the music industry.

Rebuilding his career, however, must also involve restoring himself. The moment he entered prison, he says, he left behind the trappings of Mystikal, the boastful, untouchable rap star, and became Michael Tyler once again. A failure to distinguish between the two precipitated his downfall.

"It was a case of Michael Tyler acting like Mystikal," Tyler told me in August 2010, as we sat in his Land Rover outside KLC's Baton

Rouge studio. "I don't know what he was acting like. But I know it cost both of them. It cost both personas a great deal."

That Tyler would go to prison for victimizing a woman was all the more perplexing given the unfathomable tragedy he and his family suffered one terrible night in 1994. In that case as well, the victim was a woman. His sister.

Michael Tyler was born on September 22, 1970. As a high school student, his mother, Marie Tyler, had met an older man named Al Bell. Al was married, but separated from his wife. He took up with Marie and fathered two children with her: a daughter named Michelle and, five years later, Michael.

Marie planned to marry Al once his divorce was finalized. Looking ahead to a life together, the couple bought a two-story building in the 800 block of Delachaise Street in New Orleans' hardscrabble 12th Ward. Bell opened a neighborhood grocery store on the ground floor. The family—Marie, Al, Michelle and Michael—moved into the same building. Bedrooms were upstairs; the kitchen, living and dining rooms were downstairs, behind the store.

Around the time Michael was two, Marie left Al, in part because she no longer believed he intended to divorce his wife. She and her two children moved in with one of her sisters, the first of several moves Marie initiated in an effort to improve their lot in life. "I was mother and father, trying to do the best for them and keep them out of trouble," she said.

When Michael was seven, his father died from complications following surgery, and Bell's Grocery closed. Money was tighter than ever; Marie took a job as a cashier and customer service rep at an A&P grocery on Magazine Street. In 1981, she gave birth to a second son, Maurice. By 1983, she had moved her family back into the Delachaise house, which she now owned. The empty downstairs space that formerly housed Bell's Grocery was used for storage.

Marie applied a firm hand to instill what Michael later described as a "Christian background and strong family ties." Michael was a "feisty," rambunctious child, unable to stand still for long without executing a back flip or somersault. More than once, Marie walked outside with him and "the next thing I'd know, he done flipped from the porch to the ground."

A natural entertainer, he emulated Michael Jackson, James Brown and martial arts star Bruce Lee. Michelle, meanwhile, focused on contemporary R&B star Teena Marie's repertoire. At family gatherings, relatives with video cameras in hand eagerly anticipated Michael and Michelle's performances. One Mardi Gras afternoon, young Michael popped into a neighborhood barroom and broke into his Michael Jackson routine, mimicking the superstar's moves from the "Billie Jean" and "Thriller" videos. Patrons "were throwing money at him," Marie recalled. "That let him know at an early age that he was talented. I knew he had great potential."

He burned off additional energy by breakdancing under the stage name Mystikal Mike. As rappers replaced Michael Jackson in his personal hall of fame, he hung at a buddy's house, practicing rhymes and flow until Marie arrived to collect him. "I always knew where he was—at his friend's, rapping," Marie said. "Eleven o'clock at night, I didn't want him to be away from home, where I knew he would be safe. I'd get a friend, and we'd go get him. I didn't want him walking the streets at night."

At Walter L. Cohen High School, the cheerleading squad provided an outlet for Michael's tumbling skills. He flipped girls into the air and anchored human pyramids. He signed up for the school's Junior Reserve Officers' Training Corps, a program for students considering a military career. He drew meticulous reproductions of cartoon characters and pondered astronomy and architecture.

Rap consumed his free time. At home, he listened to DJ Jazzy Jeff and Will "Fresh Prince" Smith, and covered his bedroom walls with LL Cool J posters. He sought out microphones at talent shows and school assemblies, writing raps about everything from Black History Month to Christmas. After graduating from Cohen in 1988, he worked in a grocery's meat department and as a security guard before following a cousin's example and enlisting in the Army. Because his cousin was a combat engineer, Tyler requested the same specialty.

For a young man who had barely traveled outside New Orleans save a boyhood trip to Disney World in Florida, the Army was an eye-opener. He took business and psychology classes. While stationed in Georgia, he rapped in NCO clubs as a gong show contestant. Iraq's invasion of Kuwait in August 1990 dashed his hopes for an uneventful enlistment. Tyler was eventually deployed to Iraq during the first

Gulf War. He discovered, much to his dismay, that a combat engineer's duties include mine-sweeping.

Honorably discharged after four years, he returned to New Orleans and landed a job as a plainclothes security guard at a Woolworth five-and-dime. Such was his zeal in the pursuit of shoplifters that his boss loaned him out to other stores. But rap remained his passion. He finagled himself onto the bill of an outdoor concert in the Tremé neighborhood headlined by Run-DMC and Doug E. Fresh; he performed one song, an original called "Not That Nigga." Leroy "Precise" Edwards, a staff producer for upstart local rap label Big Boy Records, was in the audience. The physicality of this unknown rapper impressed Edwards, as did the audience's enthusiastic response.

Days later, Tyler was in a recording studio with Edwards. Normally, the producer built instrumental tracks first; rappers tailored their flow to fit. But the idiosyncratic construct of Tyler's wiggedy-diggedy wordplay necessitated a reversal of the process: Tyler rapped to a scratch beat, then Edwards formed music around the vocals, a waterfall of gruff, guttural, staccato words and phrases. Tyler rapped like a drill sergeant. Rather than accent one or two words in a line, he emphasized most with a tongue-twisting dexterity. He was not dependent on the singsong, repetitive refrains of block party "bounce" rap nor the drugs and guns crime scenes of gangsta rap. Instead, his superhero-like Mystikal alter ego practiced extreme braggadocio, sexual and otherwise, and called out rivals.

At their first session, Tyler and Edwards tracked two songs, "Not That Nigga" and "Mind of Mystikal." Two weeks later, the single was in local stores, selling briskly. They soon went to work on the rapper's full-length debut.

Cheering Michael on was his twenty-nine-year-old sister, Michelle. The siblings were especially close; Michelle often wore promotional T-shirts bearing her brother's image. Deploying the same brassy voice that had once belted Teena Marie hits as a child, she contributed backing vocals to "Not That Nigga."

The Tyler home on Delachaise Street had grown crowded. Marie, Michael and Maurice lived upstairs. Michelle stayed downstairs in what was formerly the living room with her little boy, Markell. By the summer of 1994, she and Markell's father had split and she was seeing someone new: Damion Neville, the troubled son of popular New

Orleans entertainer Charmaine Neville and grandson of Neville Brothers saxophonist Charles Neville.

In the wee hours of September 22, 1994, Michael's twenty-fourth birthday, he left the house to bring a girlfriend home. When he returned around 3:30 A.M., an exterior door downstairs was open. Peering into his sister's moonlit room, at first he noticed only clothes strewn about the bed.

And then he saw Michelle. She had been strangled with the cord of a clock radio, and stabbed multiple times with a screwdriver that still protruded from her neck. Her lifeless body was clad in a Mystikal T-shirt.

Reeling from the horror, Michael drew on his military training to prevent himself from fainting. "I'm sure that God had his design," he said years later. "My mama couldn't go in there. My little brother couldn't go in there; he was too young. The best person suited for that situation, to find her, was myself. I had to be the one to find her."

Compounding the tragedy, Damion Neville was arrested and charged with Michelle's murder. Neville initially confessed to killing her in a fit of rage. But during his trial, his defense attorney argued that police coerced the confession, and that drug dealers to whom Neville owed money were likely responsible for the brutal crime. The jury acquitted him. (In 1999, after killing a man in a crack-related shootout in which he was wounded, Neville pled guilty to manslaughter; he was sentenced to eight years in prison.)

The Tyler family was devastated. Marie assumed guardianship of Michelle's son, Markell, and raised him as her own. Michael channeled his grief and rage into determination and drive. His debut album was now his mission. For the final track, he recorded a remarkably poignant seventy-second spoken-word tribute to his sister that stands in stark contrast to all that precedes it. Setting aside his Mystikal persona, he allowed himself to be Michael Tyler, grieving brother, on "Dedicated to Michelle Tyler." "Thank you for being the best sister a brother could have ever wanted—twenty-four years of laughter and joy," he speaks through barely contained sobs, his sorrow raw and real. "Sure is gonna be hard, not being able to see you smile again, baby. So I guess I'll just hold onto all the memories that we did share until we meet again. You were already an angel, so I guess you've just gone home . . . I'm gonna keep you in my heart, and my thoughts. I love you."

Such a wound never fully heals. "It doesn't matter how much I attain and how many accolades I achieve," Tyler confessed in the summer of 2010. "I'll never have it all without her."

Big Boy Records released Tyler's *Mystikal* album in late 1994. Within the bustling New Orleans rap community, *Mystikal* was a game-changer, an immediate sensation. The breakout single, "Ya'll Ain't Ready Yet," name-checked local rappers as Tyler claimed their best attributes for himself. The following spring, during the second week of the 1995 New Orleans Jazz & Heritage Festival, *Mystikal* outsold the latest releases from traditional stalwarts Aaron Neville and Dr. John. Despite limited, regional distribution, it hit No. 56 on *Billboard*'s national R&B album chart. Fans turned out in droves to see Mystikal and Partners N Crime open the Jazz Fest's Congo Square Stage at 11:20 A.M. on Sunday, April 30. Eleven days later, Mystikal became the first local rapper to headline the New Orleans House of Blues, topping a roster of fellow Big Boy artists.

National labels soon came calling. Jive Records secured Tyler's services, buying out his contract from Big Boy. Jive revamped *Mystikal* with new artwork and additional tracks, and re-released the album nationally in 1996 as *Mind of Mystikal*. It introduced him to the rap world at large, which, as the title of "Ya'll Ain't Ready Yet" suggested, didn't quite know what to make of this braided dervish from New Orleans. *Mind of Mystikal* sold respectably, but not enough to match sky-high expectations.

Tyler came to believe he'd be better off casting his lot with fellow New Orleanian Percy "Master P" Miller. Miller's No Limit Records had cornered the market on street cred. Ignored by rap's East and West Coast establishments, Miller presented himself and his artists as authentic ghetto soldiers; No Limit's logo featured a tank. Whatever he lacked in microphone prowess, Miller more than made up for in marketing genius. He owned the streets, and moved much product. With the addition of Mystikal, his roster finally boasted a rapper with skills to match the hype. "I saw the audience that they had, the fan base that they had," Tyler said of his enlistment in the No Limit army. "It was the ghetto. That's a lot of people."

Contractually, he was still bound to Jive; a deal was brokered, and his November 1997 release, *Unpredictable*, bore both the Jive and No Limit imprints. It included "Murder 2," another response to Michelle's death. If "Dedicated to Michelle Tyler" was an expression of grief, "Murder 2" was all vengeance and rage ("I tried to tell her that nigga's bad news but she ain't heard me. . . . he's gonna pay for what he did ya"). With Miller's Midas touch, *Unpredictable* hit No. 1 on *Billboard*'s national R&B chart and peaked at No. 3 on the mainstream Billboard 200 pop chart en route to selling two million copies. Mystikal had arrived aboard the No Limit tank.

To distance himself and his empire from New Orleans' troubled streets, Miller had established a base of operations eighty miles away in Baton Rouge, the capital of Louisiana. He built a sprawling nouveau riche mansion, complete with glass elevator and lake view, in the gated Country Club of Louisiana subdivision. Per Miller's wishes, several No Limit artists and executives occupied somewhat less ostentatious homes in the Country Club. Thus, the likes of Snoop Dogg, briefly a member of the No Limit family, roamed the same tranquil, manicured streets as former Louisiana governor Edwin Edwards.

In June 1998, Tyler moved his mother, brother and nephew into his handsome new three-bedroom brick home on a discrete cul-de-sac in the Country Club of Louisiana. Michelle's portrait occupied a place of honor on a mantel; her car sat in the garage. With its polished hardwood floors and a breakfast room stocked with exercise equipment, the house was the kind of upper-middle class dwelling a successful lawyer might call home. Community rules mandated neatly trimmed lawns and assigned parking. The sense of order appealed to the ex-soldier in Tyler. "They keep it uniform out here," he told me in the fall of 1998. "I respect that. If that's my problem, worrying about cutting the grass and getting the mailbox right, I'm straight."

Tyler supported his family, and then some; his mother drove a gleaming white Mercedes-Benz, a gift from her eldest son. He felt pressure to match the success of *Unpredictable* with his second No Limit release, *Ghetto Fabulous*. To that end, he enlisted veteran rappers Busta Rhymes and Naughty By Nature to make guest appearances alongside fellow No Limit soldiers. New songs covered familiar themes. "Round Out the Tank" gave a shout-out to his old Army buddies. On "The Stick Up," he, Mia X and other No Limit soldiers metaphorically "robbed" the record business of overdue money and respect. "Life Ain't Cool" saluted mothers. "Respect My Mind" was meant to impress with his lyrical skills. The title track described his social status, "Ghetto Fabulous," even though, technically, he never lived in a ghetto.

Weeks before the album dropped, Tyler and I stood in his tidy Baton Rouge den. He rummaged through his wallet and extracted a $500,000 check, an advance on *Ghetto Fabulous* royalties. His future looked exceedingly bright. "I've got the foundation. The slab is laid, the concrete is poured. God blessed me to grow to this point in my life. All the homes and the cars and the business tools, I own all those things. Now we're straight liquid; it's time to own investment things, things that work for you. Right now, I'm trying to maintain everything that I'm doing, and make all the right decisions."

Days later, he made a very public wrong decision.

On December 17, 1998, two days after the release of *Ghetto Fabulous*, Tyler drove his late sister's Monte Carlo to Kenner, a suburb at the western edge of greater New Orleans, to run errands. Police pulled him over and discovered a 9mm pistol and the remnants of a joint. Though he claimed the gun was legally registered, possessing it in conjunction with the pot resulted in a felony weapons charge.

Four days after his "mishap," Tyler described signing autographs at the police station before posting bond and driving home to Baton Rouge. The cops, he proclaimed, were *too* nice: "Don't be nice to me—I'm a criminal. This is some kind of lesson I'm supposed to be learning, so let me learn it." The arrest, he insisted, would serve as his proverbial wake-up call. "It made me realize how serious this is, that I have a lot to lose. Those few hours . . . made me realize how many people depend on me and rely on me for so many good things."

He even saw a higher power at work through the Kenner police department. "Anything that happens to me has a reason behind it. That was God telling me, 'Don't celebrate that hard. Cool it.'"

If so, God must not have spoken clearly.

By 2000, Tyler had disengaged from No Limit and was once again recording exclusively for Jive. The company aggressively promoted a new Mystikal single, "Shake Ya Ass," in advance of an album called *Let's Get Ready*. "Shake Ya Ass," with its huge hook of a chorus and svelte production by the Neptunes, was clearly influenced by the success of Juvenile's "Back That Azz Up"; it rose to the top of *Billboard*'s rap singles chart.

In October 2000, *Let's Get Ready* bumped Madonna's *Music* from the No. 1 position on the Billboard 200 en route to selling more than two million copies. Notching the best-selling album in the nation culminated Mystikal's five-year ascent. As a bonus, "Shake Ya Ass" was nominated for a Grammy as best rap solo performance.

Suddenly Tyler was in demand as a collaborator in the rap world and beyond. Pop/R&B superstar Mariah Carey featured him prominently in "Don't Stop (Funkin' 4 Jamaica)," a single from her 2001 CD *Glitter*. She even flew to New Orleans to shoot a video with him at the Maple Leaf Bar and in a swamp outside the city.

On May 5, 2001, Tyler returned to the New Orleans Jazz Fest's Congo Square stage, slotted just before the closing act, Cuban-born salsa legend Ceila Cruz. A vast crowd swamped the area around the stage and pooled with an even larger throng awaiting the Dave Matthews Band at the Acura Stage. The day's announced attendance of 160,000 was easily the largest in Jazz Fest history. Some fans of more traditional music grumbled about Mystikal's inclusion; Jazz Fest producer/director Quint Davis pronounced the booking "culturally correct. Fats Domino and Mystikal are the bookends" of New Orleans music.

Both would, at various points, cause headaches for Jazz Fest's producer. Tyler awoke in Dallas the morning of his May 5 show and boarded a private jet for Baton Rouge. He set out for New Orleans in a convoy of five vehicles but was, as Davis would later note, "a little off on his timing." At five P.M., an hour past his show's scheduled start, he still hadn't arrived at the Fair Grounds.

Jazz Fest staffers pride themselves on their extraordinary efforts to insure punctual performances. But Tyler eluded them; for much of the afternoon, they had no idea where he was, or if he was coming at all. Finally, they reached a member of his entourage as the convoy approached the corner of Tulane Avenue and South Broad Street, two miles from the Fair Grounds. Motorcycle police set out to escort the rapper through traffic; he was gone by the time they arrived. Ditto the next rendezvous point, at the Tastee Donuts at Broad and Esplanade Avenue.

Hedging his bets, Davis sent for Cruz. She exited her white limousine on the dirt track behind the Congo Square stage just as the rapper rolled up from the opposite direction at the wheel of his convoy's lead SUV. His entrance sparked a frenzy among security guards.

Decked out in black and gold athletic gear, he fired lyrics like a machine gun; his charisma held the restless crowd's attention. He was full of praise for his hometown and did his best to mind his manners. He apologized when he accidentally doused photographers with water, excised expletives from his between-song banter and instructed fans who joined him onstage during "Shake Ya Ass" not to strip and to "watch your mouth."

After thirty-five minutes, it was over. Davis marveled that "in this day and age, a hard-core rapper said, 'Watch your mouth.'"

His PG-rated Jazz Fest set aside, Mystikal inhabited an R- and sometimes X-rated world. It is difficult for ordinary mortals to comprehend the bounty and variety of sexual opportunity offered first-tier entertainers and athletes. Even if the likes of Wilt Chamberlain and Gene Simmons exaggerated their personal statistics, they still slept with an enormous number of women.

In the late '90s, Tyler fathered two children out of wedlock by two different women. ("Had to see what baby-mama-drama was all about. And Lord, did I find out.") In the summer of 2002, he appeared in *The Making of Liquid City*, a quasi-documentary about a porn film shot in New Orleans. The value of the rings, watch and necklaces Tyler wore during the shoot was likely more than the film's entire production budget. Between interview segments, he savors an on-camera lap dance from "Janet Jackme" and cavorts with "Chaos," identified as a "recording artist/porn actress." Elsewhere, male and female porn actors discuss in graphic detail embarrassing incidents suffered while practicing their craft.

For the benefit of the viewing public, Tyler offers the following observation on his chosen profession: "I don't think it's rappers doing it on purpose, trying to make it more sexual or nothing. It comes kinda natural."

That he agreed to appear in such a crude production at the height of his mainstream success says much about the risks of keeping it real.

When sex is a readily available commodity, the quest for fresh thrills can badly skew one's perspective and moral compass. In his heyday, Tyler would later confirm, sex was "to my disposal. And now you're not just doing the regular sex."

Even if attributed to the Mystikal character's quasi-comedic over-kill, his lyrics can be offensive and sexist. The especially graphic "P—y Crook" posits that he gets so much, it should be a crime. In "Shake Ya Ass," he addresses the object of his lust thusly: "Came here with my d— in my hand/Don't make me leave here with my foot in yo' ass." Such sexual entitlement is not the sort of sentiment generally found in Hallmark cards.

Tyler maintains that his sister's murder is never far from his mind, and has served as a check on his actions—to a point. "The thing that humbled me was what happened in 1994, when my sister was stolen away, brutally taken away from us. Having said that, in some instances you get that 'can't f— with me' [attitude]. I try to keep it to the music, and cut that switch off when I come off the stage or out the recording booth. 'Cause Michael Tyler can't do all that Mystikal's talking about he can do, breaststroke through lava and tiptoe across barb wire." He claims the exaggerated exploits of Mystikal, sexual and otherwise, are "like television. It's entertainment. But there is a lot of reality inter-twined in it. I rap about what's going on around me. I absorb my envi-ronment. That keeps it interesting."

The Making of Liquid City DVD was shot on July 1, 2002. Two nights later, Tyler starred in a sex tape of much different nature. It would send him to prison.

From the outset of his career, Mystikal's tightly-wound braids were essential to his image. As his hair thinned and his hairline receded, they often protruded from beneath a skull cap.

For several years, a certain hairstylist was entrusted with the care of the braids. She was a member of Team Mystikal, orbiting alongside old friends, bodyguards and managers; years later, Tyler would de-scribe her as part of the "family."

But on the night of July 3, 2002, according to police and prosecu-tors, Tyler confronted the forty-year-old woman at a Baton Rouge apartment and accused her of pilfering thousands of dollars' worth of unauthorized checks from his account, a charge she denied. He allegedly offered to not report her to police if she performed "degrading" sexual acts with him and two bodyguards. She complied, then contacted police herself.

During the course of the investigation, a videotape surfaced; Tyler and his crew had filmed their encounter with the hairstylist, surely one of the most damning sex tapes in recent history. On July 18, they turned themselves in to Baton Rouge police. Tyler was charged with aggravated rape—which carries a mandatory life sentence—and extortion. He posted $250,000 bail and was released later that day.

In the coming weeks and months, as his attorneys jockeyed to keep him out of jail, he resumed his life and career. "I had a lot of trust in my lawyers. I believed the things they were telling me. So for the most part, I slept pretty good. But it always was lurking." In January 2003, his year-old *Tarantula* CD and the single "Bouncin' Back (Bumpin' Me Against the Wall)," a sparse, potent bit of stuttering hip-hop funk that evoked James Brown as a rapper, were nominated for Grammys.

But his newfound notoriety overshadowed such achievements. In an airport, an "older white guy" approached him with, "You look familiar."

"I thought, 'Uh-oh,'" Tyler recalled. "I said, 'It's either one of two things. Either you know me because I'm on TV regularly, I'm a musician, a rap artist. Or, I just kind of made the news as of late.' He said, 'That's it. You're the guy that got in trouble.'

"Of all the places he could know me from, why did that have to be that? I care what people think about me. People said, 'You gonna get street credibility.' I don't want that kind of street credibility. That's not fire to me. I don't want to be that kind of gangsta."

Legal restrictions prevent Tyler from discussing details of the incident, but he has always disputed elements of the prosecution's narrative, even as he cops to his overall culpability. "Did I make a horrible mistake? Was it stupid? Hell, yeah. But did I do what they said I did? I can't do it like that. But I put myself in that position to make it look like that. So I've got to take my lick. 'Cause I wasn't acting like Albert Einstein, and I didn't go to jail for praying too loud in church."

He accepts that the blame is his and his alone. "Where else do I have to look? You've got to be brutally honest with yourself. And that's where all the lessons come from. You've got to say, 'Of all the ways you could have handled a situation, that's the way you handled it? What's wrong with you?' You can't lie to yourself. I was the mastermind of the whole situation. One dumb-ass decision hurt a slew of people."

Ultimately, he was unwilling to go to trial on the aggravated rape charge and risk a life sentence if convicted. "I couldn't go play down that line and fight for my life," he said. "If I lose, the stakes are too high. I had to plead out."

On June 26, 2003, he pled guilty to extortion and sexual battery of the infirmed. Months later, state district Judge Anthony Marabella, after viewing the infamous videotape—much to the consternation of Tyler's defense attorney, who deemed the tape "inflammatory"—imposed a six-year sentence, and made clear he believed the rapper deserved more.

Looking back at his court appearances, Tyler is mortified by his own arrogance, which he blames on immaturity. "When it was time for me to go to court, I was looking in the camera, fixing my sideburns. If I had to do that over, I never would have done that. If I'd been looking at that, I'd be like, 'Look at this stupid m— f—. What are you doing?' Young, rich punk—I'm sure that's how those people looked at me. I made sure they did, acting a damn fool."

Marie Tyler recalled something Michael said shortly after Damion Neville was acquitted in Michelle's murder. "He figured that boy got off because they had money," Marie said. "I remember him saying, 'Just wait. I'm going to have some money one day.' To me it sounded like he was saying, 'I'm going to have money, and I can do something and I'm gonna be able to get away with it.' Maybe that gave him a frame of mind that you can do what you want and get away with it because you've got money.

"The Lord showed him that's not true. When we do wrong, we have to pay."

Tyler spent January 14, 2004, his last night of freedom, in a studio with KLC until four A.M. Following a court appearance hours later, he was taken into custody. Mystikal is one of three high-profile residents of Baton Rouge's exclusive Country Club of Louisiana to go to prison, along with former Louisiana governor Edwin Edwards and Corey "C-Murder" Miller, Master P's younger brother. Years earlier, Master

P had lectured his No Limit charges about avoiding trouble. "He tried to tell us, but we were arrogant punks, can't tell us nothing," Tyler said. "When I saw him [in June 2010], I had to tell him, 'I wish I had listened to some of what you told me. 'Cause it could have avoided me six years of agony.'"

Before being remanded to the Louisiana Department of Public Safety and Corrections, Tyler passed through various indoctrination and holding facilities, including the privately run Riverbend Detention Center in Lake Providence, Louisiana, and the Caldwell Parish Detention Center. Along the way he was placed on routine suicide watch. The process, he said, was akin to boot camp: guards in his face, laying down the law, emphasizing that any disrespect or misstep would be dealt with severely.

"They might as well have gave me a violin and a guitar, because they tried to blues me over there. That was my shock therapy. Had I given them a reason, they would have whupped the rapper. But I never gave them a reason to put their hands on me.

"They didn't know what my mind-set was. They had me prejudged—I guess they were listening to the Mystikal records. They thought I was gonna come through there as Mystikal. 'Man, Mystikal's not in here. This is Michael Tyler.' I went in there humble, with my mind right. I was thirty-three. I wasn't no child—I was a grown-ass man."

On March 8, 2004, he arrived at the Department of Correction's maximum-security Elayn Hunt Correctional Center, a 700-acre facility carved from farmland along two-lane Highway 74 in St. Gabriel. Situated near a bend in the Mississippi River ten miles south of Louisiana State University's Tiger Stadium, Hunt is Louisiana's second-largest prison, home to 2,100 male inmates. As part of the intake process, Tyler spent two weeks in the Hunt Reception and Diagnostic Center, undergoing medical and psychological examinations, plus mandatory training on sexually transmitted diseases and the Prison Rape Elimination Act.

His orientation complete, DOC Inmate No. 469659 cycled into the general prison population. Home was an un-air-conditioned dormitory that afforded absolutely no privacy. Four wings radiated from a central guard station. Each wing contained thirty-two beds lined up in two rows of sixteen. Showers and toilets at the far end of the open room were in full view of guards and other inmates.

His celebrity afforded no particular advantages or disadvantages, other than visits from the likes of basketball great and would-be rapper Shaquille O'Neal. Hunt's warden denied all requests for interviews with Tyler, based on the nature of his crime; as a DOC official explained, "You don't want the victim to pick up an article and have it look like the offender is being glorified in prison." Fans attempted to contact him through the prison's Web site; it was not unusual for the webmaster to open messages along the lines of "I'm trying to reach my cousin Mystikal," where the "cousin" did not know Tyler's real name or date of birth. Fan mail arrived almost daily. "The letters never stopped encouraging me and lifting me up and keeping me strong and sane," Tyler said. "It reminded me that I still had something to do."

All able-bodied Hunt inmates are assigned jobs; most start off in the prison's fields, earning "incentive wages" of two cents an hour (workers with seniority can make a maximum of twenty cents an hour). Tyler was no exception. He picked potatoes and tomatoes, dug holes, worked "every job they had," earning his way to "preferred" tasks. He especially liked the seasonal nature of grass-cutting; when the grass didn't grow in winter, he had time off. "They made me earn it. When they made me earn it, I respected it. I knew where I came from."

To pass the time, he "ate iron"—i.e. lifted weights. In his dorm's day room, he watched whatever TV show the majority chose; they listened through headphones plugged into jacks in the room's benches, so as not to disturb other inmates. He bought a CD player and music through the prison canteen, as well as extra snacks to share.

Before his conviction, Tyler had started seeing a woman named Tedra Sterling, who lived near the mother of one of his children. She was the sort of woman who demanded and deserved respect, unlike some of the adult entertainers, video extras and groupies with whom he previously consorted. Their relationship deepened while Tyler was in prison. He trusted her; they got engaged. She became his primary conduit to the outside world.

He was incarcerated at Hunt when Hurricane Katrina plowed into south Louisiana. Thirty relatives from New Orleans evacuated to his house in the Country Club of Louisiana; some, including his maternal grandmother, arrived in Baton Rouge after rain had already started to fall. Air mattresses covered every available floor space; neighbors supplied the evacuees with food and clothes. "That let Mike know he didn't have anything to worry about," Marie said. "We were well taken care of." Still, Tyler felt helpless and guilty. Other than providing a refuge for relatives in absentia, "all I could do was look. I'm more hands-on than that. I was supposed to be out there splashin' around in that pissy water with my people."

The storm knocked out power at Hunt; backup generators sustained basic operations for several days. "It wasn't like the situation in *Bad Lieutenant: Port of Call New Orleans*, where [inmates] are in the cell and the water is rising," Tyler said. "It just got a little warm. The [ventilation] that circulates all that stale-ass air, all that was out." Fellow inmates "weren't trippin'. Some of them dudes were in there for life. They ain't got nothing to lose: 'Lord, I knew you'd come get me sooner or later!' "

Inmates, many of whom had family in New Orleans, devoured news reports and peppered guards with questions. Normally, prisoners use designated phone lines routed through an automated system that, among other restrictions, only allows collect calls and does not dial cell phone numbers. After Katrina disabled that system, prison staffers spent days placing calls on regular landlines for inmates desperate to learn the fate of loved ones. Given the demand for the few functioning phones, conversations were limited. Tyler eventually reached Sterling and his mother. The parties on either end of the line were relieved to know the other was safe. "He was so happy to hear my voice," Marie said, "and I was happy to hear his voice. That was a joyous occasion."

Life at Hunt eventually returned to normal; Tyler would test his limits. "I wasn't perfect. I tried to get over when I could," he said. His most serious infraction was an attempted conjugal visit with his fiancée. As he would later explain, "I'm sorry, but I'm a man, that's my woman, she loves me, I love her, we're going for it."

Prison officials were not sympathetic to his unauthorized romantic gesture. On January 12, 2006, he was transferred to David Wade Correctional Center in Homer, Louisiana, far from his family and friends. Tucked away in the pine woods near Louisiana's northern border with

Arkansas, DWCC is home to 1,200 inmates. Now classified as a maximum security inmate, Tyler was housed in a "working cellblock"—a disciplinary cellblock whose residents are still allowed the "privilege" of a job.

The entry-level job at DWCC is a tough one: Cutting grass and clearing underbrush on 1,500 acres with a hoe and sling blade. After six months, he earned a downgrade to medium custody and a bed in a seventy-nine-man dormitory; like the dorms at Hunt, all personal business is conducted in full view of guards and fellow inmates. He also landed a better job as an orderly—in other words, a janitor. For the next three-plus years, he cleaned toilets, emptied trash cans, and swept and mopped floors in administration buildings.

After his misstep at Hunt, Tyler was determined to abide by the rules at DWCC. A year without any disciplinary write-ups, coupled with his participation in sex offender therapy and other self-help and educational programs, qualified him for DWCC's honor inmate program, or HIP. HIP membership has its privileges: a later curfew, an extra hour of visitation, more phone time, a higher spending limit at the prison canteen. When inmate organizations held fundraisers for the American Heart Association, Sickle Cell Anemia Foundation, American Red Cross and other charities, Tyler typically donated a few hundred bucks anonymously. "He never wanted his name attached to it," said DWCC Warden Jerry Goodwin. "He never took any credit for it."

He still received a steady supply of fan mail, even after years of exile from the pop charts. His celebrity "may have helped him a little with the inmates," Goodwin said. "They might have looked at him a little differently. But it didn't help him with the staff at all. He had to earn everything he got."

Within the prison environment, he found small pleasures. He looked forward to the pork chops supplied by the prison's swine farm, and treated himself to Levis' jeans and $100 Timberland boots from the canteen. "I used to buy them like potato chips. If I got one scuff, I got to buy some more. I did that because it made me feel better. I'm in here, but at least I kept myself up. I can't walk around with dirty shoes." Unable to vote in the 2008 Presidential election, he nonetheless cheered on Barack Obama, whom he credits with fostering his nascent interest in politics.

Few visitors found their way north to Homer; Tyler's mother didn't see him at all during his four years at David Wade. "He said I didn't need to take that long a ride, which I would have been willing to," Marie said. "For some reason, he didn't want me to." They stayed connected through letters and phone calls, but she found the physical separation extremely difficult. Still, "there's always something good in everything," Marie said. "We felt God placed him there [in prison] for a reason. God was taking him out of an element that he needed to be out of for a while. If he had been out in that element, anything could have happened."

Incarceration severely curtailed Tyler's earnings. The tab for his conviction—legal fees, court costs, restitution, etc.—drained a six-figure sum from his bank account. His old recordings still generated some royalties; he assigned power-of-attorney to his mother so she could apply his royalty checks to household expenses. But it was not enough. After her son went off to prison, Marie went back to work. She took a job at a Baton Rouge Winn-Dixie "just to keep our heads above water."

More financial difficulties lay ahead. In the summer of 2005, the federal government charged him with two misdemeanor counts of failing to file federal tax returns on a total of $1.7 million he earned from 1998 to 1999. "I didn't have malicious intentions," Tyler said. "It was pure, unadulterated inexperience, uncut, raw stupidity. I left it up to other people, but that was on me."

He pled guilty in January 2006, and was allowed to serve his year-long federal sentence concurrently with his state sentence. To cover his delinquent tax bill, he instructed his mother to sell their house in the Country Club of Louisiana. Marie also sold the family's old home on Delachaise Street in New Orleans; with the proceeds, she bought a modest house in a Baton Rouge subdivision not far from the Country Club.

Tyler did not believe he would serve his full six-year sentence; he expected to be paroled as soon as he was eligible, in early 2006. When he wasn't, he pinned his hopes on his next parole hearing two years later. Confident about his chances, he arranged the purchase of a silver 2007 Land Rover, so he could drive away from prison in style. But he was again denied.

In hindsight, the possibility of parole at least broke up his six-year sentence into more palatable two-year increments. "Had I known that I was going to have to do the whole six-piece chicken, without no French fries or nothing to drink, that would have been a little mentally tough to digest. By the time I really adjusted [to prison], nine months had passed. So I just got a little bit and a year. Then you're denied. So now I'm waiting for two more years. I'm like, 'OK, I've seen this on TV. They deny the man the first time, the second time, if he's still doing good, they gonna let him out. It's kind of like automatic.' I was really banking on that. I had achieved every certificate I could pile up. Can't nobody tell me nothing; I was focused. The man said, 'Keep up the excellent work. You are doing great. Your outlook is right where it needs to be. But we got to deny you.'"

Tyler's sentence, at least, was finite. Unlike the lifers he befriended, he would get another shot, a chance to rebuild his life and career. And prison wasn't as bad as a war zone. "I went to Iraq. I'm a combat veteran. Just from a sanity perspective, [prison] was like day camp. But it turned into the Twilight Zone. It was like living the same day over and over, like *Groundhog Day*. The thing that helped me the most was the reality that this could be worse. I could be dead, or blind, or HIV positive—there's a lot of ugly things that life can throw at you. 'Lord I'm in jail. This ain't no pretty situation, and it's not no walk in the park, 'cause I'm not gonna go home tomorrow, or tomorrow, or tomorrow. But thank you, Lord. I'll take it.' The time could be far longer. I could have got ten years. I could have got mandatory life."

Some inmates who are denied parole drop the good-behavior facade. Not so Tyler. "It didn't have a big negative impact on him," said Warden Goodwin. "He kept doing the positive things he was doing."

During his four years at DWCC, Tyler was a model prisoner, Goodwin says. "We never had a minute's problem out of him. It was pretty obvious he was brought up in a respectful environment. He obviously had a good raising. He'd been taught right from wrong. He always seemed to have a good attitude. He did everything he was supposed to do. He was very respectful toward staff. He knew how to behave and how to follow rules. If all the inmates behaved like he did, then prison would be an easy place to work."

Tyler served every day of his six-year sentence. When his discharge day finally arrived, Warden Goodwin wished him well and sent him off with a piece of advice: "Be careful who you hang around with and who you pick for your friends and associates. You're obviously capable of staying out of prison on your own. Just don't get caught up with the wrong crowd and you'll do fine."

At 12:01 A.M. on January 14, 2010, Michael Tyler walked out of David Wade Correctional Center. His girlfriend was waiting to drive him home to Baton Rouge. From the road, he called Wild Wayne, a friend and popular deejay on New Orleans urban contemporary radio station WQUE-FM. "I'm still trying to feel this reality," Tyler said of newfound freedom. "I was gone so long, all the things I achieved felt like a dream, like I had never done that stuff."

Given the ever-growing list of incarcerated hip-hop stars, Wayne asked if rappers are unfairly targeted for prosecution. "That's an easy excuse, but we've got to take responsibility for what we do, too," Tyler said. "We've got to pay more attention to what we're doing ourselves. We can't be fools, especially when you're blessed and successful beyond your dreams. We've got to tighten up."

In Baton Rouge, Tyler was reunited with his joyful mother. "Oh my gosh, that was a happy moment," Marie said. "I might have gotten a little teary-eyed, I was so happy." Per her son's request, she prepared fried pork chops, macaroni and cheese, and stuffed bell peppers, a variation on his post–Desert Storm homecoming meal, which featured peas in place of bell peppers.

Michael going to prison "was like we were in a season, and that season had to pass," Marie said. "I thank God it's passed. I'm sure he's learned from what he did. It shouldn't have happened, but it did. When he was going off, I wasn't sad, nor was he. We were going to miss each other, but we felt something good was going to happen from that. Which it did. It looks like it made him stronger, and made him see things clearer. And I really have to believe that it was a learning experience for him.

"I just hope he continues to think right. Just do what's right, son. And stay humble."

In 2010, Tyler faced the daunting task of reentering a music industry he barely recognized. Sales of CDs had cratered, with digital music stores making up only some of the difference. Record labels had slashed budgets and staff. Social media—YouTube, MySpace, Facebook, Twitter—was now an essential marketing tool. "Most artists would not be able to sustain a blow like I took," Tyler told Wild Wayne. "Six years off the scene, for most rappers, it would be over with. It's going to be the beginning for me."

Legal restrictions would hamper his comeback. He must receive permission from his probation officers before traveling outside the Baton Rouge area. "I'm out, but you ain't all the way out," he told me seven months after his release. "You can't violate. You want to be cool. You want to avoid trouble at all costs. It's manageable. That's why I say the system worked for me, because now I don't have a choice—I have to be smart. Had they let me out and just took the leash off and said, 'Go get it!,' I would have f— something up somewhere."

To the Ascension Parish sheriff's office, "Mystikal" is nothing more than an alias of Michael Lawrence Tyler, registered sex offender. Such a stigma is not easily overcome. "Being a sex offender is almost worse than being a murderer," Tyler said. "Out of all the things that I could have allowed to happen to me, 'sex offender' is not a real good fraternity to be in. It sounds like a [man] with the van, and the curtains. However your vision of a sex offender looks, that's how people portray you.

"I'm past it, but I still have to live with it every day . . . for life. It's routine now. It's a technicality I have to go through. People have to get government assistance and dialysis . . . I got to go register." Regardless, he plans "to lead a successful, happy, strong life. Love my kids, being loved by my kids, and my fans. I can't let nothing like that stop me."

Leaving prison, he was reminded of a 1988 Keenan Ivory Wayans movie. "You got to wonder, 'Am I going to look like the guy in *I'm Gonna Git You Sucka* that came out of prison with the fish-tank shoes and the big pimp hat?' That's how it was before he left; now people were laughing at him. Do I look like that? Please don't let me look like that."

Eight months after his release, he turned forty. He had a message for the cadre of much younger rappers who were now his competition. "All you nineteen-, twenty-year-old whippersnappers, ya'll ain't ready. You gonna have trouble with me. I'm starting back from thirty-three."

He's encouraged that his old music still resonates. "Bouncin' Back" turned up in the premiere episode of *Treme*. And fans have responded enthusiastically to his live appearances. "You can imagine how humbled I was to come home and see people with their hands in the air after six years, still waiting on me. A lot of the younger kids don't know who I am, but a lot of them do, because it has been passed on."

Tyler returned to the stage a month after his release. On February 12, he substituted for a snowbound En Vogue at the annual Carnival ball hosted by Zulu, New Orleans' long-running, historically black Mardi Gras organization. Three nights later, he showcased at a nightclub in Lafayette, Louisiana, two hours west of New Orleans. On February 16, he headlined a poorly promoted, planned and produced Mardi Gras night concert at New Orleans' Mahalia Jackson Theater for the Performing Arts.

Barely five hundred of the theater's 2,200 seats were occupied. After a procession of New Orleans rappers from the 1990s—Mia X, Fiend, the Ghetto Twiinz, DJ Jubilee—Mystikal kicked off his no-frills, thirty-minute set by jumping offstage to embrace his mother in the front row. With his platinum jewelry sparkling against his black knit cap and purple shirt, he was backed by a deejay and two hype men, one of whom was his younger brother Maurice. As if no time had elapsed, he spit lines over prerecorded tracks, whipping through truncated hits: "U Would If U Could," "Here I Go," "Ya'll Ain't Ready Yet"—complete with "Thriller"-esque dance steps— "Tarantula," "I Smell Smoke," "Move Bitch," "Bouncin' Back," "Danger (Been So Long)," "Shake Ya Ass." Addressing other rappers, he declared the "competition just got stiff." The show, he promised, was "just the beginning." Perhaps "Bouncin' Back" contained the night's most apropos lyric: "Sometimes you gotta get knocked down to get up."

Following the anticlimactic Mardi Gras concert, his comeback picked up steam. On May 2, he made a surprise appearance with popular funk/jazz/rock bandleader Troy "Trombone Shorty" Andrews on the Gentilly Stage at the 2010 New Orleans Jazz Fest. In June in New York, he electrified the audience during the *VH1 Hip-Hop Honors* salute to "Master P" Miller.

Realizing that prerecorded music would not suffice for young audiences weaned on rock—and in keeping with the recent example set by Jay-Z and Eminem—he recruited musicians for a live band that included a horn section. In August, he sold out the 850-capacity New

Orleans House of Blues for his first performance fronting that band. In November, he and the band headlined a Thanksgiving night concert at the Dallas House of Blues following the Saints' victory over the Cowboys.

Before Lil Wayne entered New York's Rikers Island on a gun charge in early 2010, he recorded a backlog of music and videos. During his eight months of lockdown, his team released the material on a carefully managed schedule meant to preserve his profile on the pop landscape. As a result, Wayne exited prison in November 2010 as much of a star as when he went in.

Given Tyler's much longer sentence, orchestrating a similar style of career life support was not feasible. In August 2004, seven months after he went to prison, Jive Records assembled a Mystikal best-of collection, *Prince of the South . . . The Hits*; the album's two previously unreleased cuts was the last new music fans had heard. He still owed another studio album to Jive, but resolved to take his time. He and his team realized the all-important post-prison comeback, his first full album of new material in a decade, would largely determine whether or not he still had a career. "I'm not just jumping back in," he said. "I'm doing it double Dutch. You've got to take your time and be strategic. Professionally, I have to put my thinking cap on."

Producer KLC had mailed a CD of beats to Tyler in prison, but the demands of day-to-day life behind bars left little time or energy for creativity. He managed to write several songs at Elayn Hunt; he kept a folder of lyrics close by. But in the rush of his transfer to David Wade, he mistakenly included the lyrics with other mail; the folder never arrived at his house.

Over the years, KLC had stockpiled beats with Tyler in mind. But once they were finally reunited at KLC's compact Baton Rouge studio, they focused on fresh material. One beat originated with the distorted kick drum in a YouTube clip of Tyler performing "Bouncin' Back" at the Zulu Ball. "Whoever had the camera was standing close to the speakers," KLC said. "It was muffled. That inspired me."

Based on the half-dozen new songs screened for me in the summer of 2010, six years of lockdown did not diminish Tyler's confidence or the velocity of his flow. If anything, he compresses even more words into a measure. KLC's tracks are, for lack of a better term, especially musical—and not just the one on which Troy "Trombone Shorty"

Andrews guests. They are meticulously assembled, densely arranged sonic workouts steeped in funk.

Lyrically, Mystikal is as graphic as ever. The nature of his legal woes did not prompt him to tone down his outlandish sexual boasts. But he insists he is better able to separate Mystikal, the outrageous rapper, from Michael Tyler, the flawed but well-meaning man. "I'm drawing on everything I experienced from the last eight years, and what I see in the years to come. The true source is God. As he gives it to me, I give it to ya'll. Excuse the curse words, Lord."

Soon after his release, Tedra Sterling, his fiancée, became pregnant; in October 2010, Sterling gave birth to their daughter. Tyler says he wants to be an active, involved father, and rebuild his bond with his daughter and son from previous relationships.

His mother, having lost one child permanently to violence and another, temporarily, to prison, "constantly" prays for his well-being. "I pray that the Lord keeps him out of harm's way, and that the Lord enables him to reach all his endeavors. Because Michael is a good guy. I'm proud of him."

Heeding the DWCC warden's advice, Tyler surrounds himself with a clean-cut, low-key crew stocked with friends from years ago. He and KLC were high school breakdance rivals. Robert Shaw, Tyler's beefy, soft-spoken manager, co-founded Big Boy Records, signed Tyler to the label in the mid-1990s, and has worked with him off and on ever since. "Bees don't hang with flies," Tyler said. "You've got to be around people that have your best interests at heart. Fortunately I have something to fall back on. I have talent and charisma and I'm smart and I believe in God and I've got people that really, truly love me. Who will not tell me what I want to hear, but what I need to hear."

As with any convicted felon, Tyler's margin for error is slim. But he says he is committed to playing by the new rules—as both Michael Tyler and Mystikal. "I'm not exempt from being human. In regular, normal, every day life, I'm gonna make mistakes—regular, man mistakes. But certain areas, I can't [screw] up. And I'm not."

Along the way, he hopes to rehabilitate his image. "Now, looking back at it, everything went the way it was supposed to go, so I could be the man sitting here. I'm much more usable to God. I'm a smarter man, a better son, and am going to be a better husband and father. I'm all those things because of all that I went through." Prison, he insists, "was worth it. It was destiny. The proof is gonna be in the pudding. I plan to lead a successful, happy, strong life.

"What do you want me to do? Go crumple in the corner? I'm not going to do that. So those who are in opposition of me being out here, I'm sorry, I'm out here. And you got me wrong. You'll see."

Chapter Ten

To Hell and Back with Phil Anselmo

Pity Phil Anselmo's mother. A petite, strawberry blonde grade school regis-
trar, she has expended more than her fair share of worry, grief and mortifi-
cation over her rock star son's antics.

He once concluded a Pantera concert at New Orleans' State Palace The-
ater by suggesting, in pornographic terms, how male and female fans should,
shall we say, express affection for one another. His mother, seated in a bal-
cony box, pursed her lips and shook her head in a manner that said, "Oh,
Philip."

But she loved and supported him as best she could through some hard
times. The blackest night fell in December 2004, when guitarist Darrell
"Dimebag" Abbott, his former Pantera bandmate, was shot and killed
onstage by a deranged fan.

I had interviewed Anselmo frequently over the years, and always liked
him; he reminded me of my brother Craig, who sang in a punk band called
Flagrantz. But when I reached Anselmo on the phone soon after Abbott's
death, he was in a very bad place. That was the last I heard from him for a
long time.

Eighteen months later, I encountered a much different Anselmo back-
stage at Tipitina's. After major surgery on his back, he had finally ditched
the pain pills that ruled his life and rejoined the world of the living. He
spotted me and growled, "I'm seeing you for the first time with both eyes
open."

They've been open ever since.

It's a terrible thing when your spine betrays you, especially with so much riding on it.

As the mouthpiece for ultrahard rock band Pantera, Philip H. "Phil" Anselmo sold millions of albums and filled arenas around the globe. "Punishing" and "brutal" do not adequately describe Pantera's attack. Anselmo's voice was a hard-core howl from the abyss, riding atop the "power groove"—buzzsaw guitars grafted to a fat, rhythmic undercurrent—generated by his bandmates.

Except for a brief, unhappy, late-1980s stint in Dallas after he first joined Pantera, he has lived in and around his native New Orleans. With his first influx of cash, he bought a raised-basement home in New Orleans' middle-class Lakeview neighborhood. His was the only swimming pool in the vicinity inlaid with a pentagram.

In 1998, Anselmo purchased a second home across Lake Pontchartrain from New Orleans on seventeen wooded acres, with two white-sand beaches on a slow-moving branch of a brown-green river. The house is hidden in a bucolic swath of woods in rural St. Tammany Parish, past Baptist churches and fields studded with cattle and bales of hay. Just off a two-lane highway and beyond a gate with no address, its long gravel driveway snakes among pine trees and azalea bushes laden with pink flowers.

He moved to the country in part to escape the booming bass of car stereos and drunken fans' late-night knocks on his door. But he also sought to create a world of his own, where he could party and work as he pleased.

To that end, he modified his new lair to reflect his fascination with the dark side. The previous owners, a retired doctor and his wife, did not paint the foyer black with bloodred trim, as Anselmo did. They did not cover the den walls with posters for *The Evil Dead*, *The Thing* and other B-grade horror films. They did not post a truly disturbing blow-up of Linda Blair's face, in full *Exorcist* demonic possession mode, alongside the toilet in an upstairs bathroom. Nor did they hide life-size rubber monsters and demons throughout the surrounding woods, the better to spook unsuspecting friends and neighbors.

And they certainly did not anticipate the unholy racket that would one day emanate from the tractor barn a few paces from the main house. Anselmo converted the barn into a recording studio and headquarters for his independent Housecore Records. The soundproofing layer of sand beneath the floor did not always prevent bass vibrations from rumbling through the woods and rattling neighbors' nerves.

His success, however, could not save him from the beast on, and in, his back. In fact, success provoked it.

After years of thrashing around onstage, he suffered from three blown discs. He self-medicated with a murderer's row of pharmaceuticals: Heroin. Methadone. The muscle relaxant Soma. The pain killer OxyContin. Needles. Pills. And oceans of alcohol.

His substance abuse was partly related to the culture of excess cultivated by hard rock in general and Pantera specifically. There is much competition for the title of hardest-drinking band in hard rock, but Pantera, proudly, was a contender. Its members' specialty was the "Black Tooth," a lights-out serving of whiskey and Coke.

For years, Anselmo's spine felt like it was devouring itself. His torment stemmed from deep within, dragging him down into isolation and chemical dependency. "Not everybody can crawl out of that particular cellar," he said in the fall of 2010.

He found a way.

Phil Anselmo was born in 1968. His mother, Michelle Robards, was nineteen at the time. She and Phil's father soon divorced. Robards remarried when her son was five. The young Phil bristled under the authority of his stepfather during a turbulent early adolescence. "Since he was very little," Robards recalled, "it's always been 'me against the world.'"

Heavy metal offered an escape. The walls of his bedroom were decorated with Ozzy Osbourne and Kiss posters. In grade school, he declared that one day his face would adorn such posters.

As a student at Grace King High School in the mid-1980s, he joined a local heavy metal band called Razor White. Decked out in the spandex stage clothes and puffy hair of '80s "hair metal," Razor White intermingled Judas Priest covers with original material. Much to his mother's chagrin, Phil quit school during his senior year to focus on music.

In 1987, he auditioned for a Dallas-area band called Pantera. Pantera also hailed from the falsetto-and-fluffy hair school of heavy metal, and had already released three independent albums. Anselmo got the job, moved to Dallas—enemy territory for a committed New Orleans Saints fan—and made his recorded debut on Pantera's fourth indie album, *Power Metal*. He rocked a cascade of teased, two-tone hair, in all its glam rock glory.

But by the time Pantera made its major-label debut with 1990's *Cowboys From Hell*, the musicians and their music had transformed. The flashy stage clothes and teased hair were gone. Anselmo sported a shaved head, sleeveless flannel shirts, tattoos, an alpha-male posture, and a permanent scowl. He replaced his falsetto with a guttural, confrontational bellow even as his three bandmates—drummer Vinnie Paul Abbott, his guitarist brother Darrell "Dimebag" Abbott, and bassist Rex Brown—chiseled harder, heavier and faster grooves.

Cowboys From Hell caught on with metal fans in search of something authentic and uncompromising. A string of million-selling albums followed, even as the mainstream media and MTV ignored Pantera and detractors dismissed them as ugly music for ugly people. Thus, much of the music industry was shocked when the band's *Far Beyond Driven* debuted at No. 1 on the *Billboard* 200 album chart in 1994.

In full arenas, Anselmo lorded over a brotherhood of the damned. They proudly, fiercely pledged allegiance to a singer who, with his hacked-off shorts stitched with punk-rock patches, sleeveless T-shirts, wallet chain and sneakers that might have been snatched from a homeless person, looked like them. Chin thrust forward, lower lip protruding, he nodded in approval as Pantera's legions teetered on the brink of mayhem. "Unscarred" was tattooed across his stomach, "Strength" on the side of his skull.

For all his hard-rock cred, Anselmo did not come up through the ranks of the New Orleans metal underground, a distinct musical subculture characterized by sludgy, doomsday guitar riffs. Like more traditional genres of New Orleans music, its practitioners—Crowbar, Eyehategod, Soilent Green, Goatwhore, Exhorder—are often celebrated more enthusiastically elsewhere than at home.

Razor White had been a more conventional hair band, and Pantera was based in Texas. But once established as the most successful hard-rock vocalist to ever bust out of New Orleans, he emerged as the local metal community's primary patron. He recruited locals for such side projects as Down (a sludgier Pantera) and Superjoint Ritual (a faster, thrashier Pantera). He funded the House of Shock, an elaborate—some would say blasphemous—haunted house staffed in part by musicians (he has since disassociated himself). He founded Housecore Records to release music by likeminded bands. Those bands often recorded in Nodferatu's Lair, the barn studio on his property (the name is a play on classic horror film vampire Nosferatu, altered to reflect certain musicians' tendency to nod off). Musicians in need of a place to stay crashed on his property; Mike Williams, the singer from Eyehategod and the Anselmo side project Arson Anthem, moved in after Katrina.

Between Pantera projects, Anselmo cultivated an extreme music cottage industry in the woods of rural south Louisiana. Fans sensed he was genuine, as tormented a soul as he purported to be. The lyrics to the likes of "Good Friends and a Bottle of Pills" made clear he was no choirboy.

The fleur de lis on his right calf spoke to his fierce loyalty to the New Orleans Saints. But the frightening tableau of tattoos on his arms came from a much darker place.

On July 11, 1996, Pantera shared a bill with White Zombie at the University of New Orleans Lakefront Arena. Anselmo was under the weather, but would not miss his first chance to co-headline his hometown arena. Backstage after the show, amidst a crush of friends and fans, Anselmo's mother chased after him, as mothers often do: "Philip, did you take the aspirin?" Exasperated, as sons often are, he assured her he would.

Two nights later, following a gig at the Coca-Cola StarPlex amphitheater in Dallas, Anselmo took something far stronger than aspirin. He injected heroin, overdosed, and went into cardiac arrest. His skin turned so blue that his tattoos were barely visible. "I thought, 'Well, that's the end of the tour,'" recalled Chris Kansy, a member of the road crew who helped load the singer into an ambulance.

But Anselmo is nothing if not a survivor. In San Antonio a day later, he convened a meeting of the band and crew, apologized for jeopardizing everyone's jobs, and promised it wouldn't happen again. He released a statement that admitted his mistake but denied he was an addict. The tour continued uninterrupted.

The Dallas incident reportedly shocked his bandmates. From that point forward, Anselmo said, they were less likely to give him the benefit of the doubt as he sought to dull the source of ever more excruciating pain: his lower spine. "They saw me overdose on heroin and die. Back pain, no back pain, painkillers—once you overdose on heroin, there's no excuse anymore. All they see is a drug problem."

Onstage, he banged his head, genuflected at the waist, crashed and thrashed around. Over the years, accumulated damage took its toll. He blew out a disc in his back, destroying the cartilage around it; bone scraped on bone. He toured more, destroyed more cartilage. Another disc blew.

The end result was degenerative disc disease. "Once one disc goes, infection creeps in and creeps upward," Anselmo said. "The next disc went. That cartilage went. And then my next disc went. I can't think of a more horrific thing than your spine slowly crumbling upwards. I felt helpless."

He consulted with multiple doctors, but the surgical solutions he was offered in the 1990s were "barbaric. They wanted to cut me from the front, move my organs out of me and lay them aside, cut through all my stomach muscles. My doctor now tells me, 'Phil, if you had that surgery in the nineties, you'd be a ruined man.'"

Pink Floyd's classic "Comfortably Numb" describes a rock star whose handlers prop him up with drugs ("it's just a little pinprick . . . that'll keep you going for the show"). Though not familiar with the song, Anselmo lived it. Fearful of surgery, and pressured by those who profited off Pantera, he opted to self-medicate and keep on touring. Ticket demand was at an all-time high. Millions of dollars awaited on the road, along with mass infusions of ego gratification and the opportunity to indulge his various appetites.

"You're dealing with chronic pain that feels like you got chopped in half by machine-gun fire and they're telling you, 'Get out on stage, boy, and earn your bread. You got the number one record across the world—the U.K., Japan, Australia.'

"What am I supposed to do? *Not* take the pain killers, *don't* do the gigs, go get this barbaric surgery? I took the pills. I got onstage f— up.

There was no time for me to say, 'Fellas, I need to step back. I can't do this touring stuff anymore.' I'm in my prime, our band is never going to get bigger—I had to do the shows. I had to. Which only compounded things and led to more broken bones, more pain."

The "Evel Knievel of heavy metal" pressed on, resorting to ever-more extreme measures and becoming increasingly erratic and unfocused onstage. He injected the painkillers OxyContin and Dilaudid—and even whiskey. His post-overdose statement to the contrary, he also binged on heroin, a drug he describes as "definable evil."

However, he blames his infamous tendency to zone out on the muscle relaxant Carisoprodol, better known by the brand name Soma. "That is a drug that should, in my opinion, be yanked from the shelves. It is so much more hard-core than people give it credit for. People who pop pills and have parties, they love the Soma. They call it the Soma coma. You don't know what you're doing or how many you took or what happened and why.

"A lot of times when people would see me nodding off, they would go, 'He's on heroin. Absolutely it's heroin.' No it wasn't. Not that I didn't do heroin—I did plenty. But nine times out of ten, it would be the Soma. Matter of fact, ten times out of ten it would be the Soma."

The video for "Mouth for War," the first single from Pantera's 1992 album *Vulgar Display of Power*, captured Anselmo in his prime. Shot mostly in black and white, the clip spotlights individual bandmembers as they rage through the song. Anselmo, his head shaved, is shirtless, his neck and shoulder muscles straining with effort as he howls about channeling hate into productive action. At one point, he smashes a cinder block with a sledgehammer. The words "strength, revenge, determination, success" flash by; the singer, at that point, personified them.

Fast forward nine years to Halloween 2001. At midnight, he married girlfriend Stephanie "Opal" Weinstein in front of a roaring bonfire. He was trussed up in black leather bondage gear, complete with studded choker and sleeves. In photos, his hair is in long braids, his skin deathly pale, his cheeks sunken, his eyes weak. That he even consented to get married at all, he would say years later, demonstrates "the erosion of will drugs will bring you to."

In one of the most bizarre interviews of my career, I witnessed

Anselmo fading in and out of a "Soma coma." One night in the summer of 2002, I met him at his house in the woods. Before we talked, he wanted to go on a "short" bicycle ride with Weinstein and another friend. "We'll be right back," he promised.

Wearing his standard-issue fatigue cutoffs, sleeveless mechanic's shirt and worn tennis shoes, he pedaled off on an old-fashioned bicycle with wide fenders and fat tires, rattling down the gravel driveway and disappearing into the night.

An hour later, there was still no sign of him. As I waited outside the property's barn studio with a photographer from *The Times-Picayune*, a chorus of crickets and frogs serenaded us. Anselmo finally reappeared, stumbling along the path from the house. "How long have you been waiting?" he asked woozily.

He apologized, explaining that after the bike ride a succession of phone calls demanded his attention. But something was amiss. After leading us into the studio, he sat down in front of a drum kit. During the subsequent conversation, he couldn't keep his eyes open. More than once, he nodded off, a lit cigarette suspended between his fingers, only to come to and resume speaking.

He did not look like a drug addict. He was robust, with rippled arms and clear eyes. He blamed his grogginess on a themed, late-night photo session in which Stephanie and her friend were costumed as naughty nuns. "By the time we went to sleep it was about five A.M.," he said. "Then at ten A.M. the phone started ringing. That's how it's been. Some people may say it's not work, but they have not walked an inch in my shoes. These days people want some of my time all the time."

The words flowed out slowly, deliberately, as if his already deep voice were a 45-rpm record slowed down to 33⅓ speed. I resisted the urge to shake him out of his stupor. Days later, Down guitarist Pepper Keenan suggested pain pills were the culprit, back pain the root cause. "He should try and get this surgery soon, but the record company and everybody puts pressure on him to keep going," Keenan said. "He's been avoiding this for years."

He would continue to avoid it. That summer, Anselmo spent three weeks on the road with Superjoint Ritual, followed by two months with Down on OzzFest, Ozzy Osbourne's traveling hard-rock festival. Exercising his back and stomach muscles provided some relief. When that failed, he turned to Soma. "He hates taking them," Keenan said. "The way those damn things work is if you take one, you're fine. If you take two, you're out. Once you swallow the thing, that's it. They hit you like a ton of bricks."

Somewhere along the way, Anselmo also developed a dependency on methadone, a synthetic opioid used to treat chronic pain and to wean addicts from heroin and other narcotics.

Kurt Cobain, the troubled genius of grunge heavyweight Nirvana, was bedeviled by chronic stomach pain; drugs, legal and otherwise, did not help. Cobain's story ended badly, with a shotgun.

Anselmo, too, was on the road to oblivion, injesting Soma and/or methadone and/or injecting whatever, indiscriminately. That, he observed years later, "is suicide. How many movies do people say, 'I'm going to commit suicide' and they take a whole bottle of pills? In those years, I could have starred in every one and gotten an Academy Award.

"That got old not quick enough."

Of the major milestones in Phil Anselmo's life, joining Pantera was certainly one. So was meeting Kate Richardson.

Their paths first crossed around 2003 during a Down tour stop in Grand Rapids, Michigan. A communications major at Grand Valley State University, Richardson was also a metal fan who ran the college radio station and wrote concert and album reviews.

The New Orleans underground metal scene was of particular interest to her; she had befriended Eyehategod's Jimmy Bower and Crowbar's Kirk Windstein when they passed through Michigan on tour. Bower and Windstein were also members of Down. When Down came to town, Richardson paid a visit to her buddies, who introduced her to Anselmo.

At the time, Anselmo's mutually destructive marriage was disintegrating. He fell for Richardson immediately. She wasn't the stereotypical "metal chick." The fresh-faced co-ed appeared even younger than her years. She wore little makeup, preferred T-shirts to more revealing attire and generally sported long, braided ponytails. At a relatively young age, she had already grappled with family tragedy. "For lack of better words, she had experience in dealing with real-life stuff," Anselmo said. "I don't know of a more even-tempered, strong, strong, strong-willed person. I saw it the first time I met her."

At first, their relationship was professional: Anselmo hired her as his personal assistant for a Superjoint Ritual tour. "I was qualified for the job," Richardson said, "and everybody trusted me." Later, she would manage a Down tour. That she was a positive influence on the singer was not lost on his bandmates. "Whenever I'd come around, Philip would be more bright-eyed and straight," she said. "So they're like, 'Yes, bring Kate around.'"

By 2004, Anselmo was divorced and he and Richardson were a couple. "As cliché or even borderline cheesy as it may sound, I think I damn well fell in love with her the first time I met her," he said. "She came into my life and caught the tail end of the worst part of Philip. She laid down the line: Me or the drugs, Jack. I chose her, in good faith. And it's paid off, it really has."

She took on stewardship of Housecore Records and turned it into a functioning label. She organized the singer's affairs, and introduced him to e-mail. In perhaps the best possible endorsement, Anselmo's ever-protective mother approved.

Richardson, Anselmo says, is the reason he gave up needles. "She wasn't going to have any needles around her. There was one time where she walked into something ugly. It only took that once for me to say, 'OK, you're right. F— this s—. Let me walk toward love.'"

There were still many more hard miles ahead.

In 2003, the estranged members of Pantera had officially announced the band's dissolution. Anselmo exchanged insults and accusations in the heavy metal press with brothers Vinnie Paul and Darrell "Dimebag" Abbott, Pantera's drummer and guitarist, respectively. The feud was bitter and protracted.

Meanwhile, Anselmo's substance abuse continued to take a toll. Onstage with Down or Superjoint Ritual, he mumbled lyrics or skipped entire passages. He made bellicose, ugly statements, professing a bond with fans even as his stumbling, bumbling performances disrespected it. By 2004, Superjoint Ritual had disbanded, Down was inactive, and Anselmo was increasingly isolated.

And then the unthinkable happened.

On December 8, 2004, a twenty-five-year-old ex-Marine armed with a handgun stormed the stage during a performance by Damageplan—Darrell and Vinnie Abbott's new, post-Pantera band—in Columbus, Ohio. The gunman shot and killed Darrell and three other people before he was cut down by a police officer responding to 911 calls.

The music industry, especially the hard-rock community, was shocked. Some speculated that the killer blamed Darrell for Pantera's demise, and that Anselmo's derogatory comments about his former bandmates may have factored into the shooting.

Days after Abbott's killing, a distraught Anselmo released a home-made video in which he accused the "heavy metal media" of destroying Pantera. He lamented that he "never got a chance to say good-bye [to Abbott] in the right way and it kills me, and I'm so sorry."

He traveled to Dallas in the hopes of attending Abbott's funeral, but was not welcome. "I believe I belong there," he said later, "but I understand completely. I wish his family the least grief they could ever have, and I know it's impossible. Just bless his family, bless his friends. I love him like a brother loves a brother . . . I'm so sorry to his family and everyone else who was senselessly killed in Columbus, Ohio."

His statement concluded with an ominous line about his own uncertain future: "This has changed the entire world, and this is the last you'll be seeing of me for a long time." True to his word, he spent the next several months in seclusion.

But instead of sinking deeper into the abyss, he began to claw his way out, right through Hurricane Katrina.

By August 26, 2005, Phil Anselmo was likely the only person in south Louisiana unaware of the approaching storm. Days earlier, Richardson had borrowed his pickup truck to retrieve her belongings from storage in Detroit. Left alone on a Friday, he decided to commute the forty-five minutes to New Orleans and party with friends.

The only vehicle at his disposal was a restored, vintage Checker cab—tricked out with the skull logo of horror-punk band the Misfits—that once belonged to a relative. After crossing the twenty-four-mile-long Causeway bridge over Lake Pontchartrain, the cab overheated and stalled on Interstate 10. He coaxed it back to life, only for it to peter out as he approached his house in Lakeview. He coasted into the driveway; the cab was dead.

That evening, his mother was going to the Saints' preseason game against the Baltimore Ravens at the Superdome, so he borrowed her car. His attempts to round up friends proved unsuccessful; most were likely nervously watching the news, or already evacuating.

Anselmo still hadn't grasped that a powerful hurricane was due to make landfall in little more than forty-eight hours. Bored, he stocked up on beer and Jägermeister at a drugstore on Harrison Avenue. Driving home, he swerved to avoid a cat and clipped the steel corner of a curb, blowing out a tire. Enraged, he pressed on with the wheel's rim shooting sparks and ka-thunk-ka-thunking down the road. Home alone in Lakeview, he drank himself into a stupor.

He awoke the next morning to an incessant ringing at the opposite end of the house. "I'm reaaalllly hungover, and this phone will Not. Quit. Ringing." He dragged himself out of bed, still intoxicated. Jimmy Bower, from Down, had heard the message Anselmo left the previous night, and was now frantically trying to reach him with a warning to get out of Lakeview, fast. With no cell phone, and having not turned on a TV or radio, "I hadn't heard a damn thing about this storm," Anselmo said.

He couldn't find the spare tire to his mother's car; she dispatched her husband to fix the flat. Anselmo hustled back across Lake Pontchartrain to his country house, flipped on the TV, and met Katrina. He realized the time had come for the first hurricane evacuation of his life.

With help from his father, he secured his property, packed up his animals—Dracula the Rottweiler would ride out the storm at a friend's safe house—and took off for Houston.

Richardson drove the 1,070 miles from Louisiana to Detroit in seventeen hours. Thanks to bumper-to-bumper evacuation traffic, Anselmo required nineteen hours to cover the 350 miles to Houston.

A Comfort Inn in Texas would be his home for the next month. A cross-section of south Louisiana occupied the hotel; the rock star lived next to three generations of a family from a New Orleans housing development, crammed into a single room. Anselmo was thrilled to discover that the Comfort Inn's permanent residents included the former Super Destroyer, a star of the Mid-South Wrestling telecasts he enjoyed as a boy. "The guy lived right on the corner upstairs. He had a double room, with all this crazy wrestling memorabilia and out-fits."

In Houston, he absorbed the news of the drowning of New Or-leans. Lakeview was hit especially hard; a friend of his stepfather's snapped a photo of Anselmo's house while paddling by in a canoe. Water filled the first floor, destroying the singer's collection of rock T-shirts and posters, demo tapes and vintage gear. The second floor, he later learned, was untouched. "It looked like a maid just left."

Richardson soon joined him at the Comfort Inn, where he set out, with fresh motivation, to shake the monkey off his damaged back.

Before Katrina, Anselmo had finally found a neurosurgeon willing to operate on his spinal column—but not until the singer was drug-free. Stranded in the Houston hotel, he sought to free himself from metha-done's grip. Coming off methadone, he says, was like "falling from a fifty-story building every five minutes, and every minute in between you're getting pushed toward the edge. Your anxiety is at an all-time high."

The sickness "is massive. The anxiety that is sprinkled on top of this flu-like stuff . . . it'll make anybody go back to the drugs. A test like this will separate the men from the boys. Either you're going to fail, or you're not. Well, I wanted that back surgery. I knew what my problem was. So I was fighting."

Pain management clinics had always supplied him with metha-done, but he tended not to use his entire prescription; instead, he built up an emergency stash. "A lot of people go into methadone with no plan for coming out of it. I always had a plan to come out."

Hoping to avoid the physical symptoms of withdrawal, he devised his own detox regimen. With a fingernail clipper, he shaved down the methadone wafers into ever-smaller doses each week. As he progressed, "the mental residue of that crap was almost like having Tourette's or something. I couldn't control this overexcited thing. I knew I was overbearing, but I couldn't help it."

He was not pleasant company, as Katrina anxiety tag teamed with methadone anxiety, but Richardson stuck with him. "I don't know who else would put up with the lunacy of methadone detox," Anselmo said. "I could have done something rash, and been really sorry about it, but still not been able to help myself. She's stuck by me through everything."

After several weeks at the Comfort Inn, the couple returned to Louisiana, bunking at former Saints tight end Boo Williams's house in Mandeville, then at a friend's house in Covington. They couldn't move back into their north shore house right away, as the long driveway was blocked by 150-foot pine trees felled by the storm. "It looked like Godzilla had walked around back here," Anselmo said. Fortunately, the trees missed the house.

Standing in his kitchen weeks later, he stared down methadone for the last time. He had steadily shrunk his dosage to a crumb, but that crumb still stood between him and back surgery. "I looked at this tiny little piece in my hand—this is controlling my life? I said, 'This will control me no more.'"

He threw it in the trash.

"Katrina did this for me: It gave me the ultimatum. I came out of the thing clean, man. I came out of that storm clean.

"Everything that came out of Katrina in my life, I turned into a positive. Not that I wouldn't take back Katrina—it was like a small nuclear device going off. You have to put your life back together. But in my case, it worked."

Cleared for surgery, Anselmo entered Ochsner Medical Center, just across the Jefferson Parish line from New Orleans, in November 2005. Doctors made five incisions in his back and inserted a half-dozen titanium screws and clamps in a "three-level fusion" of his spine. His first peek at the surgeon's handiwork via an MRI came as a shock: "It looks like a mail bomb inside my body."

Even this relatively noninvasive surgery required cutting through layers of muscle. Anselmo faced an intensive rehabilitation, one that would require a boxer's focus and drive. Essentially, he had to learn how to walk again.

"There was a time when, directly after surgery, I was on a lot of drugs. My midsection was like jelly. To get up to piss at night, I had to strap on this hard plastic-and-metal thing. But without it, it felt like

I could fall and break in half. It was miserable. But you had to work it all back so you could support that spine and that clamping and the work they did inside your body."

He was prescribed pain medication, but vowed that he would use no more, for no longer, than was necessary. "I can see where it's easy for people to have the surgery and half-ass their way through rehab and just stay on pain pills for the rest of their lives . . . I can see that. It does take that extra sit-up, it does take that extra push-up, it does take that extra core work, and time, and commitment."

Physical therapy had benefits beyond the physical. The program "put regimen into my life, rule into my life. I knew I had to wake up, do my stretches, I had to be dressed and ready and out the door to work out for an hour, then leave and deal with the rest of the day. There was no more time for hangovers of any sort, booze, pills, anything."

By the spring of 2006, he was ready to raise a racket again. He visited Pepper Keenan in New Orleans—they had not seen one another since well before Katrina—and resolved to reunite Down. On May 19, 2006, Down launched its first-ever European tour in Hamburg, Germany. Barely six months after major back surgery, Anselmo returned to the stage. "That's how seriously I was taking my rehab."

He dedicated the first show to Darrell Abbott.

The tour wound its way through the Netherlands, Norway, Sweden, Denmark, Ireland, France and Scotland, concluding at the massive Donington festival in England. Richardson accompanied Anselmo in dual roles as assistant and girlfriend.

He felt "pretty raw. I was physically not even fifty percent." The lingering effects of back surgery required pain medication, but "I wasn't abusing it. I was taking it as medicine, instead of just for kicks and giggles and to knock me unconscious because I didn't want to be there. This tour, I really, really wanted to be there."

Still, he was not yet up to the task of performing sober. The 2010 DVD/CD *Diary of a Mad Band: Europe in the Year of VI*, a chronicle of the tour, shows dressing rooms littered with beer and wine bottles. Drinking, he says, "was part of the routine of going onstage." But he soon learned "that I couldn't drink like I was twenty-one anymore. I tried. I damn well tried."

Looking back, Anselmo is embarrassed by his drinking's effect on his performances. "When you see the footage, it's like, 'Oh my God,

I can't believe this is me all over again.' It doesn't come off any better than when I was f—ed up before. I don't want to see this version of me anymore. It's ugly to watch.

"You think to yourself, 'Whoa. I've never done a gig sober.' Which isn't true. The first gig I did I was thirteen. I wasn't drunk or stoned then. There were many Razor White shows where I was not drunk. But Pantera, it became a way of the band, of the creature, the personality attached to it.

"Trying to shake that, when you're trying to recreate yourself and you're taking that big step back onto the stage . . . fans will be able to see [on the DVD], as far as my performance goes, a guy going through growing pains again."

On June 24, 2006, Down performed its first hometown concert in four years at storied New Orleans music club Tipitina's. The room holds around 800 people. A line stretched up Tchoupitoulas Street as fans waited to pass through metal detectors; security was extraordinarily tight, as the memory of Darrell Abbott's murder was still vivid.

But the hometown crowd showed nothing but love. Following a brief documentary on Down's pedigree and primary influences, Anselmo, Keenan, rhythm guitarist Kirk Windstein, drummer Jimmy Bower, and former Pantera bassist Rex Brown slammed through a set of old favorites. Anselmo sipped wine, but was more focused and clear-eyed than fans had likely ever seen. He repeatedly expressed gratitude for fans, bandmates, the security guards, his life. From the balcony, his misty-eyed mother beamed. "It's like he's come back from the dead," she said.

Indicative of the new, friendlier Phil Anselmo, on November 12, 2006, he, Keenan, Windstein and Bower conducted the weekly Sunday afternoon workshop for student musicians at Tipitina's. The mother of Keenan's girlfriend at the time organized the workshop series, which generally featured more traditional New Orleans jazz, funk and blues musicians. But Anselmo and company found common ground with the kids, schooling them on the art of rocking.

Reenergized, Down released a new album, *Down III: Over the Under*, in 2007; *Rolling Stone* named it one of the best fifty albums of the year. The band spent much of 2008 touring Europe and North American with hard rock heavyweights Metallica. The run concluded with a triumphant homecoming concert at the 16,000-seat New Orleans

Arena. Metallica's James Hetfield and Robert Trujillo joined Down for the crunching "Bury Me In Smoke."

Down subsequently took another break, and Anselmo busied himself with Housecore Records. In 2010, Housecore released new albums by haarp and Arson Anthem, the hard-core punk band featuring Anselmo on guitar, Hank Williams III, grandson and son of country music legends, on drums, Collin Yeo on bass and Eyehategod vocalist Mike Williams.

Five years after surgery, his spine was doing well. "There's bone growth now, everything looks healthy." He still maintained a regimen of morning stretching, and had more or less grown accustomed to the foreign objects in his body. "Can I feel it? Sure, I can feel it. But there's a mental toughness there to where you say, 'Hey, this is what it is. I can deal with it.' I've put my hard work in."

Technically, he's not entirely sober; "'Sober' is a harsh word." He'll smoke pot, maybe drink a beer or two during Saints games. But he avoids hard liquor—"I can't do it"—and says he has learned the meaning and value of moderation. The days of the Soma coma are over.

He has, since Katrina, rebuilt his personal house of cards as "a better house of cards, with a stronger foundation." Richardson was "insanely important" to that process, Anselmo said, "maybe one of the biggest factors. I love her. She is the anchor in my life.

"I could have gone in a million different directions. But I know my nature. I'm insatiable sometimes. It's not like I look at something and the grass is greener; I'm too much of a pessimist for that. But I always think that there's something *more*. Just give me *more*. Not money, but experiences. At one point in time, being in love with one girl, there was an apprehension of, 'Is this where I want to be the rest of my life?' It's not like that now. We don't have that kind of relationship to where we hold things over our heads to keep a relationship together."

He is not nominating himself for sainthood just yet. "There's always going to be tripwires and land mines . . . none of us are a perfect machine. We're going to f— up along the way. But f—ing up along the way purposely . . . why hasten the process? None of us is immortal. Might as well do the best work we can while we're here.

"When you know what you can and can't do—more importantly, what you can't do—once you identify and eliminate that from your life, life is easier. Life is better. It really is."

His recovery has opened him up to new experiences. Indulging his passion for boxing—his collection of fights runs into the thousands—he joined the board of the Kronk Gym Foundation in Detroit. He attended a glitzy fundraiser for the gym's youth outreach programs alongside Aretha Franklin, who "had more security than Metallica." He even bought a new black suit and tie for the occasion, a replacement for the "court suit" he wore for Pantera-era lawsuits. "It was from the nineties," Richardson said, "and it looked like it was from the nineties."

In June 2010, Anselmo realized every long-suffering Saints fan's dream: he hoisted the Vince Lombardi Trophy awarded to the winners of Super Bowl XLIV. On that same visit to the Saints' training facility, he interviewed tight end and fellow tattoo enthusiast Jeremy Shockey for a video that appeared on the Housecore Web site; modeled the Super Bowl ring belonging to retired kick returner Michael "Beer Man" Lewis; and was drafted to coach a United Way twelve-and-under team for a scrimmage on the Saints' practice field.

Even as he prepared for a brief Arson Anthem tour of North America in 2011, Anselmo seemed in no hurry to leave his hideaway in the woods. At home, he and Richardson lead quiet lives. They cook gumbo, red beans and rice, and other New Orleans staples. They care for a menagerie of dogs—including Shirley, a hyperaffectionate lap dog—cats, and winged creatures. The latter include a vain, camera-shy peacock named Valentino, who shares his pen with two chickens, and a gaggle of ducks the couple raised as ducklings.

"I don't know what to say as far as success goes, or how you measure success in your life. But I'm happy. I'm relatively healthy. And when I look back on things, bands and people, I chose to look at the positives. There are negatives, there are the bad times. But even looking back at the good times . . . it's OK to look back, but I wouldn't want to get stuck there. I'm the type of guy who's ready for tomorrow. I'm ready to put that foot forward."

He may never again achieve Pantera's level of success, but he's fine with that. He would not, could not, pay the same price for it.

"I've had an unbelievably successful, lucky, storybook kind of life. Music has been so kind to me. The world has been so kind, when it is so cruel.

"It's not like I haven't seen the ugly side. That's why I can identify the good. Because I know the bad so very well."

Chapter Eleven

Mr. New Orleans: Pete Fountain

In 2000, I encountered Pete Fountain and his good-humored, long-suffering wife, Beverly, in a Biloxi, Mississippi, casino following a performance by comedian Don Rickles. The famed clarinetist had recently celebrated his seventieth birthday. Apropos of nothing, he offered to show me his new tattoo. Beverly rolled her eyes as her husband unbuttoned his shirt to reveal an owl pulling a snake out of his belly button.

An owl. Pulling a snake. Out of his belly button.

Beverly shook her head as Pete stood amid the slot machines and retirees, grinning broadly. He said the tattoo had something to do with Native American culture. A more likely explanation is that the notion of getting inked with such a grand design at his age appealed to his still-mischievous sense of fun. That's all the reason he needed.

Ten years later, I joined hundreds of well-wishers for Fountain's eightieth birthday bash at Rock 'n' Bowl, a combination bowling alley/music venue/shrine to New Orleans nostalgia. He had endured some hard years in the interim, thanks to Katrina and assorted physical ailments. He'd lost significant weight; the owl tattoo likely flew a little lower on his downsized belly.

But surrounded by family, friends and fans at Rock 'n' Bowl, his eyes still twinkled. He bent down to kiss my four-month-old son, Sam, on the head. One day I'll tell Sam about the time he received a blessing from the merry pope of New Orleans.

The old man in the checked shirt shuffles past St. Louis Cathedral, the grand house of worship at the heart of New Orleans' Jackson Square, and ducks into Pirate Alley unnoticed. In the shadow of a banana tree, he opens a black case and carefully assembles a LeBlanc clarinet with gold-plated hardware. He touches the horn's reed to his lips.

With that, he is anonymous no more. He is Pete Fountain, Mr. New Orleans, briefly restored to his natural habitat.

A rough couple of years had left him less steady on his feet. Hurricane Katrina obliterated his beloved ten-acre waterfront estate in Bay St. Louis, Mississippi; reduced the three-story, 10,000-square-foot main house, two guest cottages and storage barn to 120 truckloads of debris. Decades of memorabilia, the record of a life lived large in the name of New Orleans—all of it gone.

Aftershocks included quadruple bypass surgery, two minor strokes, and a bout of shingles. Regardless of whether they resulted from the stress and upheaval of the storm, from advanced years, or from a cruel combination of both, the result was the same: his heart now beats to the rhythm of a pacemaker. Words sometimes get lost en route to his mouth; one-liners don't tumble out quite so easily anymore. Growing old, he'll tell you, ain't easy.

Once upon a time, Fountain and Fats Domino were the most famous New Orleans musicians who actually resided in New Orleans. The clarinetist's two years on *The Lawrence Welk Show* made him a star. Welk didn't much cotton to Fountain's Big Easy attitude, but Johnny Carson did. Fountain made fifty-nine appearances on *The Tonight Show*, selling his records and himself as the mug and melody of good-time New Orleans. Along the way he entertained presidents and a pope, a jester in the courts of kings.

He and his buddy Al Hirt, a bear of a trumpeter whose dense beard was the ying to the yang of Fountain's bald dome, defined the city's nightlife with their respective Bourbon Street clubs. They lived large, laughed loud, and drank a lot. For a generation or two, Fountain was as integral to Bourbon Street as go-cups and strippers.

Closing in on eighty, his eyes still danced and his clarinet still sang, but he didn't visit the French Quarter much anymore. He usually spent the first part of each week at a new house—built a few blocks inland, rather than right on the water—in Bay St. Louis. On weekends he returned to his longtime home in New Orleans' leafy Lake Vista subdivision, near Lake Pontchartrain.

But on an overcast afternoon in April 2008, he materializes in the Quarter like the ghost of Bourbon Street's past. The LeBlanc clarinet in his hands survived Katrina because he worked a casino with it a couple nights before his evacuation and set it down near the door of his doomed house. He grabbed the horn on his way out; the instruments he left behind were washed away.

All that is required of him on this day in the Quarter is that he pose for pictures with the clarinet. But when you're Pete Fountain, you can't help but play.

In a town well-stocked with partisan characters, laying claim to the honorific "Mr. New Orleans" is no small affair. But so what if many of his favorite restaurants are outside New Orleans proper in Jefferson Parish? Or that he prefers to watch Saints games at home instead of in the Superdome with the faithful? Or that for decades he spent weekends in Mississippi, in a gigantic house where "you can run around like crazy, and nobody hears you"?

His claim to the title runs much deeper: Pete Fountain is joie de vivre personified. From humble origins—his dad drove a Dixie beer truck—he emerged as the most famous contemporary ambassador of traditional Dixieland jazz. "It snuck up on me," Fountain once said of fame. "I didn't look for it. I never did strive for anything. Through the years I just wanted to play. I enjoy playing. When you enjoy playing, and your clarinet is singing, it's stealing. You feel like, 'They give me money to do this?' But some nights when it's not working, you say, 'Boy, I wish I had taken over my daddy's beer route.'"

He idolized the great Benny Goodman and New Orleans clarinetist Irving Fazola, of the Bob Crosby Bobcats. He aspired to replicate the fat, bluesy tone of Fazola and the drive, swing and technique of Goodman. By combining the two, he hit upon a sweet sound all his own.

It was an irate teacher at Warren Easton High School who set Pierre Dewey LaFontaine Jr. on the path to glory. One day he was caught sleeping in class. His excuse was that he worked nights as a musician on Bourbon Street. The teacher asked how much he made. Fountain told him: $150 a week. "He said, 'I don't make that—go turn in your book,'" Fountain recalled with a chuckle. "He wrote my mother a note saying, 'Let this boy get some sleep so he can work at night.'"

So Fountain, a senior, quit school—although years later Warren Easton officials awarded him a diploma and class ring—to blow his horn full time. His reputation grew, especially during his tenure with the Basin Street Six. In 1957, celebrity big bandleader Lawrence Welk caught wind of this swinging clarinet player down in New Orleans and offered him a job. Fountain accepted, even though the gig required he move to Los Angeles, the first and only time he would live full-time outside the city of his birth.

As the featured soloist on ABC-TV's popular weekly *The Lawrence Welk Show*, Fountain stepped out in front of the orchestra to accompany the adorable Lennon Sisters' harmonies on "White Silver Sand." He squared off with young trumpeter Warren Luening on a hot "Jingle Bells." He soared through "Tiger Rag" and "My Blue Heaven" as coat-and-tied young men and perfectly coiffed young ladies danced chastely. "Pete, are you all ready? Swing right out," Welk instructed, and Fountain obliged.

Week in and week out, he conducted a clarinet clinic of exquisite tone and taste. Broadcast in black and white into living rooms across America, he was one of the most visible jazz artists in the world at a time when people still bought jazz albums. Three of his sold more than a half-million copies apiece. *Pete Fountain's New Orleans*, a straight-ahead 1960 recording with piano, drums, bass and clarinet, is considered a requisite Dixieland jazz album. "I did forty-five albums for one company, and mostly every one would sell a hundred, hundred-and-fifty thousand copies. Which is fantastic. I'd get some fantastic checks, which I blew."

The dreamy Champagne fantasies fostered by the rigorously conservative Welk did not always abide the Bourbon devil inside Pete Fountain. Welk strictly forbade his musicians to drink on the job. "He kept me sober—damn near killed me," Fountain complained to me forty years after the fact. "Every time they make rules to a guy from New Orleans, he'll break it. Instead of just going to the bar and getting a drink, I'd get a double."

One night at the Aragon Ballroom in Santa Monica, California, Welk discovered Fountain had snuck a nip or two. Determined to teach his wayward young musician a lesson, the taskmaster called for five consecutive songs featuring the clarinet. "He put me in the front, and made me play one after the other, waiting for me to make a mistake. The more I played, the hotter I got. So he finally backed off. He must have thought, 'This kid can drink.'"

Fountain initially introduced himself to America in his natural state: receding hairline, thick-framed eyeglasses, a modified chinstrap of a goatee. Welk's people eventually prevailed on him to ditch the glasses, downsize the chin hair, and wear a toupee. But he was still Pete. As the other members of the clarinet section flipped through playbooks on their music stands, he ogled a *Playboy*.

In 1959, two years into the Welk gig, homesickness prompted him to quit and move the family back to New Orleans. He bought a handsome home near Lake Pontchartrain and opened his first club at 800 Bourbon Street in 1960. Several years later, he moved to a larger space at 231 Bourbon. Unlike Welk, he did not prohibit his musicians from drinking. He was at the heart of Bourbon Street intrigue and action. "I went to McDonogh 28 [grade school], Warren Easton, and the conservatory of Bourbon Street."

All manner of dignitary and not-so-dignitary stopped by. "I just sat there with my mouth open, listening to him play," recalled country music outlaw Hank Williams Jr., a satisfied customer. "I really like that kind of stuff. We sat around the dressing room and shared a little toddy together. It was real special."

A dispute with his landlord sent Fountain in search of new digs in 1977. The Hilton Riverside was about to open downtown at the foot of Poydras Street, overlooking the Mississippi River. The hotel's management offered to customize a third-story club for him. Equal parts New Orleans bordello and Las Vegas lounge, the space sported crimson velvet walls, cocktail waitresses, maître d's who escorted patrons to tables, multi-tiered seating, and red vinyl handrails supported by grapevine wrought-iron posts. At the start of every show, the call rang out, "Ladies and gentlemen, will you please welcome Mr. New Orleans, Pete Fountain!"

Over the years, he made, and lost, multiple fortunes. "I'm a bad businessman. I blew some serious money. I never did gamble, I never did throw it away. Somebody would say, ' "Want to get into the hotel business?' and I'd go, 'Oh, yeah, sounds good!' I bought a hotel, I bought this, I bought that."

Among his more infamous investments was Peter's Wieners, a fast-food hot dog stand in Bay St. Louis. T-shirts trumpeted "The Wiener That Puts A Smile On Your Face!" He envisioned franchises mushrooming all over the country, like Wendy's. Instead, he took a $100,000 bath.

Nostalgia for that idea (and that money) lingered, but he has no use for regrets. "If a frog had wings, he wouldn't bump his ass. You can't go if, if, if—it'd make you sick. I say it once in a while, and that's it."

The wiener business "was fun. All these things are fun while they last. As long as I can keep tootin' . . . The day I can't keep tootin', then I'm in trouble."

Beverly, his sainted wife, contributed mightily to the effort to keep him out of trouble. "She should have left me on the honeymoon," her husband contends. "She raised me—I was her oldest boy." She mostly raised her three actual children, too, as her husband was often on the road or working late at his club. Or sauced. During the '60s, Fountain observed "the whole world going crazy—and I was in there with 'em."

He embarked on a decade-long game of chicken with whiskey. He blinked first. "Jack Daniels whipped my butt. I thought I'd beat him, but you can't beat Jack Daniels. He's too strong. My wife used to tell the kids I had the flu. Every weekend I had either the Jack Daniels flu, the Taaka flu, or the tequila flu. It's just one of those things that pass you by. It's like another life. I've gone through three or four lives."

Those lives got progressively tamer. He eventually handed down the tradition of all-nighters in hotel bars to the younger members of his band, while he turned in early. Onstage, he sipped a mild half-and-half mixture of white wine and Perrier. "Things change. Nothing stays the same. I used to be taller."

As Fountain curtailed his touring in the '90s—he mothballed his old band bus in his Bay St. Louis garage—he still logged as many as four nights a week in his club. He did short tours during the summer and occasional private engagements, gigs that paid well enough to travel by rented Lear jet. "I couldn't afford myself if I charged me."

He still had his wind, could still squeeze as many notes from a breath as ever. "The biggest thing with the clarinet is to find a good reed. If you find a good reed, you might go two months without any problems. I want it to sing, and I want the people to hear me at my best."

Regardless of how well he played, customers walked away satisfied just to be in his presence. That wasn't enough for Fountain. "I don't go for that, I never did. I think, and the people still think, that I'm still tootin'. My CDs are still selling, so something's happening. I'm still having the fun. The day I'm not having fun . . . I think I'll pack it up. And the day I really can't toot, I hope somebody tells me."

Instead of a rooster, many New Orleanians awaken to the sound of Fountain's clarinet on Mardi Gras morning. Since 1960, he and his Half-Fast Walking Club have spent the early hours of Fat Tuesday "tootin' and scootin'" along the downtown parade route, distributing kisses, paper flowers and jazz to the Carnival diehards who staked out a spot before breakfast. Over the years, "I think we've walked from here to Florida," Fountain said. And that's definitely Walking Club, not Marching Club. "We can't march. If we marched, we'd die. We'd last about four blocks."

Never averse to a good time, Fountain hit on the idea of forming his own walking club after seeing all the fun had by members of such venerable outfits as the Jefferson City Buzzards. Initially, he, Beverly, and a handful of other couples set off from Franky & Johnny's restaurant Uptown. The wives moved way too quickly for their husbands, who were inclined to make numerous stops for "refreshments." "We got to Canal Street, and the girls wanted to walk back. We told them there was no way we could walk back, because we were smashed. So we all got a ride back. The next year, we left the girls home, because they outwalked us."

Beverly suggested the "Half-Fast" name, based on the pace her husband and his friends set, as well as the half-cocked manner in which the idea was conceived and executed. They gradually fine-tuned the operation; the wives formed their own organization, the Better Halves.

By tradition, Fountain and his krewe embark from Commander's Palace, the flagship old-line New Orleans restaurant, at seven A.M. on Fat Tuesday. They make their way to St. Charles Avenue and head downtown ahead of the Zulu parade, to the French Quarter. Along the way, they are fortified by sympathetic establishments. "They used to drink us," Fountain said in 2001. "Now they feed us. I'll have maybe a glass of wine mixed with Perrier water to start with. Then during the day, if the beer wagon's close, I'll get me a draft."

Originally, they walked to a pace set by Fountain's clarinet and a drummer. More recently, a sixteen-piece ensemble rode in an official bandwagon up front, with eight more musicians in the rear. A truck hauled beads, doubloons and other essentials, replacing the individual carts that members once woozily navigated down crowded streets. They costumed as a group—pirates, gypsies, Indians, Vikings, Romans, Egyptians. Once, Fountain was a prince while the rest were frogs. Another year, he strolled the streets of his hometown in a tutu. All in the name of fun.

In the late '90s, actor John Goodman became an honorary Half-Fast member, after he showed up at Commander's Palace one Mardi Gras morning. "He adopted us," Fountain said. "He gets on the truck, people don't bother him, and he's happy up there."

Fountain started riding, rather than walking, around the same time, as he approached his seventieth birthday. In 2001, he resolved to get in shape and get back on the pavement. "I had picked up so much weight that I couldn't walk that far. I rode, and I really missed the street. So I'm leaving the band and John Goodman on the truck. He says he'll hold up my spot, and I'm going to try and walk as far as I can."

Quitting the Half-Fast club is not an option: "Once you walk, you're hooked." Fountain planned to stay on the street "as long as I can toot and scoot. And if I can't scoot, I can always toot."

In March 2003, the gold curtain came down on an era of New Orleans nightlife. With little fanfare, in front of 400 mostly invited family and friends, Fountain performed for the last time at his nightclub in the New Orleans Hilton.

For forty-three years, New Orleans boasted a club bearing Fountain's name. He spent the final twenty-six in the Hilton Riverside, where the likes of Bob Hope, Doc Severinsen and Don Rickles dropped by to lend a hand. For years he punched in five nights a week at the Hilton, but gradually scaled down to two. His graying audience didn't get out as much any more. Following the terrorist attacks of September 11, 2001, the overall downturn in tourism eroded attendance further.

He probably could have held on a while longer, but, at seventy-two, Fountain was ready to simplify his life, to rid himself of the pressures and responsibilities of running a nightclub. With his Hilton lease about to expire, he and Benny Harrell, his son-in-law and long-time manager, decided it was time to move on. "I needed a change," Fountain said. "I didn't want it, but I needed it. It's one of those things. The club was still making it, but we could see the handwriting on the wall. It's been a real good ride, and we've still got a lot of riding to do. I might get off the motorcycle and ride a little scooter now, but it's still a ride."

The club was retiring, not Fountain. He still received more offers for private and corporate engagements than he cared to accept, and had dates penciled in ten months in advance. He would soon add a twice-a-month gig at a casino near his weekend home in Bay St. Louis.

Still, the final Friday at the club felt like a farewell. The office behind the stage served as the headquarters of his working life for a quarter century. The walls amounted to a de facto hall of fame for a golden era of American entertainment. They bore autographed portraits of Frank Sinatra, Louis Armstrong, Johnny Carson, George Carlin (who, much to Fountain's amusement, wrote, "Hey Pete: F— you!") and pictures of Fountain performing for Pope John Paul II and President George H. W. Bush. Beverly Fountain scanned the overcrowded wall and wondered where they would store all the mementos. "We don't have much wall space," she said. "It's nice to have all those memories, but where do you put them?"

As showtime approached, Fountain's clarinet lay atop his desk as a lamp warmed the instrument's wood. Five of his six grandchildren—their photos lined the desk—collected quick hugs and kisses from him. His eldest granddaughter, Danielle Harrell, called from New York—where she was auditioning to dance in a Broadway musical—to wish him well.

For the last time, the club's staff, including Fountain's two sons, would fret over seating arrangements. For the last time, Dorothy M. Bradley, Fountain's secretary since 1960, would escort guests to their tables. For the last time, Paul Famiglio, a bartender in Fountain's employ for forty years, poured the drinks that made the jazz go down smoother.

And for the last time, Fountain and his six musicians gathered in his office, pulling on tuxedos and loosening up with ribald jokes. They passed through a small locker room and up five steps to the stage. A collage of naughty pictures near the steps was temporarily covered up: The Rev. Frank Coco, the chaplain for the Half-Fast Walking Club and an amateur clarinetist, was scheduled to sit in on closing night.

So, too, was New Orleans coroner/trumpeter Frank Minyard. "He sat in for the opening night," Fountain quipped. "We want to see if he got any better in twenty-six years."

As the clarinetist fidgeted behind the gold lamé curtain, the audience laughed and cheered throughout a seven-minute video retrospective of his career: The buttoned-up Welk bidding farewell to the rascal Fountain. Dolly Parton kissing his bald head. President Clinton testifying that the sound of Pete's clarinet is "one of the joys of American music."

The curtain peeled back to reveal Fountain center stage, gliding through "Clarinet Marmalade," still the embodiment of the laissez-les-bons-temps-rouler spirit at the heart of Dixieland jazz.

It was a night for old friends and old favorites. The audience sighed its collective approval at the first notes of "Just a Closer Walk With Thee" and "Basin Street Blues," beloved staples of the Fountain repertoire. Burt Boe and Greg Harrison paired their horns with the master's for a three-clarinet summit. Minyard navigated "Do You Know What It Means to Miss New Orleans?"

As the ninety-minute set drew to a close, Fountain said, "It's been twenty-six years here. It went by half-fast, and so did my liver." He introduced his grandchildren at the final curtain call. "I'd like to thank everybody. I love you, I love you, I love you. See you next time. Thank you very much."

Minutes later, he had shed his tuxedo and was out amongst friends, exchanging hugs, signing autographs, posing for pictures, accepting congratulations, and looking ahead to the next stage of his ride. "After all these years, it feels strange. But nothing stays the same. It's time to move on."

Generations of well-to-do New Orleanians have flocked to Bay St. Louis to escape the heat, demands and distractions of the city. An easy forty-five-minute commute separates the two destinations, which are light-years apart in temperament and tone. Bay St. Louis is a quaint, hospitable Southern town with a thriving arts community arrayed along a broad inlet opening into the Gulf of Mexico. From the early 1970s on, Fountain spent weekends he wasn't working on the Mississippi Gulf Coast.

He built a grand waterfront estate. He moved a two-story house to his property and set it atop a fifteen-foot-tall first-floor clubhouse. He outfitted the clubhouse with the vintage carved oak bar from Storyville, a New Orleans barroom he owned in the 1960s. On the fully stocked bar's copper top stood an antique cash register. There were pool tables, vintage pinball and video games, a sauna. Breezes blowing off the water caressed the rocking chairs on a broad, plantation-style porch. Time stood still, stress evaporated; it was the perfect setting for a peaceful retirement. It wasn't a bad place to conjure and cure a hangover, either.

On Saturday, August 27, 2005, Pete and Beverly drove to Bay St. Louis. They planned to secure the property in advance of the approaching hurricane, then drive back to New Orleans. At least, that's what Pete told Benny Harrell. "He lied to me," Harrell said, laughing. "He was going to try to stay there the whole time."

Sure enough, that night Harrell got another call from his father-in-law. He and Beverly wanted to ride out the storm in Bay St. Louis. They figured that the house was solidly built, and even if the ground floor flooded, they'd be fine on the upper two floors.

Harrell wasn't so sure. By Sunday morning, he was increasingly frightened by Katrina's destructive potential. With the storm slated to make landfall that night, he got on the phone with his in-laws and insisted they flee the coast.

Reluctantly, Fountain agreed. As he paused to set the burglar alarm—in hindsight, an almost comic precaution, given that wind and water would soon steal the *entire house*—he grabbed a clarinet from the table near the door, where he'd left it after a gig four nights earlier.

With no set destination, he and Beverly drove twenty-four miles north to Picayune, Mississippi. Incredibly, they found an available room at a Super 8 motel, and hunkered down.

The storm crashed ashore just east of New Orleans—better for New Orleans, far worse for Bay St. Louis. The punishing storm surge, ton upon ton of angry Gulf water, roared up out of the bay and bulldozed everything in its path, including the Fountain estate.

Katrina's winds roughed up Picayune as well, knocking out power and water at the Super 8. For two days, Harrell—who rode out the storm on the western edge of New Orleans in Metairie—did not know where Pete and Beverly were.

Pete's son Jeff finally reached them. Picking his way around downed trees on back roads, he collected his parents at the darkened motel and drove them to Winnsboro, in central Louisiana.

The Bay St. Louis house, they later learned, was crushed, obliterated. Had the Fountains stayed, in all likelihood they would have perished.

Weeks later, they returned to pick through the rubble. There wasn't much to find. The game room, Pete's Porsche, the antique 1930s-era Ford, the 1940s pickup truck, the antique furniture, all the other toys, everything . . . gone.

His house near Lake Pontchartrain in New Orleans did not flood, but wind damaged the roof, admitting rain, then mold. Power would not be restored for many weeks. His Lake Vista neighborhood was in bad shape, but the adjacent Lakeview, which flooded badly, was far worse. It was no place for a couple in their seventies.

So the Fountains hopscotched across south Louisiana on an odyssey of borrowed and rented dwellings. They stayed for a time in Lafayette, where their first great-granddaughter, Isabella, born two weeks before the storm, was christened. They borrowed a fishing camp in Vacherie, Louisiana, from their banker; in return, Fountain appeared in a TV commercial for the bank. They finally settled in Hammond, a college town north of Lake Pontchartrain, for the remainder of their months-long exile.

Even ever-sunny Mr. New Orleans was not impervious to storm-related depression. He lost so much, not the least of which was his way of life and sense of security and home. He had always been healthy, except for booze-induced "flu"; perhaps, his son-in-law theorized, all the drinking over the years killed off other bugs.

But Katrina didn't claim all victims immediately. The difficult months that followed chipped away at sanity, triggering suicides and overdoses. The stress, strain and upheaval took an especially physical toll on elderly Gulf Coast residents.

Mardi Gras 2006 fell on February 28, six months after Katrina nearly to the day. Fountain generally spends the night before the Half-Fast Walking Club parade at Hotel Monteleone in the French Quarter. On February 27, he was in his room, resting. But something didn't feel right. He looked terrible by the time Harrell arrived to check on him. At a nearby hospital, doctors discovered blocked arteries. The next day, the Half-Fast Walking Club walked without Fountain for the first time in forty-five years, much to his dismay.

He went under the knife for a quadruple bypass days later. Doctors recommended he rest for at least six weeks. Fountain was still in the hospital when Harrell asked him what he wanted to do about his scheduled gig at the New Orleans Jazz & Heritage Festival—which was six weeks away.

This would be the first Jazz Fest after Katrina. It would also be Fountain's first performance since the storm, and his first following quadruple bypass surgery.

"He basically said, 'I have to do Jazz Fest. If I don't do Jazz Fest, I might not play again,'" Harrell recalled. "It was a big thing for him. It was a pivotal moment."

And so, with his cardiologist in attendance just in case, Fountain eased onto the stage of Jazz Fest's Economy Hall Tent to rapturous applause.

More troubles followed. In the coming months, two strokes, one minor, one more serious, left him with limited speech—but did not hinder his ability to make a clarinet sing. In January 2007, he underwent an operation to relieve lingering pain caused by shingles.

A month later, he returned to the streets, riding in front of the Half-Fast Walking Club. Mr. New Orleans, back where he belonged.

The following spring, Fountain was the featured attraction on opening day of the twenty-fifth annual French Quarter Festival, the self-described largest free music festival in the South. Established in 1984 to lure visitors and business back to the Quarter after the disruption caused by a sidewalk reconstruction project, the French Quarter Festival initially focused on traditional jazz. It has since grown to encompass most forms of New Orleans music except rap, and draw hundreds of thousands of attendees each April.

Fountain appeared at the first French Quarter Festival. The 2008 festival would be only his third formal concert in New Orleans since Katrina three years earlier.

Days ahead of the festival, he showed up in Jackson Square for a photo shoot. As a photographer clicked away in Pirate Alley, Fountain trailed surprised and delighted fans in his wake like a Big Easy Pied Piper. Two couples from northern Virginia stopped and stared.

"What an honor to meet you after all these years," said one man.

"You make beautiful music," said another.

Mimi Richard, a local, approached with a cell-phone camera. "You're my dad's favorite! He's just gonna die."

"Can you play for us?" asked another woman.

"Can you give me a dollar?" said Pete, grinning.

Bald, bearded Tony Seville, owner of the Pirates Alley Café, confided, "You gave me my look." While trying to buy the café, Seville caught the clarinetist's show in Mississippi. He returned to New Orleans and the sale went through. "You brought me luck."

Terry Cowman of Los Angeles fawned over Fountain. "It's a pleasure, an absolute pleasure! Oh my God, I can't believe it! Here we are in this little place . . . I think my heart is gonna crush."

Fountain finally emerged from Pirate Alley and settled on a bench facing Jackson Square. Nearby, local trombonist Glen David Andrews fronted a brass band entertaining tourists outside the Cabildo, the onetime seat of Spanish municipal government in colonial Louisiana. Not one to miss an opportunity, Andrews played his way over to where Fountain rested.

"Ladies and gentlemen, Mr. Pete Fountain!" he announced.

The old man rose to his feet to toot along to "High Society," thrilling the tourists. A man prodded his four young daughters to pose for a photo near the legend; the girls clearly had no idea who he was.

"High Society" wound down and Fountain turned to leave. In a bid to prolong the moment, Andrews broke into "Just a Closer Walk With Thee." Just as Andrews suspected, Fountain couldn't resist, and hoisted his clarinet once again.

"What you got to say about that, Uncle Pete?" Andrews exclaimed.

The tourists clapped and cheered; Fountain waved and walked off.

Roger Bird and Chico Thomas couldn't believe their good fortune. They had traveled to New Orleans from Oakland, California, with their wives to watch the Golden State Warriors take on the New Orleans Hornets at the New Orleans Arena. Moments ago, they posed alongside the bronze Pete Fountain statue several blocks away in the New Orleans Musical Legends Park on Bourbon Street. "And then, holy cow, it's the real thing," Bird said. "This made our trip."

At the northeast corner of Jackson Square, the sight of Fountain rendered veteran tarot card reader Norman Oaks thunderstruck. As a boy growing up in the French Quarter, he peeped into Fountain's old club and marveled as the legend roamed the streets.

And now, on a Friday afternoon in the spring of 2008, Fountain had appeared in Jackson Square once again. A positive omen, for sure. "It brought back a lot of good memories," Oaks said. "You go through life and start missing things, and then you go around a corner and there it is again, and life isn't as screwed up. That's what seeing him did for me.

"It's like everything from the past is not gone. That's really encouraging."

In the summer of 2009, the Blue Room reopened in the Roosevelt Hotel, the newly restored former Fairmont Hotel on Baronne Street in downtown New Orleans. For decades, the Blue Room was a first-class supper club on the national circuit, hosting all manner of marquee entertainers: Louis Armstrong. Frank Sinatra. Sonny & Cher. Tony Bennett. Ella Fitzgerald. Marlene Dietrich. Jimmy Durante. Bette Midler. It was where real-life "Mad Men" would squire wives and/or mistresses for a classy night on the town. Many a New Orleanian harbors fond memories of special occasions spent there.

The Blue Room closed long before Katrina shuttered the Fairmont. After the storm, the 504-room hotel was acquired by the Hilton Hotel Corporation as part of its Waldorf-Astoria portfolio. The new owners restored the Roosevelt name and refurbished the Blue Room. They wanted opening night to harken back to the Blue Room's glory years.

Paging Pete Fountain.

Fountain first played the Blue Room in the 1940s, and returned dozens of times over the years. On reopening night, he would be paired with clarinetist Tim Laughlin, his heir apparent. As a young man, Laughlin attended a handful of shows at the old Blue Room, including the Mills Brothers and Mel Tormé. But he had never graced the stage until he shared it with Pete, his mentor and close friend. "It was almost spiritual in a way," Laughlin would say later. "One of the biggest honors I've ever had. And to do it with Pete is a notch above that."

The new Blue Room altered the classic appearance only slightly. Tables are set on two tiers, per tradition. But the low stage on which performers once ventured out among tables has been replaced by a herringbone-patterned dance floor. Musicians now occupy a raised stage set into the room's back wall.

Take away the iPhones and opening night could have passed for the Blue Room circa 1963. Water glasses reflected blue stage lights. A massive chandelier sparkled. Elegantly attired guests who paid $195 a ticket dined on lobster and filet mignon. Laughlin and an expanded edition of his band unspooled a program of jazz standards and original compositions. The latter included "For Pete's Sake," a song Laughlin wrote in honor of Fountain. Every musician but Fountain wore tuxedos; he opted for a dark suit and tie.

Men in suits and women in cocktail dresses crowded the dance floor. They danced right on through the spiritual "Just a Closer Walk With Thee" ("It's done in a tempo where you can get away with it," Laughlin said). Fountain tooted alongside Laughlin, passing the torch even as his own flame continued to burn.

After a final "Struttin' with Some Barbecue," fans pressed against the stage to shake Fountain's hand, collect an autograph on blue souvenir menus, or just be near him. As he made his escape, grinning broadly, speaking little, a man exclaimed, "The whole city loves you."

Of course it does. He is Mr. New Orleans, continuing on his merry way, as long as he is able.

Chapter Twelve

Bouncing with Juvenile

Regardless of their gangsta fantasies and real-life legal entanglements, the protagonists of New Orleans' Cash Money and No Limit rap empires have been unfailingly courteous whenever our paths have crossed. Terius "Juvenile" Gray, especially, is a gracious host. I joined him for a tour of his old neighborhood soon after his "Back That Azz Up" introduced New Orleans bounce to the nation in the late '90s. We wandered into a corner grocery and he treated me to a cold drink—a small gesture, but an indication that he was not, like so many pop stars flush with fresh success, completely self-absorbed.

In December 2005, much of New Orleans was still abandoned and desolate following Katrina. In a departure from his usual escapist fantasies, Juvenile shot the video for his song "Get Ya Hustle On" in the devastated Lower 9th Ward. The shoot was decidedly low-budget; there was no catering. No restaurants or fast food joints were open for miles around. Consequently, most of us on the authentic urban wasteland set were both cold and hungry.

Thus, I was astonished to find Juvenile in his SUV, chowing down on a box of piping hot Popeyes fried chicken. He had dispatched a production assistant fifteen miles to Jefferson Parish on a quest for food. The PA found what was, three months after the storm, possibly the only open Popeyes in greater New Orleans.

Juvenile offered to send the guy on another forty-five-minute round trip to procure a chicken dinner for me. I assured him that wasn't necessary.

On an ugly, frigid morning in December 2005, Juvenile's tour bus idles alongside a Forstall Street sidewalk littered with roofing shingles, discarded shoes and the rotting carcass of a brown dog.

Hours earlier, the rapper, his wife and his seven-year-old son had returned to New Orleans from their post-Katrina exile in Atlanta for the first time. They had come to check on their home on the north shore of Lake Pontchartrain, but also to crisscross the Lower 9th Ward with a camera crew in tow.

The rapper who encouraged women to "Back That Azz Up" sold millions of records by perpetuating a fantasy of sleek cars, ornate mansions, buxom babes and an abundance of bling. But his "Get Ya Hustle On" video would be built around what was, for him, a previously unexplored topic: reality.

Most of *Reality Check*, Juvenile's 2006 album on Atlantic Records, was finished before Katrina. "Rodeo," the first single, involved strippers—familiar territory for Juvenile. But days after Katrina, he recorded three additional songs that referenced the storm. "Get Ya Hustle On" urged Katrina's victims to motivate in the face of upheaval.

"I know y'all got shipped away to other parts of the country," Juvenile, born Terius Gray, said during a break in the video shoot, as if addressing fellow evacuees. "I know y'all been cheated out of things. But you don't have a right to pull a gun on the next person and take it.

"My point is stop feeling sorry for yourself and start doing things for yourself. OK, the government did nothing for us, everything didn't go the way we wanted. What you gonna do? Keep crying? Nah. Get a job. Do whatever you do. Get your hustle on."

To illustrate that point, James Lopez, Atlantic Records' head of urban music marketing, suggested that Juvenile shoot the "Get Ya Hustle On" video on location in the Lower 9th Ward. "Juvenile has very strong opinions on the aftermath of the situation," Lopez said. "I thought this could be his way of speaking out, protesting or just plain making sure that people do not forget."

Echoing proprietors of "disaster tours"—guided minibus journeys through hard-hit neighborhoods, which some residents came to resent—Juvenile believed that filming authentic destruction was instructive, not exploitative. "What I got from city officials is that they needed somebody, a face of New Orleans, to come down here and expose this. I want people to see what these people went through. We're shooting where people actually lost their lives, and people [outside of New Orleans] are not even talking about it. It's like it's over with.

"I could have sent the camera crews down here to get the footage. I don't see me gaining from this video. All I see me doing is exposing it. This really ain't a normal Juvy record for me to put out. By me being here, I want people to see what these people went through."

With the video shoot, "I'm not promoting a record. I'm promoting a movement, a message. It's about the state of mind we have right now. My message is, 'Don't sit around and wait. Get your hustle on. Do whatever you do.' I'm not putting a gun to nobody's head and saying, 'Go out there and sell drugs.' You could go to jail if you don't know what you're doing.

"Live. Don't give up on yourself. That's what I'm saying."

This from the very same Juvenile who, in the years before the storm, spent more time in courtrooms than recording studios. Several very public scrapes with the law generated tawdry headlines: allegedly striking a man with a champagne bottle outside a Miami comedy club; busted after police found marijuana and a small amount of cocaine in a car in which he was a passenger; chasing strippers through a quiet subdivision outside New Orleans late one infamous summer night.

To date, Juvenile's most prominent artistic statement was an inducement/celebration of the female posterior.

But Katrina changed everyone, at least temporarily.

Terius Gray spent part of his youth in the Magnolia projects, an affiliation he would later celebrate in lyrics, videos and album artwork. But his family sent him to Our Lady of Grace, a Catholic grade school in LaPlace, a community west of New Orleans in St. Charles Parish. "My people wanted me to go to a good school," he said.

He later returned to Orleans Parish to attend Fortier and Booker T. Washington high schools, avoiding any serious trouble along the way. "I had my problems. I used to smoke weed and get loaded and all that, but I had to let that go because I wanted to be successful with my career. I was like, 'I ain't with that no more.' Everybody respects that.

"I learned how to lead my own trail instead of just following behind somebody. Because a lot of times you get caught up following the wrong person, or you'll be around somebody that did something, and you don't know nothing about it, but you wind up involved and you might get killed or go to jail or have things said about you. You are who you hang with; birds of a feather flock together. That's why I always stood alone."

In high school, he fell in with T. Tucker, Everlasting Hitman, DJ Jimi and other pioneering "bounce" rappers and deejays, purveyors of a local, highly danceable form of rap featuring singsong melodies, call-and-response choruses and rhythms sampled from second-lines and other traditional sources. He wrote lyrics for DJ Jimi and, in 1992, rapped "Bounce (For the Juvenile)" on Jimi's *It's Jimi* album. The track, like much early bounce, features simple, straightforward production, with a repetitive if irresistible beat. He sounds young, if not quite as young as the high school student he was, as he salutes Reebok sneakers and Girbaud shirts and shorts, busts out a decent Jamaican dancehall patois and suggests to listeners, "Hey diddle with the cat in the middle/check out the Juvenile while I bust this riddle." "Bounce (For the Juvenile)" was a regional smash, popular at both housing development block parties and private school dances.

Gray would say later that he did not earn his fair share of royalties for his work with Jimi. He issued his first full-length album, *Being Myself*, in 1995 on Warlock Records. But it wasn't until he signed with Cash Money Records, a fast-rising local rap label, that his career skyrocketed.

Cash Money was co-founded by Ronald "Slim" Williams—tall, sleepy-eyed and soft-spoken—and his shorter, stockier, younger brother, Bryan "Baby" Williams. The brothers grew up near New Orleans' Magnolia projects. In the early '90s, they bought into the rap game. Each brother represented half of a yin-yang partnership. Slim, the good cop, handled the behind-the-scenes business. Baby, the bad cop, was out front, dealing directly with artists and shoring up the label's street credibility.

At the time of Cash Money's founding, bounce dominated local clubs and dances. Few observers outside New Orleans expected bounce to move beyond its regional base and muscle in on rap's dominant East and West Coast power bases. But a clever entrepreneur willing to hustle and grind could still make a pile of cash selling CDs by the thousands across the Gulf South.

For a while, the Williams brothers operated out of a small office on a seedy stretch of Tulane Avenue, not far from Orleans Parish Prison. They served as their own distributors, selling CDs to mom-and-pop record stores directly from the trunks of their cars.

Among their earliest discoveries was B.G., then all of eleven years old. Born Christopher Dorsey, B.G. was headed for trouble at an early age. After the death of his father, his mother asked the Williams brothers, family friends from the neighborhood, to help look after her boy. Despite their guidance, he was soon earning his nickname, Baby Gangsta (later abbreviated to B.G.). His family moved to eastern New Orleans, where he enrolled in and later dropped out of Abramson High School. He dealt drugs and dabbled in heroin.

For a multitude of personal and professional reasons, in the mid-1990s the Williams brothers cleaned house and dropped every other artist but B.G. from the Cash Money roster. He would be the foundation on which they would rebuild their label. B.G.'s alliance with Baby and Slim helped sustain the label, even as the brothers and their label helped sustain him.

They signed other promising young rappers. As a junior high student, Dwayne "Lil Wayne" Carter met Baby Williams at another rapper's autograph signing, spit a few lines for him, exchanged phone numbers and was soon admitted to the Cash Money stable. Tab "Turk" Virgil Jr. grew up in the Magnolia projects with Juvenile, and met the Cash Money crew at a party. He auditioned on the spot, then doggedly followed up with nonstop phone calls.

Together, Juvenile, Lil Wayne, Turk and B.G. formed the Hot Boys, Cash Money's all-star team. But it was Juvenile who emerged as the most personable and bankable star in Cash Money's early history. His 1997 Cash Money debut, *Solja Rags*, sold well across the South. In 1998, Cash Money inked a lucrative manufacturing and distribution deal with Universal Records, part of the Seagrams entertainment empire. In what was regarded as a landmark arrangement for an independent, privately owned company, Cash Money retained creative control and ownership of the music; Universal would essentially be paid a commission to make, move and market Cash Money CDs.

Juvenile's second album, *400 Degreez*, was the first Cash Money release funneled through Universal. With guest appearances from his
fellow Hot Boys and production by Mannie Fresh, Cash Money's in-
house studio wizard, *400 Degreez* announced this New Orleans label to
the nation. The mix of fat-bottomed tracks, humor and street smarts
earned praise from not only the rap press, but mainstream rock publications. Thanks to the hit singles "Ha" and "Back That Azz Up," *400
Degreez* sold over four million copies, making it one of the most successful rap albums of 1998. *Billboard* magazine named it the best R&B
album of the year; *Spin* picked "Ha" as one of the year's best singles.
A video for "Back That Azz Up" filmed in the Magnolia projects aired
repeatedly on MTV, BET and other channels, introducing the world
at large to the peculiar locomotive talents contained in the derrieres of
a segment of New Orleans' female population.

Contrary to predictions of its parochialism, bounce blew up; Cash
Money lit the fuse. "It happened," Juvenile told me in 1999. "Everybody's bouncing now, like a chain reaction. I expected it to be big,
but I didn't think it would take off as quick."

In November 1999, Cash Money owned four of the Top 20 slots in
Billboard's R&B/rap album chart, far outpacing rival No Limit Records. The Williams brothers raked in millions of dollars; they literally
could not spend it all, despite acquiring every sort of mechanized vehicle save a submarine. As Cash Money duplicated its regional success
nationally, the operation's inner workings remained largely unchanged.
Everyone understood and accepted his role; the rappers were the
Indians under big chiefs Baby and Slim. No interviews, recording sessions or public appearances happened without first consulting Baby.

But 1999 proved to be the Cash Money high-water mark, at least
until Lil Wayne's ascendance to pop superstardom a decade later. *Tha
G-Code*, Juvenile's follow-up to *400 Degreez*, failed to generate as much
excitement as its predecessor. Rumors spread that all was not well in
the Cash Money camp. By the time Cash Money released Juvenile's
Project English in 2001, he was estranged from the label; the CD, he
later said, was made largely without his cooperation.

The Cash Money "family" fractured along an all-too-common
fault line: money. Artists came to believe the Williams brothers did
not fairly compensate them for their efforts, shortchanging them on
royalties, tour income and other revenues. By the end of 2002, three

of the four Hot Boys—Juvenile, Turk and B.G.—were no longer actively recording for Cash Money. Juvenile said his contract essentially made the Williams brothers his managers as well as the heads of the record label—an arrangement generally perceived as an inherent conflict of interest. "That's the trickery of paperwork, when you don't know what you're writing your name on," Gray said in 2004. "It's a conflict of interest to manage and be a [record company] CEO, because then you're not looking out for the artist's best interest—you're looking out for the best interests of the company."

Juvenile launched a legal battle to free himself from his Cash Money contract and reclaim millions of dollars he believed he was owed. "A lot of people can't afford to fight that. I'm one of the people that can stand here and tell you that I fought it." He sued Cash Money in Louisiana state court. The two sides settled the case in the spring of 2003. Terms of the settlement were confidential, though the deal required Juvenile release one more album through Cash Money. "It was public knowledge that there were some serious complaints on the part of Juvenile," said Tim Fry, the New York attorney who represented him. "Juvenile stood up for his position. We reached a settlement in the spring, we were pleased with it, and we agreed to do another album."

Of the strained relationship with his former mentors, Gray said, "It's just business, that's all it is. I'm not mad. I wish it never would have happened, but it happened, and that's life. You suck it up and you move on."

During his three-year absence from the pop charts, Juvenile was no stranger to court dockets. He introduced himself to his new neighbors in a Mandeville subdivision in July 2000 when a late-night party at the rapper's house went awry. Media reports at the time incorrectly described the gathering as a housewarming; it was, Juvenile says, a bachelor party for a friend. And yes, he did get angry and eject a gaggle of strippers after one of them overflowed an upstairs bathtub. "Water was coming out of the light fixtures [downstairs]. After it was over and I thought about it, it was funny."

But he says he never chased anyone with an icepick. "I don't have an icepick," he said. After booting out the strippers, he also kicked out his male friends, which is when the strippers started banging on a neighbor's door for help. "When the girls saw them coming out of the house, they thought they were coming out to finish them, so they started running. I'm sorry I messed up my dawg's bachelor party, but hey—I didn't strike them. And I didn't chase them with an ice pick."

He did not show up in court to answer charges, and so was convicted of several misdemeanor assault charges.

In March 2001, Juvenile notched his second major tabloid-worthy incident when he was arrested in Miami for allegedly striking a man with a champagne bottle during a melee outside the Improv comedy club. He pleaded guilty to felony battery in February 2003, and received a sentence of seventy-five hours of community service. The Florida courts allowed him to complete his community service in New Orleans with the Velocity Center, an after-school program. "I liked the community service they gave me. I'd read books, play games. It was cool for me to play with [the students]—I've got kids. If that was supposed to be punishment, it's not punishment."

The alleged victim also filed a $5 million civil suit against the rapper. He settled the suit for "around $80,000," he said, an amount he could quickly recoup. "That's, like, two concerts."

In January 2003, Juvenile and three other men were arrested when police stopped their rented Lincoln Town Car at the intersection of North Claiborne Avenue and Bienville Street in New Orleans and discovered two marijuana cigarettes in the ashtray and a small amount of cocaine in the trunk. "I was in a vehicle with somebody that had something. I was like, 'Drug test me. I know what's in my system.' Marijuana? I'll be honest—you got me. But cocaine? I can't do that. That ain't my thing. I watch too many star [documentaries] and see what happens in the long run. I've watched cocaine tear a bunch of stars up, and I'm not about to be one of them."

The incident taught him a lesson about being more careful when choosing associates. "It's a thing my daddy tells me: You tighten your circle. When you're with me, something small will be made big, just because it's me. I can't tell you what to do with your life. But keep it away from me if you know it's going to be something that's going to jeopardize mine."

The tumult cost him dearly in legal fees. He faced the loss of another sizable fortune in a federal courthouse in 2003. The popular local rapper DJ Jubilee, another "bounce" veteran, released a song called "Back That Ass Up" in 1997, around the time of Juvenile's "Back That Azz Up." Juvenile's song was a huge national hit; Jubilee's wasn't. Jubilee and his record label, Take Fo' Records, sued Juvenile, alleging that Juvenile's song was an unauthorized rip-off.

Juvenile countered that the songs were different, but if anyone stole the song and its "back that ass up" catchphrase, it was Jubilee. In one of the more unusual cases on the court docket that year, both sides called music experts to discuss the songs' similarities and differences. Jubilee, a special education instructor at West Jefferson High School, wore a suit to court. Juvenile opted for warm-up suits, a deliberate strategy. "I wasn't going to wear a suit, for one reason: that's not me, and I wanted them to see me, not the suit. There are places you go where you do wear a suit. But in this case, a suit was the last thing you wanted to do. Nobody had on a suit in the jury."

In the end, the federal jury came down heavily in Juvenile's favor, ruling that his "Back That Azz Up" was his own creation. Juvenile had been "more than confident" that he would prevail. "That situation was a character thing. If I had just let Jubilee win that case, it would have destroyed my character."

In his line of work, tawdry headlines are not necessarily a bad thing, but he'd prefer to make do without such publicity. "Sometimes in the type of music I'm doing, people portray that that's cool," he said. "It's not cool. I've got kids, man. I don't want to be on the news with [people] looking at me like I'm crazy. I'm regular. We all have our [bad] days, but when you're a star, it's ten times larger."

Which is not to say that he believes bad press is the media's fault. "If I was a reporter and I heard about 'Juvenile runs behind strippers in Mandeville with an ice pick,' that's a good story. That's something to write about."

That said, Juvenile was ready to talk about music again.

To fulfill his Cash Money contractual obligations and become a free agent, Juvenile released one final album for the Williams brothers. That album, *Juve the Great*, dropped in December 2004. Reclaiming his place among rap's elite wouldn't be easy. *Juve the Great* entered *Billboard*'s pop charts at No. 32, selling around 100,000 copies its first week. Reviews were mixed; *Entertainment Weekly* graded it a C minus.

Many lyrics on *Juve the Great* were lifted directly from his life. In one, the narrator is "in courtrooms beatin' felonies." Elsewhere, he dismisses a woman who falsely claims that he fathered her child: "Don't be that 'Billie Jean' on me." In the single "In My Life," he boasts that his "rap sheet is several pages longer."

"Each song, I say something that's personal and relates to me, but I always speak in third person. You can say something that relates to people and ease their mind. That's what I try to do. I might say something real humorous, I might say something real sexual, I might say something that would have [social critic and anti-rap crusader] C. Dolores Tucker after me tomorrow. But I try to make it all fun."

"Slow Motion," the last track on *Juve the Great,* featured a guest appearance by New Orleans gangsta rapper Soulja Slim, aka James Tapp. Tapp was shot to death on November 26, 2003, outside the house he shared with his mother and her longtime companion, Rebirth Brass Band founder Philip Frazier. Tapp and Gray had met in the early 1990s, when Juvenile mentored the younger, easygoing Slim in the ways of the rap game. "He used to play a lot and crack jokes. He'd crack a joke and have everybody laughing—that was Slim's thing."

As Soulja Slim, Tapp eventually landed a deal with No Limit Records; the company released his *Give It 2 'Em Raw* album in 1998. But his career was hamstrung by jail stints. Over the last year of his life, he and Gray rekindled their professional and personal friendship. Tapp planned to use his appearance on Juvenile's record to give his own career a boost, which, given the success of the single, was certainly plausible. "He had a lot of plans, and those plans are destroyed now," Juvenile said. "It hurts to see him go like that. I feel like I was cheated. I lost one of my best friends."

Tapp's death, as well as Gray's own exile from the pop world, reinforced his appreciation for his success. "I always look at the big picture: Where would I be if I didn't have this opportunity? If I'd been one of those people that had all the talent in the world, but nobody ever heard me, or I was never in the right position to be heard? I always think of the big 'what if.' And I'm blessed. I lost a lot, but I feel like I gained more than I lost. I don't have to look over my shoulder and feel like I did somebody something.

"The last three years, I really took control of my life. Everybody that beat me out of something that I could go back and salvage and save, and everything I could change around me and change about me, I tried to do that. Not that I'm the most perfect person in the world, but I do see a change in myself, because I see a change in the people around me."

"Slow Motion," released after Tapp's death, yielded an unexpected dividend: The song hit No. 1 on the Billboard Hot 100 singles chart. Additionally, Juvenile and his brother, Corey Gray, launched their own label, UTP Records, short for "Uptown Players" and "Uptown Pimps," among other slogans. Soon after "Slow Motion," Juvenile scored another national hit, "Nolia Clap," with his UTP comrades Skip and Wacko.

Fueled by that momentum, he was a hot property again. Atlantic Records signed him to a solo deal, and also agreed to distribute albums from UTP Records.

Having earned his freedom, he made the most of it. During his years as Cash Money's primary cash cow, Gray primarily played by the label's rules. He rapped to tracks supplied by Mannie Fresh and largely limited his collaborations to other Cash Money artists.

On his 2006 Atlantic Records release *Reality Check*, his first solo album after parting ways with Cash Money, he worked with a range of new producers, collaborators and samples. The result was his strongest, most sonically ambitious effort in years. From the turntable scratches of "Around the Way" to the chiming, old-school R&B guitar of the first single, "Rodeo," the nineteen tracks on *Reality Check* showcased a confident, clearheaded Juvenile, one still connected to his New Orleans roots even as he branched out beyond them.

Fresh crafted some beats on *Reality Check*, but other hip-hop producers, primarily Sinista, dominated. Juvenile prominently featured his own UTP crew, specifically Wacko and Skip. He also shared the mic with such special guests as R&B crooner Brian McKnight—the surprise guest vocalist at Juvenile's 2004 wedding—and the rapper Ludacris. Producers Cool & Dre constructed a chill groove for "Rodeo," setting the chorus against lush female backing vocals and a sample of R. Kelly's "Bump N' Grind (Remix)." The subject matter—strippers— is familiar to Juvenile fans. But the tone of the track, a look at the struggles of the stripper lifestyle, was sympathetic. By contrast, "Loose Booty," with its tumbledown percussion break, was the thematic successor to "Back That Azz Up."

A sneaky synthesizer riff juiced "Why Not," an album highlight produced by Lil Jon. The singalong "Rock Like That" and "Sets Go Up" featured classic Juvenile hooks and catch phrases. New Orleans percussion is generally built from the bottom up, and so is "Sets Go Up": The track's foundation is a stark, four-beat bass drum pattern.

Houston rappers Mike Jones and Paul Wall join Skip, Wacko and a sample of Jay-Z's "Dirt Off Your Shoulder" on "Way I Be Leanin'." Fat Joe and Ludacris guest on "Pop U." The fanfare of the intricately produced, lascivious "Who's Ya Daddy" halts for a series of breaks; Juvenile drags out and emphasizes the second-to-last syllable in most lines, a twist on his rugged flow.

He generally avoids glorifying gunplay, though "Around the Way" urged his homeboys from the 3rd Ward to "put your trigger fingers up." The UTP's Skip and Redd Eyezz take over for "Keep Talkin'," threatening to "smack the taste right up out your mouth." Shifting gears, Brian McKnight dominated the lush "Addicted." Juvenile spoke the verses as McKnight crooned the chorus.

He managed to hold off on addressing his former Cash Money bosses and comrades until the album's last track, "Say It To Me Now." The ominous tone recalled Eminem's darker musings. In the chorus, Juve, backed by Partners-N-Crime's Kango, throws down a challenge from his new position of strength. He calls out those who sided against him in his legal dispute with the Williams brothers. Later, he quotes the Lord's Prayer and its imperative to forgive those who trespass against us, even as he engaged in an inner dialogue laying out the case against Cash Money. "They're saying that I betrayed them/They're asking if I could save them . . ."

Had he stopped there and shipped *Reality Check* to the manufacturer, the result would have qualified as a solid Juvenile CD. But just before he finished recording, Hurricane Katrina roared ashore, destroying his newly constructed mansion just outside New Orleans on the shore of Lake Pontchartrain. He returned to the studio to respond to the storm and its aftermath.

That the likes of jazz trumpeter Terence Blanchard, blues-folk guitarist Spencer Bohren, and blues guitarist Chris Thomas King reacted to Katrina in song did not surprise anyone; such artists routinely address matters of consequence, and are equipped with the skills to do so. But Juvenile? The guy best known for rapping about "azzes"?

In "Get Ya Hustle On," he criticized everyone from Fox News to New Orleans Mayor Ray Nagin ("the mayor ain't your friend, he's the enemy"), even as he urged storm victims to use whatever means necessary to speed their own recoveries. The song, Juvenile told me, expressed "anger toward the mayor and the system, the way they went about helping the people."

It would be his first-ever political statement. "I'm kind of scared about it, too. Because I don't want my people to think that I'm political. I'm not. It's just that I'm one of those people that actually lost. I'm one of the people that hasn't received insurance money, that was promised help from the government and didn't receive that help. So I'm just speaking from that point of view."

In December 2005, he agreed to shoot a video for "Get Ya Hustle On" amid the all-too-real destruction of the Lower 9th Ward. *Reality Check* was about to get real.

As the production hopscotched through Fats Domino's neighborhood, the rapper drove himself and his family in his own midnight-blue 2006 Range Rover. The modest "Get Ya Hustle On" budget allowed for only one camera, no trailers, no large entourage and no catering. City officials had sanctioned the shoot; a New Orleans police escort accompanied the crew. They worked on the fly, scouting locations on a "living set" that did not lack dramatic backdrops. "We're laying the track in front of the train," said director Ben Mor.

To Mor, shooting in the Lower 9th Ward was "a unique opportunity to do something very powerful in a historical location. I'm very aware of the significance. It's a living graveyard; a lot of people died there. It's Ground Zero, to the tenth power. I'm hoping to be as delicate as possible."

The day's first stop was the corner of Burgundy and Jourdan, near the broad green expanse of levee where the Industrial Canal meets the Mississippi River. The streets were mostly deserted. Roofers hammered atop one home. An insurance adjuster passed in an SUV. A woman searched in vain for a lost dog. Some members of the crew donned protective masks.

Juvenile emerged from his Range Rover. White diamonds covered a large silver cross necklace; blue diamonds sparkled from a designer watch and matching ring. Still, his attire was relatively low-key for a millionaire rapper. Prior to the storm, he was acquainted with some folks from the Lower 9th. "I knew a lot of people. If you were somebody that hung in the clubs, you pretty much knew everybody. And I'm an herb smoker. Anybody that sold herb, I pretty much knew. This was one of the areas."

On Mor's cue, a portable sound system cranked "Get Ya Hustle On." In front of a house cleaved in half by a pecan tree, Juvenile went to work, mouthing the lyrics for the camera: "Man, I'm trying to live, I lost it all in Katrina . . . We're livin' like Haiti without no government."

Later, child extras would hold up masks of President Bush, Vice President Dick Cheney, and Nagin; all made empty promises to send help. A lyric called out helicopter news crews for not assisting stranded victims. "I was like, 'Damn, ya'll actually giving us footage of people that might lose their life.' They did nothing to help these people."

As the crew set up near a collapsed Jourdan Street house, Juvenile wandered east along Burgundy Street, skirting a beige slipper, a vacuum cleaner, a *Snow White* VCR tape, and a ruined computer monitor. A photographer apologized for posing him in the destruction. The rapper waved off his concern: "People need to see it."

He spotted a familiar green shotgun double, now abandoned, doors and windows agape, contents scattered. "I think my brother stayed around here back in the day. This is unbelievable, man. The things that people lost, the words that I'm seeing on some of these houses. People actually died. It's not a beautiful sight. I wish I could just change this picture right now."

Compared to news reports in Atlanta, the reality "is actually worse. I thought they had gotten along a little further than this. I thought they would have at least knocked the houses down by now. We should see trucks out here right now, tearing all this down, getting ready to rebuild. You don't see that."

Ten blocks farther north, across North Claiborne Avenue, the destruction was more extreme. Rushing water from a breach in the Industrial Canal wall reduced twenty square blocks to cement slabs and debris piles; an enormous barge had come to rest where houses once stood. On Tennessee Street, a light blue house sat cockeyed. The screen door still swung on its hinges, the front porch light was unbroken, an air-conditioner balanced on a window frame. And yet the entire house was parked atop a pickup truck. The hood jutted out beneath the front door.

Aubrey Francis, Juvenile's manager, shook his head: "That's like *The Wizard of Oz*."

The rapper agreed: "Like the Wicked Witch of the West."

As the crew framed a shot, Mor marveled at the apocalyptic destruction.

"And to think," the director said, "that all this was underwater."

Each time Juvenile rapped the line "I lost it all in Katrina," he gestured at the all-too-real devastation around him.

The long, gray day ended with a final shoot at the corner of Claiborne and Forstall. Workers gutting a nearby Chicken Box franchise paused to watch. Two former soldiers working as private contractors asked Juvenile to autograph dollar bills. He obliged.

The cataclysmic surge of water from the nearby breach pushed a beige, wood-frame house into the street. A black wreath was affixed to an exterior wall marked "1 DOA." Someone died inside. Juvenile quietly contemplated the scene. "That s— is crazy."

Because *Reality Check* was nearly finished and locked into a marketing schedule when Katrina struck, Juvenile could only address the storm with three, last-minute additions. "I wish I could go back and really repaint the picture. I could show them even more, now that I'm down here seeing it."

The storm and aftermath changed him, he insisted. "This hurricane was my reality check. I really understand now. I know that this country is nothing but a big business venture. Everything is for sale."

Later, he would visit his own home on the shore of Lake Pontchartrain. The tony neighborhood is thirty minutes and several socioeconomic rungs removed from the Lower 9th Ward. That distance was not enough to spare his house. He moved into the newly constructed mansion not long before Katrina revoked its eligibility for *MTV Cribs*, the garish chronicle of how well the hip and famous live.

"It's flooded, destroyed, looted, everything," he said. "I can show them how it would have been: 'Well, it was going to be one of the best houses around here. Then a bitch named Katrina came through and ruined all that.'"

He planned to rebuild. "My wife says I don't have a choice. I'm so much of a believer that it's going to come back; I'm never selling my property.

"I could spend the next six months feeling sorry for myself. I lost my house, too. But . . . I'm trying to move on, and make ways for everybody else to help themselves."

Time to get his hustle on.

Chapter Thirteen

Rebirth, Now and Forever

If you need to stamp an unequivocal "New Orleans" on anything from a backyard barbecue to a national telecast, few entities do so as effectively as the Rebirth Brass Band. They are Mardi Gras to go.

Special event planners often stage faux parades to give conventioneers a taste of the "real" New Orleans, and brass bands are an essential ingredient. Years ago, my wife booked Rebirth for a corporate event at the wax museum in the French Quarter. As showtime approached, there was no sign of the musicians. Getting nervous, she called Phil Frazier, Rebirth's irrepressible tuba player and leader. She got his voice mail: "Hi, this is Phil Frazier with the Rebirth Brass Band. We're in Cuba . . ."

Apparently, before Frazier flew off to Cuba with Rebirth's A-team, he sublet the wax museum gig to a Rebirth B-team; the tourists wouldn't know the difference. But in this case, the details were somehow lost in transition.

It was a minor blip in the grand scheme of nearly thirty years of Rebirth drama. Phil Frazier is among the friendliest, hardest-working guys in all of New Orleans music; his constant enthusiasm is contagious. And it is impossible to remain still when Rebirth's drums and horns are going full tilt. Frazier and company can be counted on to turn up and turn it out.

Sometimes in two places at once.

Rebirth is New Orleans. New Orleans is Rebirth.

Since 1983, Phil Frazier has sustained the Rebirth Brass Band as its founder, captain, sousaphonist and spirit. He and his bandmates have persevered through dramas large and small across multiple New Orleans storylines, from crime to Carnival, gangsta rap to Kermit Ruffins.

Members have gone to jail and died young. They have also generated immeasurable joy around the globe, shaking up far flung locales with a joyous cacophony of surging brass and stuttering rhythms, the latter rendered by a single snare and bass drum.

Individually and collectively, the men of Rebirth struggled through Hurricane Katrina and its aftermath alongside fellow New Orleanians, even as they contributed to the soundtrack of recovery.

But Katrina, as it turned out, would not be the defining crisis for Phil Frazier. That would come later.

His personal crisis would follow a plot line familiar to Katrina veterans. It struck with little warning. It exposed and exploited areas of neglect. It was terrifying, debilitating, apocalyptic. For a time, all appeared lost.

Friends, family and strangers would rally in support. Recovery would start slowly, haltingly, then pick up speed. Much progress would be made. But Frazier, like his city, would never be quite the same. The legacy of the crisis remains, demanding vigilance to insure history does not repeat itself.

Through it all, Frazier, like his city, drew comfort, strength and inspiration from a familiar source.

From Rebirth.

On a rare day off in August 2010, Frazier settled in at the dining room table of a tidy two-story duplex in the mixed-income Gentilly Terrace neighborhood. He had married and divorced young and, at forty-four, was already a grandfather. The youngest of his children had recently graduated from high school. The gold star on his front tooth salutes his father, who sported one just like it.

He wore a twentieth anniversary Rebirth T-shirt decorated with the band's first logo—a horn busting out of an egg, drawn by Ruffins. Even on a day off, his cell phone—his number, in part, spells "TUBA"—buzzes constantly. He is Rebirth's nerve center, organizing the band's affairs with a new iPad.

He and his younger brother, bass drummer Keith Frazier, founded the Rebirth Brass Band with Ruffins while still students at Joseph S. Clark Senior High School. They played for change in the French Quarter, aspiring to be like the mighty Dirty Dozen Brass Band, the city's preeminent brass band.

Rebirth, Frazier says, specializes in "junk music—jazz and funk put together. It's clean, but unclean." Pop tunes, rap tunes, TV theme songs—anything is eligible for Rebirth.

They paid their dues in social aide and pleasure club parades and late-night gigs at neighborhood bars. Eventually they toured the globe—Japan, Turkey, Africa, Europe more times than they can remember. They visited Syria by mistake. They have traveled to forty-six states.

They released albums on local and national labels and made decent livings as musicians. They opened concerts for the Grateful Dead and toured amphitheaters with folk-punk singer-songwriter Ani DiFranco. She became a convert one night at New Orleans' Maple Leaf, where Rebirth has performed most Tuesdays for more than fifteen years on a shin-high stage lit by beer signs and a single bare bulb. Their "Do What-cha Wanna" and "Feel Like Funkin' It Up" are Mardi Gras standards.

The backline rhythm section drives the band, and Phil Frazier drives the rhythm section. "It's a spontaneous thing. I play from the heart." Onstage, he percolates and pumps like a piston. His tuba—technically it is a sousaphone—weighs around twenty-eight pounds. "I play the horn so much, it's part of my body now. It probably affects me in some way that I don't know."

He is indefatigable, and unflappable. He can blow and go for eight hours a day, if given the proper breaks. "In New Orleans, they've got all kinds of gigs to do. A half hour here, a half hour there, four hours there. It's New Orleans." As one of the city's senior brass bands, they decline most offers for Social Aid and Pleasure Club parades, which can stretch for four hours, because they "take a toll on the trumpet players. We let the newcomers do it."

As a young musician, Frazier sometimes slept alongside his tuba. His current instrument came courtesy of MusiCares, the charitable arm of the Grammy organization, one of many entities to shower musicians with largesse after Katrina. In the spirit of passing down music to the next generation, he bequeathed his battered old silver tuba to the New Birth Brass Band. Years ago, Ruffins spelled out "Rebirth

Brass Band" on its bell with black electrical tape. Frazier decided his shiny new brass tuba deserved a more upscale logo: stick-on letters from Home Depot.

Two days before Katrina made landfall, the Frazier brothers and their families evacuated. At first they drove toward Georgia, then reversed course for Houston. Phil had reserved space in the car for his tuba: "Always take your horn with you. And it paid off."

Days later, he gathered his scattered bandmates from Baton Rouge, Baltimore, Alabama, New York. At Houston's Gypsy Tea Room, they lit it up for New Orleanians desperate for a taste of home. "It was so awesome. People were crying on us: 'Man, Rebirth's playing!' They was happy. We brought part of the city back to them."

By October 2005, they were back in New Orleans, performing at the reopening of the Cabildo—the former seat of Spanish municipal government in colonial New Orleans, it is now a state museum—and venerable music club Tipitina's on the same day. Ten days later, in early November, they reestablished their residency at the Maple Leaf, before leaving on yet another tour.

Displaced New Orleanians came to regard Rebirth as a touchstone, a piece of culture uncorrupted by the storm. Ongoing repairs to New Orleans' Superdome forced the Essence Music Festival to move to Houston's Reliant Stadium in 2006. On the closing night, Rebirth presided over an impromptu family reunion. New Orleans City Councilman Oliver Thomas—who would later go to prison on bribery charges—danced and sweat onstage as fellow New Orleanians waved hands, handkerchiefs and umbrellas with abandon.

"It was still a New Orleans crowd, so that made the vibe right on time," Frazier said that night. "But," he continued, likely speaking for all in attendance, "there's no place like home."

Over the years, members came and went, sometimes under tragic circumstances. Founding snare drummer Kenneth "Eyes" Austin was hit in the head while trying to break up a fight, and died. After drinking steadily during a September 2003 gig at the Maple Leaf, saxophonist James "Phat Nasty" Durant went home with his girlfriend. She found him still in the car the next morning, dead, after he apparently suffered a seizure.

Frazier maintains that he has never fired anybody. "You fire your-self," he says. "You know you're fired if you mess up." One surefire way to fire yourself: fight with another member of the band. "That's my number-one rule. We can fuss like cats and dogs all day. If you fight, you're fired."

After Katrina, Shamarr Allen, one of Rebirth's trumpet players, was the focus of considerable media attention; he had lived in the hard-hit Lower 9th Ward, and his story resonated well. His band-mates, he came to believe, were not so keen on his newfound celeb-rity; at some point, he was no longer a member of Rebirth.

Frazier notes that, however Allen departed, he has gone on to con-siderable success with his own band, the Underdawgs, and as a tour-ing member of country icon Willie Nelson's band. Fellow Rebirth alumnus Kermit Ruffins has also thrived since leaving in 1994. "Re-birth is like a university," Frazier said. "Once you're in Rebirth, you become a star."

The level of commitment is intense. Nine days before the Rebirth Brass Band celebrated its twentieth anniversary, snare drummer Der-rick Tabb was shot in the shoulder, the result of an altercation follow-ing his half-brother's funeral. Yet Tabb performed the scheduled anniversary shows, resting a padded cushion between the strap of his snare drum and his perforated shoulder. "His heart is bigger than his body," Frazier theorized. "It's never a dull moment in Rebirth. Some-thing is always happening. I guess that's our mystique."

Several members have been arrested for something or other. "Even I've been arrested," Frazier said, laughing. The night the 2000 Saints won the first playoff game in franchise history, he celebrated by pounding Jack Daniels and Coke at Joe's Cozy Corner, a bar in the Tremé neighborhood. While sitting in his car, "feeling so good, smil-ing that big ol' smile," a cop responding to a nearby domestic dispute approached and asked if Frazier intended to drive. Frazier responded with, "The Saints won a playoff game! Take me to jail!"

The officer obliged.

If a member leaves Rebirth, either by choice or misfortune, the band doesn't miss a beat. Trumpeters, trombonists and saxophonists are relatively easy to replace, as many of the city's young musicians school themselves on Rebirth music.

"It's almost like a family thing," Frazier said. "If somebody says, 'I need a break from it for a while,' we'll get a person who used to play to step right back in. So we've got our little rotation. Plus we've got people waiting in line to get in the band."

One day, Frazier may need to pass on the torch, or tuba.

"I think I'm going to die with a tuba in my hand," he said. "I might be in the middle of a second-line.

"But don't stop—keep on rollin' for me."

Since the mid-1990s, Frazier's companion has been Linda Tapp Porter. She is the president of the Lady Buckjumpers Social Aid & Pleasure Club, a marching organization that often hires Rebirth for second-line parades.

In 1999, the couple moved into the ground floor unit of the Gentilly Terrace duplex purchased by Porter's son James Tapp Jr., better known as the gangsta rapper Soulja Slim. Frazier watched Tapp mature into "the Tupac of New Orleans"; he thought of him as his stepson and recruited him to guest on the Rebirth album *Hot Venom*.

Tapp lived above his mother and Frazier. He bought the duplex a year after he released *Give It 2 'Em Raw* on Master P's No Limit Records. His career was hamstrung on account of his being too real; he was in and out of trouble and jail. On the evening of November 26, 2003, he pulled up to the house on Lafaye Street, exited his Cadillac Escalade, and was shot multiple times in the face and chest, at pointblank range. Police characterized the killing as a "hit." He was twenty-six years old. His truncated career yielded its biggest hit, a No. 1 single with Juvenile titled "Slow Motion," months after his death.

At the time of the shooting, Frazier was at a barbershop. He received the call and raced home in time to see Tapp's body on the sidewalk. There was no question in his mind that he and the rest of Rebirth would lead the funeral second-line. "That's my boy. I'd do it for him."

It was a raucous affair, as jazz funerals for young murder victims often are. Tapp was laid out in his signature camouflage ensemble. Rebirth played only one dirge as the procession exited the church, then lit into uptempo romps, all surging horns and stuttering beats. Along Washington Avenue, mourners removed Tapp's casket from the horse-drawn carriage and danced with it above their heads. "The

funeral was perfect," Frazier said. "It happened the way it was supposed to happen."

A small memorial sits on the front lawn of the Lafaye Street house;
fans often drive by. On the fifth anniversary of Tapp's death, Rebirth
performed in the front yard, as his mother danced on the spot where
her son was slain.

As it was built on the relatively high ground of Gentilly Ridge, the
house stayed dry during Katrina. In November 2005, Phil arrived as
one of the first returning residents to his neighborhood. There was no
electricity, and he had to drive several miles to find an open store. But
he never doubted.

"I knew the city was going to come back. My heart told me. My
head was telling me the city was gonna come back. Head and heart.
I had faith. You can take me out the city, but you can't take New Orleans out my heart."

In the ensuing months and years, that relationship worked both
ways. Rebirth was present, horns and drums in hand, at high-profile
milestones in the recovery, inlcuding the September 2006 reopening
of the Superdome and the Hornets' homecoming party in October
2007. For the 2008 NBA All-star Game at the New Orleans Arena,
Rebirth joined an all-star cast of New Orleans musicians: Allen Toussaint, Ellis Marsalis, Harry Connick Jr., and Dr. John. At the time,
Frazier's kids were still living in Katrina exile in Arkansas. That night,
he hoped they were watching, as "this might be the only time you see
the Rebirth Brass Band in suits." Dressed up in black suits, Rebirth
pumped out "Oh Casanova" and "Do Whatcha Wanna" during player
introductions.

Frazier and his tuba were even featured on the 2007 New Orleans
Jazz & Heritage Festival Presented by Shell's popular Congo Square
poster. The Rebirth Brass Band is what the Neville Brothers once
were: a band born of, and still bound up in, New Orleans street culture, representing it to world. The Nevilles eventually graduated
from the smoky clubs where they cut their teeth. They rarely perform
in their hometown anymore, except for an annual Jazz Fest gig. Rebirth does its share of globetrotting, but still grinds it out at local parties, weddings, funerals, grand openings, second-lines and barrooms.

"As long as I got breath in my body, we'll still do the grind," Frazier said. "It keeps us real. It keeps us close to the city." The idea is to keep it simple. So the people can feel where it's coming from."

The Rebirth saga, when broken down to individual members, touches on all the hazards that many young black men in New Orleans face: Drugs. Jail. Premature death. Individually and collectively, bad decisions have been made, business has not been handled. Sometimes there has been a failure to understand how the rest of the world works.

In 1994, at age nineteen, trumpeter Derrick Shezbie released *Spodie's Back* through Qwest Records, a Warner Bros. Records imprint founded by super-producer Quincy Jones. Backed by a crack jazz band featuring saxophonist Branford Marsalis, Shezbie, declared All Music Guide, appeared "well on his way into developing into an Armstrong for the next century."

But unlike Armstrong, Shezbie could not escape the pull of the New Orleans streets. His manager quickly alienated record company staffers, journalists and most everyone else who could have aided Shezbie's career. After one album, Qwest dropped him.

Back in the Tremé neighborhood, he quickly found trouble and was arrested for illegally carrying a firearm. Rebirth offered him a measure of redemption and a way to make a living. But after years of playing with an unconventional technique—onstage, he reinforces his inflated cheek with a hand—he risked not being able to play at all. If he's unable to play music, he has no backup plan.

Neither does Phil Frazier.

On December 11, 2008, Frazier woke up to his own personal disaster. His right side was paralyzed. He tried to get out of bed, and fell.

He called Porter, who sounded the alarm for Frazier's mother, brother and others to meet her at the house. Frazier managed to walk to the car for the ride to the hospital.

Doctors thought he might have suffered a mild stroke. He was feeling better, so they sent him home. That night, Frazier suffered a far more severe episode. He returned to the hospital. This time, he stayed.

High blood pressure had indeed triggered a mild stroke. He remembers crying, "My career's over! I can't play my horn! Why'd this happen to my crazy ass?"

High blood pressure runs in his family. Fourteen months before Frazier's episode, his brother Kerwin James, the tuba player in the New Birth Brass Band, died of complications from a stroke—at age thirty-four. (It was during a spontaneous Tremé second-line for James that trombonist Glen David Andrews and the Rebirth's Derrick Tabb were arrested for disturbing the peace, setting off yet another debate about cultural caretaking in New Orleans. The charges were eventually dropped.)

With his prognosis uncertain, Frazier's bandmates convened a meeting at the Howlin' Wolf, the Warehouse District club owned by the band's manager, Howie Kaplan. They resolved to employ a substitute tuba player and carry on—with Frazier's blessing. "I told them, 'Please do. Don't stop the band.' The band is bigger than any one member."

Keith Frazier, who moved his family to Ft. Worth, Texas, after Katrina flooded his home in Gentilly, assumed temporary leadership of the band. To the shock of their manager, they actually rehearsed with the substitute tuba player.

But Phil was determined to rebuild himself and regain his ability to play. At Touro Infirmary's rehabilitation center, a therapist suggested he try to play his tuba. When his fingers touched the brass for the first time in days, "I was so happy. It was like I was reborn."

His head remembered what to do. His fingers, however, had temporarily forgotten. By the third day, he rediscovered the riff to "Feel Like Funkin' It Up," and was rolling once again.

At first, he only allowed his therapist to listen—he did not want his bandmates to hear his sloppy riffs. Soon, he was staging one-man concerts for fellow patients.

A month after his stroke, on January 12, 2009, Frazier checked out of Touro.

The next month, he tentatively returned to the stage. Before reclaiming his place in Rebirth, he tested the waters with the New Birth Brass Band. "They said, 'C'mon, Phil, we gonna help your therapy.'"

He only endured for thirty minutes at that first show. When he finally rejoined Rebirth for a Maple Leaf gig, he lasted for the first set, with the Lil Rascals' Jeffrey Hill, his stand-in, playing alongside him.

Three weeks later, Frazier declared, "I got this," and went back to work full-time.

Was he as confident in his own ability to come back as he was the city's? "Most definitely. Same thing. I'm a confident man."

Still, the episode "scared the s— out of me," Frazier says. It was "a good wake-up call. Not good, but it woke me up."

He says he was a good therapy patient, willing to work hard and obey instructions. When a member of the Pinstripe Brass Band suffered a stroke, the therapist called in Frazier to deliver a pep talk.

Per doctors' orders, he has adjusted his lifestyle. No fried foods or pork. No salt. Remove skin from chicken. And no more Jack Daniels and Coke. The changes were necessary, Frazier says, "if I want to live."

Always motivated, always busy, now he is even moreso.

"I'm trying to do it all now. I want to win a Grammy before I die. I'd rather win a Grammy than get rich."

Since Katrina, Rebirth has felt the love like never before. New fans sometimes assume the name "Rebirth" was concocted after the storm. They do not realize twenty-two years of Rebirth history preceded Katrina.

"People say, 'Where ya'll been?'" Frazier said, laughing. "We've been right here, every day."

The band's profile has never been higher. Derrick Tabb has won national acclaim for The Roots of Music, an after-school program that tutors 125 young students, free of charge, in music and academics.

In April 2010, the first episode of the first season of HBO's *Treme* opened with the Rebirth Brass Band at a second-line. The Davis McAlary character hears the distant music and observes, "Sounds like Rebirth."

Sharp-eared viewers realized he could have meant "Rebirth," with a capital R, or "rebirth," in lowercase—they are essentially interchangeable.

Moments after being sworn in as mayor of New Orleans on May 3, 2010, Mitch Landrieu second-lined down the steps of Gallier Hall to the sound of Rebirth.

The band, like Frazier, continues to renew itself. Rebirth signed a contract with Basin Street Records in the summer of 2010. In the spring of 2011, Basin Street released the band's *Rebirth of New Orleans*.

Through it all, Rebirth has never been in danger of fading away. Once Frazier started the band, "that was it. For life. Rebirth for life." He plans to spend Tuesdays at the Maple Leaf forever.

His speech retains only a hint of his stroke. He still walks with a slight limp, which does not hinder his ability to march in parades or stand onstage at the Maple Leaf for hours on end. Giving up, he makes clear, was never an option.

"Every day, I keep getting stronger," he says. "I think about everything I've been through, and the band . . ."

He hesitates, searching for the correct word. Finally, he makes a simple declaration for himself, and his city: "I've come a long way."

He, like Rebirth—like New Orleans—has found a way to carry on.

Acknowledgments

As market surveys confirm, New Orleanians, at least, continue to read actual newspapers. In a blogged and tweeted universe, *The Times-Picayune* and its editors still encourage creative writing. Over the years, I've chronicled the subjects of the thirteen *Groove Interrupted* chapters in the pages of the *Picayune*. Publisher Ashton Phelps Jr. and editor Jim Amoss kindly allowed me to repurpose, revamp, and expand on that material in this book.

Features section editors Mark Lorando and Ann Maloney, along with former editor and current NOLA.com director of content James O'Byrne, guided those stories through their initial incarnations; they also afforded me the time to write this much longer piece of prose. Ex–entertainment editor Renee Peck set me on the path with my first-ever freelance assignment (a 1989 review of Hall & Oates at Tipitina's, no less). In 1996, Karen Taylor-Gist brought me onboard as a full-time *Picayune* staffer. Former book editor Susan Larson, a partisan for the printed word, offered encouragement and sage advice as *Groove Interrupted* took shape.

Creative Conduit's Swanna MacNair, a brass band and po-boy enthusiast, was a friend long before she was my agent. She believed in this project from the get-go, and made good on her promise to find it a home. Thanks also to Christy Fletcher and Mink Choi at Fletcher & Company.

Michael Flamini, my editor at St. Martin's Press, nurtured the book to fruition. Thanks also to Vicki Lame, Rachel Ekstrom, Jason Ramirez, and the rest of the St. Martin's team, as well as attorney Mark Fowler.

For inspiration by example, kudos to Michael Tisserand, Tom Piazza, Sara Roahen, and Jeff Duncan, all of whom wrote excellent books about essential elements of south Louisiana (zydeco, New Orleans culture, food, and the Saints, respectively).

Jan Ramsey, publisher of *OffBeat* magazine, gave me my first bonafide job in journalism, which provided my initial backstage access to the world of New Orleans music. She remains an outspoken advocate for the perpetuation of that music, as does community radio station WWOZ (90.7 FM).

Octavia Books, the Garden District Book Shop, and the Maple Street Book Shop service New Orleans' robust community of writers and readers. The Louisiana Music Factory performs a similar function for fans of indigenous music.

Thanks in general to Eric Paulsen, Sally-Ann Roberts, Dionne Butler and the WWL-TV crew, David Fricke, Chris Granger, Alison Fensterstock, Kenny Martinez, Lisa Maurer, Charles Driebe, Matt Goldman, Rich Collins, Dave Poche, Scott "Smitty" Smith, Scott Durbin, Lyle Lovett, and Renee Pfefer.

Harry Shearer and Judith Owen bring their considerable talents and energies to bear on behalf of New Orleans, their adopted home. Shearer graciously took time out from a frenetic schedule to pen the book's foreword.

Adam Levin's cover photograph, featuring trombonist Glen David Andrews, captures the uninhibited joy, defiance and resolve that sustain New Orleans musicians specifically, and New Orleanians in general. Do yourself a favor and catch Glen in action next time you visit the city, and check out www.glendavidandrewsband.com. Also standing tall on the cover are Kenny Terry, Dewon "Itchy" Scott, and Reginald Stewart.

A special tip o' the hat is due Geddy, Alex, and Neil for decades of inspiration, motivation and companionship.

On a personal note . . . My father, Frank, first introduced me to the joys of New Orleans music. My late mother, Mary Ann, encouraged reading and writing by shuttling my brothers and I to the public library in eastern New Orleans each summer. The extended Spera and Giblin clans also offered unfailing support.

And finally, my name appears on the cover, but this book wasn't written alone. To Mary, thanks . . . for everything.